Chicken Soup for the Soul®

Angels and Miracles

Chicken Soup for the Soul: Angels and Miracles
101 Inspirational Stories about Hope, Answered Prayers, and Divine Intervention
Amy Newmark

Published by Chicken Soup for the Soul, LLC www.chickensoup.com
Copyright ©2016 by Chicken Soup for the Soul, LLC. All Rights Reserved.

The publisher gratefully acknowledges the many publishers and individuals who
granted Chicken Soup for the Soul permission to reprint the cited material.

Front cover illustration courtesy of iStockphoto.com/IgorZhuravlov (©Igor Zhuravlov)
Back cover and Interior photo courtesy of iStockphoto.com/Tobias Helbig
(©Tobias Helbig)
Photo of Amy Newmark courtesy of Susan Morrow at SwickPix

Cover and Interior by Daniel Zaccari

Distributed to the booktrade by Simon & Schuster. SAN: 200-2442

Publisher's Cataloging-In-Publication Data
(Prepared by The Donohue Group, Inc.)

Names: Newmark, Amy, compiler.
Title: Chicken Soup for the Soul : angels and miracles : 101 inspirational
     stories about hope, answered prayers, and divine intervention /
     [compiled by] Amy Newmark.
Other Titles: Angels and miracles : 101 inspirational stories about hope, answered
     prayers, and divine intervention
Description: [Cos Cob, Connecticut] : Chicken Soup for the Soul, LLC [2016]
Identifiers: LCCN 2016950843 | ISBN 978-1-61159-964-0 (print) | ISBN 978-
     1-61159-263-4 (ebook)
Subjects: LCSH: Miracles--Literary collections. | Miracles--Anecdotes. |
     Angels--Literary collections. | Angels--Anecdotes. | Prayer--Literary
     collections. | Prayer--Anecdotes. | LCGFT: Anecdotes.
Classification: LCC BL487 .C45 2016 (print) | LCC BL487 (ebook) | DDC
     202/.117--dc23

PRINTED IN THE UNITED STATES OF AMERICA
on acid∞free paper

25 24 23 22 21 20 19 18 17 16   01 02 03 04 05 06 07 08 09 10 11

Angels and Miracles

101 Inspirational Stories about Hope, Answered Prayers, and Divine Intervention

Amy Newmark

Chicken Soup for the Soul, LLC
Cos Cob, CT

Changing your world one story at a time®
www.chickensoup.com

Table of Contents

❶
~Angels Among Us~

❷
~Miracles Happen~

❸

~Messages from Heaven~

❹

~Miraculous Healing~

❺

~Divine Intervention~

❻

~Dreams and Premonitions~

❼

~Touched by an Angel~

8

~Answered Prayers~

9

~Faith in Action~

❿
~Love that Doesn't Die~

Chapter 1

Angels and Miracles

Angels Among Us

My First Responder

We can only be said to be alive in those moments when
our hearts are conscious of our treasures.
~Thornton Wilder

I was driving home from an audition to sing as a church cantor in a local Catholic church. The audition went very well and they had hired me on the spot. I felt blessed.

It wasn't far to the highway that would take me home. I had a green arrow indicating that I could make a left turn, so I turned toward the entrance ramp. Then, seemingly out of nowhere, a speeding Suburban blew through a red light and plowed into my little Neon. I saw it coming and there was nothing I could do.

Glass shattered around me, the airbags deployed and something heavy pushed against my legs. It was the car's engine. To make matters worse, the engine was in flames. I frantically tried my door, only to find it was completely caved in. I couldn't budge it. I'm pretty sure I was screaming by then.

The police came quite quickly and one officer put out the flames with a fire extinguisher. The car was still smoldering under the crushed hood, though, and I could smell gasoline.

When the firefighters and rescue team finally arrived, they couldn't get the door open either. Flames began spreading out from under the hood again. I was crying now as the firemen scrambled to get something to cut me out. I could see on their faces that things looked rather grim. I kept calling for someone to help me. The adrenaline had started to wear off and I was almost certain that my left ankle was broken.

A man suddenly appeared at the side of my car. I remember he was very handsome and had a comforting smile. He said, "I've got you, sweetheart. Hang on."

Before I knew it, he had opened the door effortlessly and helped me out of the burning wreck. Then he let me lean against him and he guided me to the side of the road, out of harm's way. The front end of the car was engulfed in flames by then. The firemen rushed over with a foam spray to put out the fire, frantic to rescue me from where I was stuck—except I wasn't there anymore.

One of the astonished firefighters walked over to where I was sitting. The man who helped me had disappeared so I assumed he had gone back to his own vehicle.

I asked the firefighter if he could thank the man for me. He shook his head, and said, "Lady there was *no* man. We went for the Jaws of Life to get you out of the car, only to find you sitting on the curb. Lady, we couldn't open that door. It's so damaged, the only way to free you was to cut you out."

I knew I had seen him. That man helped me walk to the curb. I couldn't have done it myself because I couldn't even put any weight on my injured foot. I argued with the firefighter: The man who had saved me had been there. I held onto him. He was real. I felt him guiding me out of the car and across the road. I leaned on him when I could not walk.

The fireman responded, "Trust me, Miss, there was no one there. I have no idea how you got out, but I can assure you there was no man."

I was pretty shaken up, as you can imagine, and as the paramedics came and put me in the ambulance, I insisted that I wanted to thank the kind stranger who had risked his life to save me. I think they just thought I was hysterical from the trauma of the accident.

A few days later, I was hobbling on crutches with a bad sprain. My ankle was not broken and somehow, even with all the glass from the windshield that had splintered around me, I only had superficial cuts on my neck and hands. I had a couple of black eyes from the impact of the airbags, but all in all, I was in pretty good shape, considering the magnitude of the accident. The Suburban that hit my little car was speeding at eighty miles per hour, according to the police.

I had to go to the junkyard to more or less "identify" my car and retrieve whatever items I could salvage from the wreck. Of course the car was totaled. When I saw the extent of the damage, my knees buckled. I could not believe I survived that crash. I looked inside the burnt shell of the car and spotted my purse on the floor, damaged, but salvageable. I took it with me and rifled through it. Inside the charred remains of my purse was a silver Celtic cross that I had never seen before. Not only that, it was a crucifix. Normally, Celtic crosses do not have the body of Christ on them. There was a little heart dangling from it with the Mother of God imprinted on it. It also said, "Erin" on the back, which means Ireland. Now, I am not Irish, but of all the music I love singing, Irish music rates at the top.

I don't know how that cross got into my purse and I don't know who my rescuer was. But I keep the cross with me at all times as a reminder that I was protected and blessed many times that fateful day.

~Ria Cantrell

The First Time
He Picked Me Up

Be still, and know that I am God.
~Psalms 46:10

When I was five years old we lived in Brussels. Dad's work with Pan American World Airways took us to many parts of the world, but for the first six years of my life, we lived in Belgium. Our house was a three-story, brick-fronted place on a little cobblestone street. Entrance into and out of that dead-end street was through an enormous stone archway.

From the windows of our house I could look toward the end of that street, through the archway, to the ever-busy four-lane roadway that lay just beyond. Trolley cars on tracks used to speed to and fro on that road, and the automobile traffic was endless. Under the shadows of the archway was a candy shop run by an elderly couple.

I used to walk to the little shop on my own several times each week, and each time one of the elderly proprietors must have wondered how I had managed to leave my house without being seen by my parents.

One gray and gloomy morning, I snuck out again. Dad was at work at the airport and Mom must have been upstairs doing something. That busy roadway beckoned me. This time I didn't go to the little shop. Instead, I stood on the curb of that four-lane road, wondering what lay beyond.

I started to run across the road and over the trolley tracks. But I hadn't looked both ways, and a trolley was speeding down the second set of tracks from the opposite direction. I actually ran right into the side of one of the trolley carriages. The force of the impact threw me backwards several feet, right back onto the first set of tracks I had just crossed and into the path of yet another speeding trolley. I remember seeing the growing red stain on the front of my shirt and the stream of blood as it gushed from my nose. It felt as if my face had been shattered. I also remember looking up to my left and seeing the oncoming trolley's driver, his face frozen in fear. He couldn't stop in time.

Just then a strong pair of arms lifted me from the tracks and held me tight, right between the two speeding trolleys, in the middle of those two sets of tracks. The voice was clear and distinct, sounding as if it emanated from the inside of a hollow tunnel, yet somehow soothing and calming, "Be still," it said, "Be still." A car slammed on its brakes and came to a screeching halt somewhere on the road behind me. I thought I heard someone shouting something in French in the distance.

Once the trolleys had passed, those arms carried me back to the sidewalk and put me down right at the door of the little candy shop. I looked up to see the man who had saved me, but no one was there. No one was anywhere for at least a full block all the way around. A few pedestrians could be seen walking about a hundred feet away. One of them was pointing at me and whispering to her companion, but that was it. Another female pedestrian started to run in my direction, her arms outstretched, her mouth wide open in a silent scream, the look of shock and utter befuddlement clearly written on her countenance, but she stopped short and stared, unable to fathom what she had just witnessed.

I was stunned and unable to speak. There was no blood at all, not even on my shirt. I touched my face, my nose, felt inside my mouth with my hand. Everything felt normal, with no pain or discomfort of any kind. I opened the door to the candy shop and the little bell tinkled as I walked inside.

The elderly shop owner had his hand over his mouth and his eyes were as wide as saucers. "*Comme?*" he asked, "How?" He quickly walked around from behind the counter and took my hand. He let me fill a paper bag with as many sweets as I could carry and walked me back to my parents' house at the end of the street.

I saw him looking up and down the cobblestone road in all directions, as if for an explanation. Tears were running down his face. It was the first time I ever remember seeing a man openly crying. He and my mother spoke for several minutes, and from that moment on my movements were severely restricted. I was never again allowed to venture out onto that four-lane roadway with those two trolley tracks. Then he leaned down and hugged me closely before slowly walking back to his shop under the shadows of the archway.

"How?" the sweet shop owner had asked. The answer is obvious to me. Those strong arms comforted me and that voice said, "Be still." My injuries disappeared.

I have felt that protection many times in my life, and very probably many more times that I'm not even aware of. That was only the first time that my angel picked me up and saved me.

~John Elliott

The White Dog

I have found that when you are deeply troubled,
there are things you get from the silent devoted
companionship of a dog that you can get
from no other source.
~Doris Day

My wife, Betsy, had been diagnosed with breast cancer less than a month earlier. That morning, I would be taking her to the hospital for a lumpec-tomy and the removal of some lymph nodes.

I'd just stepped out onto the back porch with my coffee mug to take a few deep breaths and try to stop the panic I felt. I couldn't stop from worrying that she wouldn't make it. Our daughter, Emily, was only two and a half at the time. We'd been married ten years and felt as if we'd known each other all our lives.

There I stood, trying to control the panic. Suddenly, I saw a dog sitting in the back yard near the east corner of the garage — a medium-sized white dog, maybe a Labrador mix. I didn't see him enter the yard from anywhere but I'd been distracted, lost in thought, and I wouldn't have noticed him walking in from another yard on the street.

The strange thing was the way he looked at me. He wasn't moving and he looked steadily at me with warm brown eyes. Once our eyes connected, he dipped his head slightly and walked off toward the trees behind our garage.

I suddenly felt much calmer.

We'd only moved into our house two months before and had been concentrating on fixing it up. I didn't know the neighbors on the street, and I certainly didn't know who had a white Labrador or any other kind of dog. Even though it didn't have a collar, I assumed it belonged to someone nearby.

I couldn't explain what I was feeling, though. Somehow that dog had made me feel confident that everything would be all right.

On the way to the hospital that morning I asked Betsy, "Do you believe in totems?"

"Maybe I would," she said, "if I knew what one was."

"Oh. You know, messengers from the spirit world, like angels, from God. As in totem poles."

"What messages do they bring?"

"Messages about our lives. Life, death, love, changes, hope — those sorts of things."

"I guess God can send a message anyway he likes. Why?"

"Nothing. It's just… I saw this white dog out back this morning and… and I just felt… better somehow. He was there and then he was gone but he let me know it would all be all right. Everything with you. Sounds crazy, I know."

She smiled at me and patted my leg.

The surgery was a success and we found ourselves trying to walk steadily on this uneven path; the next step was chemotherapy. The only problem was that Betsy couldn't take needles. The oncologists decided the best way around this was to implant a sub-cutaneous port-a-cath in her chest to administer the chemo.

And so there came another morning of another surgery and, again, my stomach kept flipping around inside me and my head felt light and tingling and I kept wanting to cry or hit something. I stepped out onto the back porch with my coffee to see the white dog sitting in the exact same spot as before, looking directly at me.

I actually wanted to ask him a question. I wanted to ask him "Why?" I wanted this dog to tell me why all of this was going on and how it would all end. The dog just sat there gazing at me and I felt instantly ashamed I'd forgotten the reassurance I'd been given before.

No sooner did I remind myself of that than he turned and walked off in the same direction he'd gone earlier.

And the second surgery went just as fine as the first.

I went around the neighborhood asking people if they owned a white dog. There was one neighbor with a small white Poodle but that wasn't *my* dog. No one on the street over had a white dog matching *my* dog either. As I'd drive around on my various errands or to work I became especially attentive to people walking dogs; but none of the dogs in the village was the white dog.

The morning of the first dose of Adriamycin I felt tired. Betsy hadn't been sleeping well, worrying about how she would react to the chemo, and I had been up most of the night. Stepping out onto the back porch that morning I was silently praying the dog would be there; and he was.

In the same spot, with the same look in his eyes, the white dog gazed steadily across the short expanse of lawn at me and I looked back, sighed gratefully and nodded at him. He seemed to almost nod back but, I was sure, it was just that dip of the head he would do just before leaving. He started off in the same direction he always did, heading east toward the tree line.

I almost felt like crying in gratitude.

The feeling this dog gave me — that everything was going to be all right — was not a guarantee that Betsy would not die of cancer nor that we weren't going to suffer; rather it seemed the assurance that, whatever happened, we were not going through it alone.

Betsy responded well to chemo and, when those treatments were done, she went through radiation. Months were measured in chemo treatments, trips to the oncologists and diet regimens. We found ourselves closer than we'd even been before; we talked more, took more chances, went more places, and had more fun. Nights in our house were like three kids at a sleepover as we'd play hide and seek with Emily or just dance to music in the kitchen, the three of us together.

And so a year passed and there came a morning when I was going to take Betsy to the hospital for another surgery: to have the port-a-cath removed. She was cancer free, at least for now; and I'd come to recognize that "for now" is really all any of us have.

I half expected to see the white dog that morning as I stepped out onto the back porch; but then, I also knew, I didn't need to. He'd already delivered the message three times and, finally, I'd understood it.

~Joshua J. Mark

The Arms of God

A hug delights and warms and charms, that must be
why God gave us arms.
~Author Unknown

I was sitting at the table, hunched over my checkbook, agonizing about my unpaid bills. "Ugh! We might as well go to church."

"Kids! We're going to church. Get your shoes on."

Being a single mother was frustrating enough. Add my nonexistent love life, stomach problems, and mounting financial woes, and church seemed the best place to be.

It was Wednesday night and the children's programs would entertain my kids while I sat in peace, hopefully receiving encouragement through the pastor's sermon.

I was twenty-three and hadn't learned money management skills. Consequently, late notices appeared in my mailbox regularly.

I also knew nothing about stress management. Years of partying had taken a toll on my body and my mounting anxiety seemed to make my stomach problems worse. I carried a large bottle of antacid in my purse. I was thin and growing more pale and fragile each week.

Driving to church, my children chattered excitedly in the back seat. Sadly, I didn't share their enthusiasm. I felt defeated.

Why was I going tonight? It was the middle of the week and it'd be past the kids' bedtime when we got home. I had to work in the morning, and I was wasting gas.

Entering the building, the kids ran toward their classroom. I followed and greeted their teachers. "Hi there! Thanks for serving tonight!"

"You kids behave and have fun," I tried to sound cheery as I hung up their little jackets.

Walking down the hall toward the sanctuary, I grew more pessimistic with each step. They'd need new coats in the winter. Where would I get the money for that?

The large room was dimly lit. The sermon didn't lift my spirits and I sat motionless when the pastor dismissed the congregation. It was time to get the kids and head home, I silently groused, dreading the long, dark drive into the country.

Slowly I stood up and looked around. A few groups of people greeted one another here and there across the large auditorium. I had no friends there. Why was I even there? I'd wasted enough time and money coming in the middle of a workweek. I felt like an idiot.

Chastising myself, I turned to leave. About six feet away to my left, a large, older woman stood alone. I felt her staring at me. My head was hung low but I glanced up and smiled at her. She held my gaze and stared into my eyes.

"How ya doin'?"

I was surprised she spoke to me; she didn't know me. I stepped toward her and sighed heavily, "Oh, I'm okay." I forced a smile, "Gotta go get my kids." She wasn't fooled by my fake cheerfulness.

Turning toward me, she held out her arms. "Come here, baby."

Without even thinking about it, I entered her opened arms. "You look like you need a hug, sweetie." Her large arms enveloped me and I melted into her bosom.

Uncharacteristically, I stayed there for several seconds, my head resting peacefully on her chest. Beyond her physical warmth, she radiated the love of God. Confidence, strength, joy, and wellness flowed from this large, lovely woman into my little, sickly frame.

As I backed away, she held onto my upper arms. "You go get your babies now and you have a good week, ya hear?" I nodded, still surprised at my own reactions.

Peace overwhelmed me as I walked to my children's classroom.

I was overcome with a profound love for my kids.

I helped them put on their jackets as they excitedly told me what they'd done in class that evening. I found it hard to listen and couldn't shake the feeling that someone intensely close to God had embraced me.

Suddenly I snapped to attention. "Come on kids, there's someone I want you to meet." I hurried my children back into the sanctuary. "Aw, she's gone."

I stopped two ladies who had sat behind me. "Excuse me. Do you know that lady who was in the pew right there?" I pointed to where she had been sitting.

"We didn't see anyone there. What did she look like?"

Smiling, I described the large woman with the simple dress and cardigan sweater. "No, I didn't see her," they each responded.

"Well, we'll find her Sunday. Let's head home kids."

I left church that night feeling well physically, emotionally, mentally, and spiritually. The adoration that poured out of me onto my children was a renewed, unconditional love from God.

For the next several weeks I searched for that sweet lady. I looked on Wednesday evenings, Sunday mornings and even Sunday evenings, but never saw her again. It felt like she was a messenger sent just for me.

The love that was infused in me when I was encircled by her arms was affection straight from heaven. It was life-transforming and contagious. Living with renewed hope, my cheerfulness was genuine and it was easy to lavish unconditional love on my children and others.

~Kelly J. Stigliano

That Last Goodbye

We laughed until we had to cry, we loved right down to
our last goodbye, we were the best.
~St. Elmo's Fire

The letter is dog-eared and forever creased because I've had it for decades. The message was written in pencil by a young, passionate soldier who looked a lot like Richard Gere.

Mark was flying back to his Army post on the eastern seaboard when he wrote it. In simple, transparent words, he put his heart on paper, and mailed it off to me.

Later I wondered if he stood before the Atlantic's crashing surf and relived the turmoil of our last days together. It had not been smooth sailing, but that's what we were — a wonderful, terrible, volatile explosion. It was heady stuff, being eighteen and head over heels in love with someone who was anything but safe.

He wrote that he wanted to talk with my dad and work out their differences. Mark was an optimist. He was young, unconquerable, and full of dreams. Dad, on the other hand, had plenty of hard times in his rear view mirror. He was a little too worn down by the world that Mark was ready to meet head-on. Dad wanted his only daughter to be happy. He didn't envision a whirlwind named Mark making me happy.

I unfold the familiar paper, and trace his words. I close my eyes and step back in time.

Weeks had passed since he left. I had just graduated from high school and was working for a CPA. On lunch break, I backed my 1967 Firebird out of the long alley. Then my breath caught in my throat. Was that Mark, sitting right there, in the empty parking lot?

The motorcycle was polished — just like he kept it. From the back, it looked like his familiar posture. He was just sitting there on his beloved bike. But it couldn't be... he'd flown away weeks ago. I felt like I was hallucinating.

My foot hesitated between the brake and the gas. My hand fumbled, confused by what gear I should be in. Then he looked at me. I was ready to run to him.

I started to back up again, because I knew I had to be seeing things. Mark's motorcycle wasn't here; it was in South Carolina. But I had to look back, and when I did, my eyes were filled with Mark. Logic shouted no; it could only be an incredible imitation — right down to his resolute jaw, his smoldering eyes, the exact color of his hair — and, of course, the exact motorcycle that he had. It couldn't be him. Mark would've smiled that great crooked smile of his by now, so smug about surprising me.

Finding the brake pedal, my car was still, my stare locked. He looked so intently into my eyes, and looked so strangely sad. So very, very sad.

Drawn to him, I shifted out of reverse and inched forward, then pulled over and parked. My hand had found the familiar door handle, but when I looked up again I'll never know if it was logic, or apprehension, or simple doubt that persuaded me that the man on the bike looked less familiar. Mark was in South Carolina. My heart had to be playing tricks on me. So I put the car into gear, backed away, and drove home.

All through lunch, I listened for the sound of a throaty motorcycle careening into the drive with a furious Mark aboard. I wanted it more than anything, because I wanted him to be real. I wanted the man in the parking lot to be mine. I promised myself I'd call him that night. I hugged the stuffed animal he won for me at a carnival when he was on leave. When I drove back to work, there was no sign of a handsome motorcycle rider.

Hoping for a message, I raced home after work. Nothing prepared me for what was waiting for me.

My father met me at the door with three words and tears in his eyes. "Mark is dead." He spoke those words softly; he could barely get them out. I felt my legs go weak and my head began to spin. "He was killed in a traffic accident in South Carolina," my father whispered.

The hard concrete driveway accepted my tears. It doesn't matter how many you cry, you can't fill up a concrete driveway.

I cried because I had lost him.

I cried because I had seen him.

I cried because I had passed by the powerful, pensive image of the man I loved, the man who had written about us starting to buy furniture.

He had somehow reached across a continent, so we could look into each other's eyes one final time.

Forty years later, I still visit his grave, in the same military cemetery as my father, for the sake of a bittersweet memory and a faded letter. I sweep the debris from his headstone — and the years with it — and I remember and I thank him for that last goodbye.

~Christy A. Caballero

Seaside Surprise

I think that someone is watching out for me, God, my
guardian angel, I'm not sure who that is, but
they really work hard.
~Mattie Stepanek

The bed and breakfast I was visiting in Newport, Rhode Island was a couple of blocks from the beach. I'm not an avid swimmer or sunbather but I love being near the ocean. Its beauty, energy, and timelessness have always been draws for me. I picked up a lunch at a local deli, grabbed a book and a folding chair, and drove to the high cliffs that famously drop down to the ocean from the "cottages" of Newport.

I found an isolated path descending from the road to the ocean's edge. As I headed down toward the water I realized that the waves were really angry. I backtracked and settled myself in a small clearing among the rocks halfway between the road and the sea.

No people. No noise. Wonderful isolation. A perfect place to read, meditate, and contemplate nature at its best — I was in heaven.

After a short while the waves seemed to calm a bit. So I picked myself up, gathered my belongings, and headed further down the rocky path toward the ocean.

Seagulls had been flying by periodically, briefly alighting—I hadn't paid any particular attention to them. I'd glimpsed one with a bent leg and another with a wing at an awkward angle. Still another had some uncharacteristic dark markings. But suddenly a huge, completely white seagull flew directly in front of me, landed in my path, and blocked my way down to the sea. Each time I attempted to shoo it away or walk past it the bird became really aggressive. It refused to move from the path and let me pass. Even pieces of bread broken off from my lunch sandwich, thrown a couple feet away, couldn't persuade this obstinate creature to move. Disgusted, I headed back up the path and settled into the spot I had previously occupied.

I was shocked when the gull followed me and alighted on a rock outcropping about three feet from my chair. It just sat there, as if it were watching over me. Other seagulls flew by — occasionally one would land at some distance and after a while take flight again. But this huge bird never left my side. At first he was a bit intimidating, but as time passed I was able to ignore him.

At one point a family with a little girl came down the path. Headed for the ocean, they walked by me and I wondered if the huge seagull would block their way as well.

Nope, he continued to sit there, still as a stone, three feet from me.

"Well," I reasoned, "If they can do it, so can I."

I got up from my chair and darn that bird — he immediately flew into the path once more, blocking my way again. Perplexed, I returned to my chair. He returned to his same rocky ledge, and continued to sit by my side for over three hours. It seemed like a vigil.

During that time the waves below became increasingly violent. The tide started to come in, and suddenly the location I had previously coveted further down on the rocks was completely inundated by a tremendous, powerful wave. I was stunned. Then there was a second, and yet a third massive wave.

Surprised by the ferocity of the ocean, I decided to drive over to the beach to see what was going on. Something really unusual seemed to be happening. As I packed to leave, the huge seagull finally flew off. He startled me by doubling back and swooping right in front of my face. I actually had to duck my head to make certain there would be no collision. And when I had climbed to the top of the cliff and was about to enter the road, this strange bird made yet another turn and swooped back right over my head. It almost seemed like a farewell.

I headed for the beach and was surprised to find it was closed. However, that didn't mean there weren't any people there. Hundreds, held back by the police and barricades, lined the roadside watching violent twelve-foot waves roar and crash onto the shore.

And then I learned that a massive hurricane had struck down in the Carolinas. A few deaths had already occurred. All the beaches along the Atlantic coast had been closed. Mother Nature was certainly putting on an extraordinary—albeit dangerous—show.

I had spent the day entirely alone, never speaking to anyone, on the rocks by the ocean's edge, completely unaware of the impending danger. Had I moved further down the path from where I was sitting I would have been swept into the ocean by the rogue waves I'd seen. This had already happened to two people south of us. They had both drowned. That would have been me as well—if not for the giant bird that spent all afternoon keeping me at a safe distance.

The following day, with the ocean still far from normal, I returned to the location of the rocky path down to the sea. But this time, instead of carrying my lunch, a book, and a folding chair, I brought a few bags of bread purchased at a local supermarket. I climbed down the path, opened the bags, and tore the bread into small pieces. I sprinkled them near where I'd been sitting the day before—all the while giving thanks to the seagulls wildly flying about over the still agitated ocean. I stayed a while, perched on the rocks, scanning the skies and my surroundings. Yes, the gulls with the crooked leg, odd wing, and strange markings were still in the area—they all seemed to hang out here together. But the huge all-white bird was nowhere to be seen.

To this day I have no idea why that big obstinate seagull was there watching out for me. What I do know is that without its mysterious intervention, I wouldn't be here to tell this tale.

~Marsha Warren Mittman

Just After Seven

It was possible that a miracle was not something that
happened to you, but rather something that didn't.
~Jodi Picoult, The Tenth Circle

It was April 1968. Dr. Martin Luther King, Jr. had just been slain and there was civil unrest in Wilmington, Delaware. From our second-floor apartment we saw fires across the skyline, and we heard the sound of breaking glass nearby from looters and rioters. There were National Guard troops in our streets and there was a strict curfew in effect.

As if that weren't enough, there was a serial rapist at large in the city. He had already raped five young girls. It was a frightening time for me as a fifteen-year-old girl.

On this particular night, my mother had gone to complete her daily welfare check on the elderly widow across the hall. Since my grandmother's passing, it seemed my mother created many projects to keep herself occupied — Mrs. Pope being her latest. Poor Mrs. Pope was so terrified since the riots began that she neglected to fill her Digitalis prescription. My mother volunteered to go pick it up but Mrs. Pope became distraught at being left alone — not ideal for someone suffering from a heart condition. My mother called to me, instructing me to get my sweater — I was going instead.

I was afraid to go. It was dark, I might be stopped for violating the curfew, and that serial rapist was out there. But Mom assured me that it would be okay and that I should just show the prescription if

I were stopped. So with prescription in hand, I grabbed my favorite red sweater with the pretty covered buttons and off I went.

The drugstore was two blocks away but it seemed like miles. At the first corner outside our building, I was stopped and allowed to pass after showing the prescription. The next two corners were repeats. I felt relieved. I finished my errand and was on my way home when I realized that the guards changed every two hours during the evening, beginning at five p.m. It was just after seven o' clock now, so I would be seeing new guards. And I no longer had the prescription to show them.

The first guard refused to let me pass. I begged him to let me go, explaining our neighbor desperately needed the medication I was carrying. His refusal was final.

I was afraid. Would he take me to the Armory where curfew violators were detained? The night skyline was already glowing with the fires being set by looters. I was scared and desperate to get home. So when the guard's focus shifted briefly away from me, I ran. The guard wasn't allowed to leave his post, so I escaped. I entered a dark, isolated alley that I typically would not have entered even in broad daylight. The alley was in the middle of the block and just north of my apartment building. I felt relieved that I would only need to pass one checkpoint to get home from there.

About a third of the way down the alley I felt such terrible fear well up inside me that I immediately got sick to my stomach. I didn't know what was wrong; I just knew I felt overwhelmed. I prayed to God for help and protection. I asked Him to please protect me and get me home safely. I kept repeating the prayer over and over.

I didn't see anyone the entire length of the alley. It was lined with metal trashcans while tall wooden fences and shrubs obscured the adjoining yards from view. My fear increased the further into the alley I went but I kept praying and moving along. Minutes later, I was safe inside our apartment.

A few weeks later, Mrs. Pope brought the morning newspaper to my mother. She suggested my mother read the article about the capture of the serial rapist. After finishing, tears welled up in Mom's eyes.

The suspect had confessed to all the attacks, giving accounts of the incidents and specific details that were known only to the police detectives working the case. He told detectives that there was one girl he really wanted but didn't get, one who was wearing a red sweater with covered buttons. The detectives thought this strange, considering his attacks had been escalating.

What made him back down from this would-be-victim that he so clearly wanted? He said that he was afraid to try and get the red-sweater girl, as he called her, the girl he had seen just after seven the same night that I was out, in an alley just north of our apartment.

Why? He said that two tall men dressed in long, white choir robes were walking on either side of her.

~Ruth Barmore

Saving Jordan

One thing you can say for guardian angels: they guard.
They give warning when danger approaches.
~Emily Hahn

Washing dishes has always been my pondering, preparing and praising time. The winter of 1987 was only different because washing dishes was not a choice, but an everyday reality in Kitzingen, Germany, where we did not have a dishwasher. Evenings tended to be very quiet after the boys were down because we were also television-less and basically radio-less since our apartment was out of signal range for the American AFN station, and I didn't speak German well enough to bother with the German stations.

This particular winter evening, I was looking out the window, washing the day's dishes and thinking about our life and how grateful I was for it. My husband, Jesse, was a U.S. Army tank company commander on maneuvers in the south, and his job allowed us to live in a beautiful village in Germany and gave me the privilege of staying home with our sons. Just that day, I had bundled up both boys in their winter gear, strapped them into the stroller, and rumbled over the cobblestones down to the village to buy our seasonal vegetables.

The ladies at the local greenhouse twittered over two-year-old Jacob and newborn Jordan. The ladies enjoyed spoiling the boys, teaching them German words just as I taught them English ones.

When we came back from our errands, I fed the boys their dinner and settled them down to sleep. Then I lowered the stack of plates into the hot sudsy water, figuring I would get the washing out of the way and then spend a cozy evening reading.

"Check the baby." It was just a fleeting thought, as I put plates in the drain board. I ignored it and started to wash the glasses.

"Check the baby!" This time, I felt it whispered in my ear. Even though I knew that I was alone, I still turned around to see who had spoken. No one. A still small voice, easily brushed aside as imagination. I picked up the first glass, swishing the cloth inside to clean it.

"CHECK THE BABY!" Crash! I dropped the glass on the floor as the louder than audible voice thundered in my heart. There was no ignoring this messenger.

I ran into the nursery and turned on the light to find that six-week-old Jordan was still and blue. His chest was not rising and I couldn't feel any breath coming from his nose. I picked him up and checked his airway, then started infant CPR while running across the hall to my neighbor's apartment. Jordan took his first gasp as Anita opened her door.

When living in the United States, I knew that in a medical emergency to call 911. In Germany, I had no idea how to call for an ambulance. I knew that we needed to go to the hospital, but the fastest way to get there was to drive. While I drove, Anita kept watch over Jordan, prepared to start CPR again, as I raced through the cobblestoned villages to the American hospital in Würzburg. All the while, the same voice whispered, "Peace, peace, peace. I am with you."

That calming voice stayed with me during the whole time that we were at the hospital. We were one of the lucky families. Jordan was diagnosed a SIDS baby (Sudden Infant Death) but he survived and went on to play football, marry his high school sweetheart, serve his country in Afghanistan and Iraq, and graduate from law school. Through many instances in his life I continued to hear that voice whisper to me, "Peace, peace, peace. I love him more than you ever could." I always listen.

~Sharon Carpenter

My Heroes

Dogs are miracles with paws.
~Attributed to Susan Ariel Rainbow Kennedy

Many years ago, I was a student at the University of Alabama in Tuscaloosa, where I lived on campus. I had an evening class that was a fifteen-minute walk from my dorm. No one in my dorm was taking the same class and neither were any of my friends, so I walked to and from class alone, returning in the dark.

One evening, I noticed two very large, black and tan Doberman Pinschers following about twenty feet behind me. I have always been an animal lover and I have never been afraid of dogs, so I stopped walking, turned around, and talked to them. They refused to come to me and when I tried to walk toward them, they backed up, keeping their distance. They were not threatening in any way — they did not growl or flatten their ears the way dogs do when they are about to attack — they just wouldn't allow me to get close to them.

For weeks, every time I walked to this particular class, the two dogs appeared and followed me. I was very comfortable with the situation, even though the dogs would not interact with me.

One night, a car with three young men slowly pulled up beside me, paused, and then sped ahead and stopped. The boys were loud and rowdy, and I remember wondering if they were intoxicated. As the young men emerged from the car, I heard one of them say, "Let's get her." As they walked toward me, before I had time to react, the two Dobermans charged at them, snarling and barking. You never saw three people get into a car so fast and pull away!

I spent the rest of the semester looking over my shoulder, hoping to see those heroic dogs again. Strangely, after that one night when I needed their protection, my guardians never reappeared.

~Sandy Alexander Reid

Embassy Miracle

Prayer is where the action is.
~John Wesley

W e were crazy to think we could pull it off again. We had adopted our first child from Romania a few years before, but now the doors were closed. The U.S. State Department warned us not to try, saying they would deny our child's visa. Without that we couldn't bring a child home.

Even though our Romanian lawyer identified a child for us, we felt conflicted over what to do. We desperately wanted this beautiful child, but we wondered if we could pull it off when government officials were telling us to stay home. We were tormented by thoughts of her crying in the orphanage without anyone to hold her and love her. We thought about her not having food, clothes, or toys. We remembered what we had seen when we adopted our first child. We already felt like this new little girl, Andrea, was ours, and we had to rescue her.

I began praying to God to send an angel to safeguard Andrea until we could get her out of the deplorable orphanage. Our Romanian attorney sent us a photograph of her lying in a chipped white metal crib; I kissed it every time I walked by the refrigerator where it was displayed. Looking at this picture and constantly thinking about her made us determined to get her. With heavy hearts we packed our bags and flew halfway around the world to try to bring Andrea home.

The first time I saw her I ached. I could see the fear in her tiny emaciated face as she sat silently and helplessly in the attorney's office. At ten months, she only weighed ten pounds! The effects of orphanage life were apparent and I couldn't wait to get her home and introduce her to Juliana, her sister.

Miraculously, when we first saw her, she was clutching a little stuffed dog with spots, the exact one that Juliana had insisted we send to her little sister "Annie" months before we ever knew about this new little girl, Andrea. Somehow, Juliana's gift for her wished-for sister had made it to the exact baby we hoped to bring home.

The moment our attorney gave us the necessary documents, we hurried to the U.S. Embassy to apply for Andrea's visa. Behind the counter of the consular section was a pleasant looking man who smiled when we approached him. I prayed again, asking God for a miracle at the Embassy.

The memories of Juliana's adoption haunted me. In 1991, dozens of prospective adoptive parents had their children's visas denied for minor technicalities. Everything hinged on this appointment. If Andrea's visa was denied, we couldn't bring her home and that would break my heart.

I nervously shuffled through the documents. I managed a weak smile. "Everything's in order," I began. "We have met all of the requirements," I said, nodding more to convince myself than him.

He examined each form and glanced at Andrea held tightly in my arms. "I don't see the agency paperwork. Where is that?"

I swallowed hard. "We didn't use an agency."

"We adopted Andrea privately using a Romanian attorney," my husband Pat said, pointing to the supporting documentation.

"Oh," he said, looking grim. "No agency?"

"No," we both said quietly.

"Now that's interesting," he murmured.

I reached across the counter and fanned the documents before him. "The law requires each one of these certificates, which we have provided."

He shook his head. "Yes, you have." He fingered through them methodically and nodded. He marked each one with an official purple stamp, and sealed them in a large brown envelope. "Here you go," he said. "Have a safe journey home."

Pat nervously took the package from him. "Thank you, Mr. Smith."

He nodded politely, accepted our thanks and watched us leave.

Pat and I held hands as we exited through the security gate past the U.S. Marine who faithfully manned his post. When we stepped outside, the bright sunshine warmed us. "That was too easy," I whispered.

Pat's forehead wrinkled as he squinted in thought. "I agree." Pat examined the envelope. "I know I'm not dreaming because I'm holding it." He leaned into me and kissed me. "Let's go home."

"Yes," I said holding Andrea a little tighter. I missed Juliana terribly and couldn't wait to introduce her to her new sister. We headed for the Swiss Air office and got seats on the next available flight.

"Let's go back and thank him again on our way home tomorrow," I urged. "We'll be near the Embassy. It's on our way."

Patrick nodded. "Okay. Mr. Smith made it incredibly easy for us. We really should tell him how much we appreciated his kindness."

I pointed to his signature on the packet reading his name, "Mr. John Smith."

The following day we entered the Embassy with our plane tickets in hand. A woman behind the counter greeted us. "May I help you?" she asked.

"Yes, we would like to see Mr. John Smith," I said smiling.

"Oh, I'm sorry," she began, "he's been on vacation all month and isn't scheduled to return until next week."

My smile faded. "He wasn't here yesterday?"

"No," she said. "I'm afraid not."

"You're sure. He wasn't here yesterday?"

She cinched her lips tightly. "I'm sorry." She checked a log, scanning the pages with her fingers. "No," she muttered. "Everyone who enters the Embassy is required to sign in. You can check for yourself if you'd like."

I scanned it and couldn't see anything that resembled the signature I had on Andrea's visa.

"You can leave a message for him. I'll make sure he gets it when he returns."

"No," I said. I bit my lip as my mind raced. "Thank you anyway."

Patrick and I walked to the end of the street. "What just happened in there?"

"I don't know." He sighed deeply. "If I didn't know better I'd say I was dreaming, or just stepped into the twilight zone." Pat rubbed his temples. "It took forever to get Juliana's visa."

"There really isn't an explanation, unless..."

"Unless what?"

"I think we met an angel," I mumbled.

~Barbara S. Canale

Chapter 2

Angels and Miracles

Miracles Happen

11

The Voice

When you get to your wit's end, you will find,
God lives there.
~Author Unknown

My husband had been out of work for months. We'd borrowed money from family members for groceries, gas and utilities. Bill collectors were calling every day and treating us as if we were criminals. Stress was eating away at our family.

One day, as I was driving to work, enjoying the silence and the beautiful Vermont spring scenery, I heard a voice. It said, "Turn on the radio." Weird, but I did it. Then I listened as the voice on the radio told listeners about a contest the local shoe store was having. This was the last day to enter. They were also giving away free pieces of pizza. All you had to do was fill out an entry form and you could win a cruise to Bermuda and $25,000.

I decided to stop at the shoe store on my way home. My son would enjoy the pizza and I would enter the contest.

It was a busy day at work and I ended up forgetting about the shoe store. Then I heard that voice again: "Turn on the radio." I did, and I heard the same announcement about the contest. I had one hour to get there.

What were the chances that I would hear a voice twice in one day telling me to listen to the radio so that I could hear the same pitch twice? I actually said out loud, "Thank you, God, for the reminder." Then I drove to pick up my son. He was hot, tired and a bit cranky. He just wanted to go home, but he gave in when I told him about the pizza.

A storm was coming in when we got to the shoe store, and the radio personality who was conducting the contest outside the shoe store was packing up his equipment when we got there. I quickly filled out the form he handed me. Then I drew a cross in the upper right hand corner of the small white square of paper and said a silent prayer.

By that time, the pizza was all gone, my son was disappointed and it had started to rain. We drove home.

That night, as we were all catching up on how our days went, I mentioned what I had done on the way home. My husband was a bit perplexed, as I didn't normally participate in contests.

I explained about the voice and my family looked at me like I had two heads. I warned them, directing my comment to my husband: "When my name is called tomorrow, I won't be able to hear it as I will be walking across the street to my job. Would you be able to listen for me and let me know?" He had a funny look on his face and said, "When your name is called?"

I laughed, stunned that I had said that and used the *Angels in the Outfield* movie quote, "It could happen," in my defense. I didn't think any more of it.

My husband didn't call me the next morning, but a coworker excitedly ran over to me when she got to work and said, "Kris, the radio station just called your name — you won the cruise to Bermuda!"

I was floored. I don't win things. My life had been hard lately. I get seasick on boats. I didn't know what I was going to do with the trip. I didn't know if I was on a timer to call back, so I called the radio station to confirm they actually called my name and sure enough, I won the trip! Because I won for my local station, the station was entering my name into the second contest nationally to win a gift card for $25,000.

I didn't think any more of it. I didn't hear any more voices.

Two weeks later I was sitting in a meeting with someone I supervise and the phone rang. During meetings, I typically ignore the phone but I had the sudden urge to pick it up. I apologized. It was the DJ from the radio station. I had won the $25,000 gift card!

My coworker sitting across from me looked at my face and was worried. All I could say over and over was, "Oh my God, Oh my God!" My supervisee was worried something bad had happened and I gave her a thumbs up assuring her it was a good "Oh my God."

We were able to pay back my family and get the bill collectors off our backs. Stranger things have happened to others, I am sure, but I listened to the voice and was rewarded. I still get goose bumps when I think about this.

~Kristine Benevento

12

An Interruption for a Miracle

Miracles come in moments. Be ready and willing.
~Dr. Wayne Dyer

I pinched myself to make sure I wasn't dreaming as Christy and I sped down the road with the "Just Married" sign flapping behind us. Who would have believed that our wedding day would end like this, I thought, as I glanced at my beautiful bride still dressed in her wedding gown.

As the miles faded behind us, I relived that initial moment of shock when I saw the police car coming up the long driveway of my uncle's estate where we were holding our outdoor wedding and reception. At first, I'd thought it was a joke that my brother, our best man, was playing on me, but I soon realized this was no joke. The officer was looking for me.

Leaving my place at the table, where Christy and I were enjoying the savory barbecued meat and other delicacies, I'd gone to find out what the officer wanted. He handed me a piece of paper with a woman's name and phone number on it. "You're supposed to call this number as soon as possible."

The woman's name meant nothing to me and I wondered again whether this was a joke. "But I don't know this woman," I protested. "Why should I call her? We're in the middle of our wedding reception!"

"The message is from your dialysis unit. They asked us to deliver it because the phone number here is unlisted."

The only message important enough to interrupt our wedding would be that the hospital had a kidney for me. I'd been waiting for a kidney transplant for five years.

As we walked into the house to make the call, I couldn't help but think of all the times the hospital had called me with good news, only to find out later that for some reason or other, the surgery could not take place. I didn't want to interrupt our wedding for another false alarm.

The hospital assured me that they had a kidney for me, but they added, "Your blood work on file is a day older than required so we'll need to do new blood work to be sure the kidney is a match."

"I'm at my wedding," I interrupted. "Do I have to come right now?"

"The sooner, the better."

"What do you want to do, Christy?" I asked my bride. "It could be another false alarm."

Christy looked at me and smiled. "Of course we're going! Why are you even asking?"

So here we were, on our way to the hospital, while our guests and families continued to celebrate at the reception without us.

Life on dialysis hadn't been easy. It meant getting up at 5:30 a.m. three days a week to spend five or six hours at the dialysis unit, then coming home and sleeping a lot. It meant watching what I ate and how much I drank, and sometimes getting itchy and puffy.

Unpleasant as that sounds, I'd reached the point where I was content with my circumstances, but was it fair to ask someone else to adjust to that kind of life? I couldn't hold a full-time job, and with all my limitations, I didn't think I'd make a very exciting husband.

Meanwhile, Christy was a rock. Her faith never wavered. "By our honeymoon, you'll have a new kidney," she kept telling me.

The last time they'd called me to come to the hospital, they'd taken me off the transplant waiting list because my white blood cell count had been too low. I wasn't sure if they had even put me back on the list later after my blood work checked out. Our honeymoon was to be two months after the wedding. I was so afraid Christy was going to be disappointed.

I glanced at my wife sitting in the passenger seat, a serene smile on her face. Apparently, someone had put me back on the list.

It was a strange trip, with my emotions vacillating between excitement and fear of being disappointed. When we finally arrived, and walked into the hospital in our wedding garb, I couldn't resist saying to the receptionist, "We'd like the Honeymoon Suite, please."

One of our guests had called the television stations and, after the lab did my blood work, the reporters and cameras started hunting us down on the ninth floor—the floor for celebrities and transplants. Our parents and our pastor arrived, too, as we continued to wait for the final word. Was the kidney a match?

I kept asking the nurse, "Any word yet?"

Finally, at 8:00 p.m., she came in and said the words we'd all been waiting to hear, "It's a go!"

Our pastor jumped out of his chair shouting, "Praise the Lord!"

Always before, when we'd reached this point, as we parted at the operating room doors we'd say, "If something should go wrong during surgery, I love you." Tonight our faith was so strong, Christy just said, "Sweet dreams," as they pushed me through the doors.

In spite of all my previous doubts and fears about what kind of a life I could provide for Christy, her statement about me having a new kidney by our honeymoon proved to be prophetic—even though its arrival interrupted our wedding! Our pastor summed it up well when he said, "Jesus performed His first miracle during an interruption at a wedding, but for Dwight and Christy, He interrupted a wedding to perform a miracle."

~Dwight Crocker

13

Divine Engineering

Family is the most important thing in the world.
~Princess Diana

My husband and I were driving to Los Angeles when I received a call from my sister. Bev and I had been playing telephone tag for several days. That wasn't uncommon. We were both very busy, and there was a three-hour time difference between us.

But this time she was calling with news so devastating that I motioned for my husband to pull the car over to the side of the road, so I could concentrate on what she was saying and not lose her call. I felt kicked in the gut as Bev informed me that she had been diagnosed with chronic lymphocytic leukemia. As she shared her diagnosis and prognosis, I tried to subdue my sobs so that I could be there for her.

"I can't believe this is happening," I thought to myself. Bev wasn't just my sister; she was my identical twin. Those stories you hear about twins reading each other's minds and feeling each other's feelings are true. But we didn't just share the twin connection. Our parents divorced when we were five years old, and life got pretty crazy at our house. The only constant we had was each other. We watched each other's backs through some pretty tough times growing up.

Between the two of us Bev and I were blessed to have five beautiful kids. Our kids were close even though distance separated them. When they would get together, it was like no time had passed since they had seen each other. I read an article many years earlier saying that because identical twins have the same DNA, their children have the same DNA as half-siblings. Our kids thought that was great, and they told it to anyone who would listen. They became delightful distractions when Bev got busy with her treatment. But worry about my sister's health was always lurking in the back of my mind.

"Help her, Lord. I still need her," I prayed often in the quiet of my mind.

My older daughter, Sarah was in the middle of her doctoral studies in psychology when she decided to join the military. Her husband, Shaun, served two terms in Iraq in the Air Force, and my daughter wanted to do her part to help soldiers returning from war with post traumatic stress disorder. After officer training, she was stationed in Ohio for an internship for a year.

When it came time for her to be assigned a base, I prayed hard that she would be stationed closer to home in California. After years of education, I knew my daughter planned to start a family. I didn't want to be that far away from my pregnant daughter, not to mention my new grandchild. My heart sank when I found out that Sarah had received orders to report to a base 2,800 miles away.

With all of the bases on the West Coast that need psychologists, my daughter got stationed in North Carolina. It didn't seem quite fair. I comforted myself with the fact that Sarah would only be two hours away from Bev. If I couldn't be close to my grandchild, at least there would be a wonderful aunt to spoil the tyke.

My kids weren't the only busy ones. Bev's younger daughter Nicole was getting married in Colorado. Not only was Bev busy planning a wedding, she had to travel back and forth from Charlotte to Denver to do it. During that time, she let her visits to the doctor go by the wayside. "Quite honestly," she told me, "I wanted to enjoy my daughter's wedding and not even think about cancer while I was doing that." I understood. He doctor wasn't quite as understanding.

After the wedding, she went in for her check-up. "Your blood numbers look terrible," the doctor scolded. "I told you that we have to keep them under control to keep this cancer under control," he chided. "What have you been doing?"

When Bev told him about the wedding, his comment was, "Too bad that daughter of yours isn't pregnant. You could use the blood from her umbilical chord to create new, healthy blood cells should your numbers get any worse than they already are."

"Doctor," Bev responded. "You know that I have an identical twin sister, right? And her daughter is pregnant and living two hours from me."

"You are one incredibly blessed woman," the doctor offered. "Genetics will make that blood a match for yours. We can harvest the cord-blood from your niece's child, and we will have stem cells for a blood transfusion that can turn your condition around."

During the birth of my granddaughter, my daughter Sarah assigned me the job of monitoring the amazing team that came in to harvest Eva's umbilical cord and save it in case my sister needed it.

I had no idea why God moved my daughter so far away from me. But he had a plan all along. I couldn't imagine in a million years that God was planning on using the granddaughter that wasn't even born at the time to save the life of the sister that I couldn't live without.

Today, my sister is still going strong, and I am grateful for the amazing divinely engineered back-up plan that is in place should all of that change. God answered my prayer in a way I could never have imagined. I don't always know what is best, but he does and he comes through.

~Linda Newton

14

Frozen

*Miracles are instantaneous, they cannot be summoned,
but come of themselves, usually at unlikely moments
and to those who least expect them.*
~Katherine Porter

My husband drove our sixth grader to the bus stop every morning because it was where our road intersected with a busy highway, with two lanes in each direction. One particular morning, my husband had to work early, so I took Joey.

When we arrived at the end of the street, I parked my car even further back than my husband might have. My husband usually pulled right out to the shoulder of the road. But I was thinking of my own father's warning that this was a dangerous location, because our road intersected the highway at the bottom of a large hill. You never knew if someone would lose control coming down that hill.

The bus approached and Joey gathered his belongings and attempted to climb from the car. However, his book bag strap became entangled in the car door.

The bus waited while Joey struggled to free his bag. A UPS truck came to a stop in the left lane, next to the bus, following the rules.

"Hurry," I said to Joey, "the bus is waiting."

But after Joey freed the bag and began to approach the bus, he stopped dead in his tracks.

I stared at Joey, dumbfounded as to what was keeping him. The bus was waiting along with the delivery truck. "Get moving, Joey," I thought.

Then, out of the blue, a loaded tractor-trailer came barreling down the hill, on our side of the road. The weight of his truck more than likely pulled him forward faster and faster. With both lanes of traffic blocked before him and no time to stop, the driver of the big rig had to make a decision. He decided to swerved right, onto the shoulder, and pass the stopped UPS truck and stopped school bus that way.

It was still a little dark, and there was no way the driver would have seen Joey walking on the shoulder approaching the bus.

Joey, strangely, didn't see the truck either. He just stood there, frozen, not moving a muscle, as the truck sped by right in front of his face.

In a flash, the truck was gone. The driver seemed to slow momentarily but never stopped.

Neither did Joey, for long. He unfroze, resumed his walk to the bus, and walked up the steps. The doors closed behind him, and the bus pulled away with my son safely inside.

As I turned to head back home, the scene replayed in my mind. Shocked, I started to cry.

I wasn't home but a few minutes when my phone rang. The bus driver called me and asked if I was able to get the license plate number of the truck driver that had nearly hit my son.

"No, it was too dark," was all I could say.

He said he couldn't see it either. I asked him how Joey was doing, and he said he was fine but very quiet during the ride to school.

"Did you see the truck coming?" I asked the driver, "Because I never did."

"I did," he said. "And I warned the kids, already seated, to hold on. I knew he would never stop in time. He was going too fast."

When I got my wits about me, I called the guidance counselor at the school and asked to speak to Joey.

They called him to the office.

I suspected all along that Joey saw the truck coming and that was why he stopped, but he had another story to tell.

"I didn't see it, Mom," he said. "But I felt like I hit a brick wall, and I couldn't take another step. It was if something was holding me in that spot."

To this very day, we thank God for His intervention that early January morning: first, for my husband's work meeting keeping him from being parked close to that shoulder where he might have been killed; secondly, for an entangled book bag on a door handle; and, third, for an angel to hold him frozen in place as a tractor trailer passed within inches of his face.

~Debbie Pinskey

15

The Mysterious Shield

Miracles do not, in fact, break the laws of nature.
~C.S. Lewis

It was a typical weekday morning, and I was looking forward to it. Since my husband had passed away the year before, I had only myself to feed. Although I still missed cooking a hefty morning meal of eggs, bacon, and toast for him, breakfast for me was quite simple. A steaming bowl of rolled oats, fruit, and milk, coupled with a cup of green tea was fine — then it was off into my office to work on some new articles, standard procedure for me.

That morning, the sun was shining, there wasn't a cloud in the brilliant blue sky, and the neighborhood hummingbirds were busily jousting with each other for positions on my outside feeder. It would be another pleasant day.

As I always did, I stood casually leafing through the pages of my morning paper at the kitchen counter, with my back to the stove, my teakettle steadily warming water for my tea.

Suddenly, with no warning — I heard a horrendous violent explosion! It shook the entire house! Whirling around, I couldn't believe what I saw! There stood the remains of my sturdy cast-iron stove, the top now shattered into tiny black shards! My eyes darted rapidly around the kitchen; I saw destruction everywhere! All the walls were splattered and damaged with bits of black particles, more pieces of my sturdy cast-iron stove. Tiny pieces of other kitchen items now littered the entire floor. The kitchen window was broken and the lid from a glass canister had somehow become completely unscrewed and blown down onto the floor.

And then I noticed something even stranger — there was insulation scattered on the floor! Where could that have come from? The attic? How? Glancing up, I found my answer. There were three large jagged holes in my kitchen ceiling; the metal trim on the ceiling light was now twisted and badly bent. Glancing down again, I saw remnants of my teakettle scattered over the floor, where they had fallen after piercing the ceiling!

As I stood there trying to make sense of it all, my nose detected an ominous smell — gas — now rapidly leaking from my shattered stove! For a split second, I paused, and then sanity set in. Rushing, I opened all the doors and windows to dilute the gas with fresh air, and then I ran for the phone.

"Hurry, please," I shouted to the 911 dispatcher. "Gas is leaking in my home. I need it shut off — now — before my house blows up!" I raced out of the house and called my son, Richard.

Thankfully, the gas company and fire department arrived in minutes; the gas was quickly turned off and my home was saved — but my kitchen was in a shambles.

After everyone left, I began picking through the damage. I discovered that the remains of the teakettle perfectly matched the holes in the ceiling. It had burst into pieces with such force that those pieces had almost gone through the roof — but why?

Everything was a total mess — glass was hanging in the shattered front window, held together only by the tinted sun protection film that stuck to it. I also found that the intense concussion of that explosion had broken another window, far over in my dining area. Surveying it all, I could only feel numb.

But then reality — and sheer puzzlement — set in. What if I had been struck by those flying pieces of metal and knocked unconscious? Or even worse — killed? My home would have filled up with that gas and blown to smithereens, with me inside. I began to shake all over, realizing the danger that I and my whole neighborhood had avoided.

Just then, my son arrived, checking to see if I'd been harmed. Other than being in tremendous shock — and still hearing loud ringing in my ears — I appeared to be all right.

Slowly, he and I began to check the full extent of the disaster — the damaged walls, the gaping holes in the ceiling. With great care, we began gathering up the shattered pieces of my stove, insulation, and loads of other debris littering the entire kitchen. It was everywhere.

As we placed the broken pieces of the teakettle and other debris into a box, my son suddenly looked at me.

"Show me exactly where you were standing when this explosion happened, Mom."

"Right here," I pointed, "three feet from the stove, by the counter, as I always do."

Then he pointed something out to me, which in my panic I had not even noticed.

"Look at that spot where you were standing," he said. "There is not one tiny bit of splatter or debris stuck in the wall, nor any debris anywhere else in the space where you were. The rest of this kitchen is a disaster."

To further demonstrate, he measured that section with his long outstretched arms, forming a semi-circle.

I realized he was absolutely right! That small area where I had stood was pristine; there was not even one tiny piece of damage in that area, not a particle, nor black shards in that wall anywhere!

Like a solid invisible shield surrounding the location where I'd been standing, I had been completely — and mysteriously — protected from any jagged flying pieces or deadly harm.

It made no sense. The pieces of debris had spread in a wide arc everywhere except where I stood, with my back to the stove, innocently reading the paper. I don't know how or why, but some kind of unusual force had formed an invisible shield of protection that protected me from injury, and maybe even death, that day.

~Kay Presto

16

A Husband's Magic Words

Here is the test to find whether your mission on earth
is finished. If you're alive, it isn't.
~Richard Bach

I was a nineteen-year-old college junior at the University of Michigan and my fiancé, John, was a twenty-two-year-old in his first year of medical school. We anticipated spending summer vacations working to save money for the next school year. We'd set an early September wedding date.

How excited we were planning for our special day! Then came a shocking diagnosis from my doctor at the Student Health Service. On a beautiful April day, I heard her chilling words: "You have multiple sclerosis. Your symptoms are consistent with a diagnosis of MS, and that's confirmed by the results of your spinal tap."

I immediately recalled a line I'd heard in television spots about funding for MS research: "Multiple Sclerosis is a crippler of young adults." I was terrified.

Mild symptoms had surfaced after a bout of springtime flu. I'd not thought much about the slight tingling in my hands, nor had I really considered that my occasional blurry vision might signal something serious. I mentioned both as minor complaints to my doctor on a routine visit.

"We'd better check into that. I'm going to order a spinal tap right away," she said with some urgency.

I wondered why the hurry but complied anyway. Later I learned my symptoms were classic early indicators of MS.

What about our wedding plans? Was marriage in my future at all, and what about our plans for a big family? Could I even have children, and could I raise them from a wheelchair? How long would I live? If I had children, would I live to see them grow up? And the scariest question of all at that precise moment: Would John still want to marry me?

I needed a miracle.

When I told John of the diagnosis, he didn't hesitate. That's when my sixty-year-long miracle began. And that's when I first heard John utter those magic words: "Of course we're still getting married! We'll live as though you don't have it and go ahead with our lives expecting the best. If we expect the worst, we'll probably get it. But if we hope for the best we're more likely to get that. Attitude is a very powerful medicine."

What a great and wise man I'd picked to marry! His response to the news of my diagnosis was upbeat and positive. I couldn't help but respond in kind.

As a medical student who planned to specialize in neurology, John knew well what the risks were. Yet he was ready to face those risks with me. He was ready to hold my hand as we climbed life's hills and staggered off life's cliffs.

John's been close by my side, ready to help hold me up when I needed him, but also letting me do things myself when I'm able. His steadfastness was the first part of my sixty-year miracle, but there was more to come. We followed John's plan to live our lives one day at a time, not brooding about my having an incurable disease. Instead, he insisted we look ahead to our future together and to what we might achieve. Between the two of us, we accomplished more than I could ever have dreamed we would.

In the years after our marriage, John finished medical school, internship, and residency training in neurology. Much more followed for both of us. We agreed to proceed with our plans for a large family.

"We'll just face the pregnancies one at a time. If all goes well, we can plan for the next," advised my very wise husband.

Over the years we had five children: part two of my sixty-year miracle. They all turned out to be terrific, talented individuals. With their spouses, they have given us nine grandchildren, all equally talented and terrific. My grandkids would be glad to know I refer to them as My Miracle, Part Three.

Did I have setbacks during those years of child producing and child-rearing? Yes. That's what life is like, even without illness. But each time, I recovered. After our middle child was born I lost the vision in one eye. After a few months of feeling like a one-eyed pirate, my vision returned completely. Over the years I had increasing bouts of leg weakness and fatigue. But what mother of five active children doesn't? I continued to heed John's advice: "We'll just go ahead with our lives and expect the best."

During the sixty years since my diagnosis of multiple sclerosis I've had a wonderful, exciting life. Because of John's work experiences we've lived in many places: Large cities; medium-sized college towns; twenty-five years on a 185-acre farm where we raised our brood of children along with dogs, cats and ponies; ten years on Mustang Island, a barrier island off the Texas coast; and now back to peaceful living in Missouri's Ozark hills. The variety of people and places in my life has contributed a satisfying blend of flavors to my sixty-year miracle.

On a personal level, many other facets of my life have produced incredible memories to treasure: finishing a college degree in studio art at age fifty; owning and running a photography studio for ten years; teaching guitar to youngsters during the 1960's and learning all the Beatles, Baez, and Belafonte songs they asked me to teach them; running for the local school board and making a difference in children's lives; teaching art to seniors; and tutoring high school dropouts in their quests for GED certificates. What a great ride it's been! And all because, as I approached each new challenge, I had a husband, friend, lover, cheerleader, coach, and advisor by my side who repeated his magic words as often as I needed to hear them: "We'll live as though you don't have it. We'll expect the best."

My miracle began in 1954 when I was nineteen years old. It's continued until now. I'm no longer symptom free. I use a cane now, and sometimes I need a walker or power wheelchair for longer distances, but so do many people my age. But I still play guitar and sing old folk songs for seniors at an assisted living facility. Recently I helped a young single mother study for and pass the GED test. Like I said, it's been a great ride and a great sixty years of a continuing miracle. I still listen to John as he repeats those magic words when I need to hear them.

"We'll just go ahead with our lives and expect the best."

I listened. I always expected the best. And I received the best!

~Toni Somers

17

The Messenger Daughter

Faith is like radar that sees through the fog.
~Corrie Ten Boom

"**G**o home!" the voice in my head commanded. I heard it as clearly as if someone were standing next to me. I didn't recognize the voice, and yet it was authoritative enough to make me rethink my schedule.

Again, the voice demanded, "Go home. Go home!"

I apologized to my friends who had made luncheon arrangements to celebrate my upcoming wedding, explaining that something urgent had happened. I had no clue what to expect as I raced home, but I knew something was wrong.

My dad was home recuperating from the amputation of his right leg, so I was imagining the worst. Despite his faith and his indomitable spirit, his diabetes was slowly taking its toll.

He never complained. He was a proud man, a hard worker, the best father, and someone who always lent a helping hand. He never made much money, but we always seemed to have whatever was necessary to make us happy and comfortable.

I saw my father's face in the front window as I pulled into the driveway. He looked good, but now I felt a little sick. Did I just imagine this voice? Was this some kind of mind game or pre-wedding panic? After all, I was getting married in two weeks.

As I walked through the front door, my dad looked surprised.

"What are you doing home?" he asked. "I thought you were having a special lunch with your friends."

I didn't want to upset him, so I said that I hadn't really felt like going. He accepted my story as part of "wedding day" anxieties. I was relieved to find him well but still confused by the power of the haunting voice I heard earlier.

"Well Dad, let's have lunch," I said as I made my way to the kitchen.

"Sounds like a plan," he responded. "Let's split a sandwich. I'm not too hungry today!"

He rolled his wheelchair to the table as I made our sandwich. As we ate, I noticed how good he looked, with clear eyes and good skin color. He was as handsome as ever. We talked about my wedding and his plan to use his prosthesis to walk me down the aisle.

He wanted to wear a white suit instead of the gray tuxedos the men were renting. "I just see myself in a white suit. Would it bother you if I didn't wear gray?" he asked.

"Dad," I said, "you can wear whatever makes you comfortable." He gave me one of his big smiles.

And then, for some reason, I blurted out, "Dad, do you ever fear dying?"

It was a question totally out of context. Yet, he answered without hesitation: "No, never. I've had many close encounters with death throughout my life, but I've lived long enough to see all four of my children grown and capable of taking care of themselves. I've had an incredible job, not much money, but I've traveled all around this beautiful country and made so many friends. And then, there is your mother, my best friend and lover of forty-one years; she is my lifeline and we are blessed to share an incredible love."

He paused and smiled. "However," he continued, "the most important reason I don't fear death is that I will see my mother again. I was only nine months old when she died. They say she held me in her arms as she took her final breath. I never got to know her, but I know when I take my final breath she will be there holding me again. That will be some reunion!"

Trying to hold back tears, I thought how blessed I was to have such a treasure of a father. With a hug and a kiss, I quickly cleaned up our dishes and headed back to work. I was thankful that I had that quick lunch with my dad.

That Friday night, my whole family was running crazy. Mom and my younger brother rushed out to pick up a pizza and get a car from the repair shop. Mom and Dad blew each other kisses as she hurried out. My sister and I were home with my father, talking on the phone with my older brother.

My dad pointed to a wedding gift that had arrived for me from a dear friend who loved to play practical jokes. The box was huge, and as my sister and I began unwrapping what seemed to be reams of brown paper, we were interrupted by a snoring, gurgling, awful sound. We looked up and saw Dad slumped in the chair, unconscious. My sister called 911 while I ran frantically up and down the street for help. One of our neighbors, a nurse, attempted CPR without success.

I went in the ambulance with my dad and I noticed, with concern, that we were moving slowly and with no siren. That told me he was already gone. The medics did take him into the hospital though, and it took another forty-five minutes before a doctor came out and told me what I already knew.

There lay that beautiful man, with one hand still open, inviting me to grasp it. It was then I remembered the voice that ordered me to "Go home!" Now I understood why. Miraculously, I had that conversation with him over lunch, when he revealed that he was not afraid of dying and that he believed he would be reunited with his mother. I would be his messenger for the rest of the family. I closed my eyes and saw my father dressed in his white suit, his mom embracing him, and I knew Dad had heard a voice calling him to go home, too.

~Lainie Belcastro

By a Hair

*Love is the one thing we're capable of perceiving that
transcends dimensions of time and space.*
~Interstellar

One weekday morning I pulled into the Great Clips parking lot for my normal quarter-inch trim. Then I looked in the rearview mirror and started second-guessing myself. Did I really need a haircut? I had driven fifteen minutes to get there and I don't know why I suddenly questioned my plan.

After staring into the mirror for a long time, I opted not to go inside. I would go pick up a prescription instead, at the pharmacy twenty blocks due north of Great Clips, on the same street in fact.

But then, I made my second unexplained decision of the morning; I started to drive east, back toward home, instead of up the road toward the pharmacy.

When I realized I was heading in the wrong direction, I decided to turn at the next intersection and head north. But then, for some reason I don't understand, I started zigzagging through the streets, not taking a direct route to the pharmacy. I felt like something was tugging at me now.

As I worked my way haphazardly toward the pharmacy, I came upon a sizeable traffic jam. It looked like it might be a wreck of some sort. I spotted a small street that would lead me around the slowdown and put me back on course in no time. The other drivers were taking the same detour, and as I began to follow them, I felt another tug, to get back in the traffic jam and head straight toward the wreck.

When I finally got to the accident that was causing the traffic jam, I saw a damaged white Acura SUV on the side of the road, right next to a police car and people milling about. My daughter Lauren had a car just like that. But it wouldn't be her — nothing bad could happen to my Lauren — the star athlete, tough dynamic mother of two little kids.

And then I saw her. It was Lauren. I parked across the street and walked over as casually as I could so as not to startle her. She was as stunned as I was. She had cuts and burns from the airbag but was displaying her legendary athletic toughness to be strong for her kids.

Thankfully they were solidly restrained in car seats and not hurt. I held three-year-old Ava while Lauren talked to the police. Ava wondered aloud why her car was so "dirty!" Little baby Drew was unaware of the upset, now dozing in his mother's arms.

Lauren kept asking me, "Why are you here?" I started to explain my haircut plans and my weird driving route but felt the whole story was too complicated and unbelievable. So I said, "I just thought you might need my help." As soon as I spoke I asked myself if that made sense. Did she understand what I meant? I later found out that she did.

My no-haircut day was over a year ago. I have often wondered how my meandering drive could lead me right to the crumpled SUV. I'm still puzzled why I didn't get that haircut in the first place.

~Doug Couch

Just in Time

*May your dreams be larger than mountains and may
you have the courage to scale their summits.*
~Harley King

I woke up at 2 a.m. on April 25, 2015, in the High Camp of Lobuche East Mountain in Nepal. I had to use the bathroom so I got out of the tent, did my business and got back into the sleeping bag. About an hour later we were woken up to prepare for our climb to the summit.

On my way toward the summit I had an uneasy feeling, thinking I should not continue. The climb was an acclimatization climb, a preparation for climbing Mt. Everest. Two years prior I had been physically ill from working too much. I therefore had a discussion with myself: Where did this uneasy feeling come from? Was I afraid the climb would exhaust me so I would not have the energy to climb Everest afterwards? Was my stomach causing problems? I really could not find the answer.

I told one of my team members that I was thinking of turning around, and she told me to do what I felt was best for me. Normally I'm eager to summit a new mountain, but the uneasy feeling continued. I started to climb slower and slower, letting the rest of the team go ahead. I told my climbing Sherpa that I was wondering if I should turn around. He asked if I was sure and I said I wasn't, so we continued to climb. A little while later I again said to him, "I'm thinking to turn around," He again asked if I was sure. I was not, so we continued.

This happened three times.

My team members had reached the summit and I was very close. Then I suddenly knew. I had to turn around.

I told my Sherpa, "I'm turning around." This time I meant it.

He said, "You cannot turn around now. We are almost at the summit."

I turned around anyway and started my descent. He did not say much, but I knew he was not happy that I turned around so close to the summit. I did not care; I just knew this was the right thing to do. The team members noticed I had turned around and also started on their way down.

We reached our High Camp, had some soup, packed our gear and stood there for a few seconds, watching our Sherpas pack our tents. We agreed to slowly start our descent; the Sherpas would quickly catch up with us when they finished packing up the camp.

From the High Camp and down, it's steep and full of rocks and sand. We walked slowly to avoid any accidents. Halfway down the Sherpas caught up with us, and just as we got down to the first place where it starts to flatten out, still with lots of big rocks, we felt the earth start to move — first just a little, then more and more. It was like time stopped. As the ground started to shake one of the Sherpas said, "Earthquake." I now understood what it was. The ground was moving so much we had to stand with our legs spread just to be able to stand. It was unbelievable.

We could hear rocks falling behind us. There was so much fog that we couldn't see them, but we knew they were coming our way. I looked for a second into the eyes of one of the Sherpas. We didn't have to say anything. We both knew: RUN!

Adrenaline kicked in and we were running like crazy, with backpacks and all. Throwing ourselves into safety behind a huge rock. Looking back at where we were standing when the earthquake started there were now big rocks. I still can't believe how lucky we were. If we'd been just a minute further up the hill I'm not sure how this would have gone.

Later that afternoon we heard that the earthquake had a magnitude of 7.9 on the Richter scale. It had caused tremendous devastation and damage around the country. The earthquake also had kicked off an avalanche that hit Everest Base Camp, only ten kilometers from us, killing twenty and injuring seventy.

Some of our team members were in Everest Base Camp when this happened. When we talked to them we found out they all had been sitting in our kitchen tent having a cup of tea as it happened. Our camp was originally supposed to have been closer to where the avalanche came from, but due to a disagreement it had been moved a little farther away. This caused our camp to be "behind" a little hill that more or less functioned as a jump for the avalanche — it practically jumped over our team and hit and damaged our tents that were more distant. Just meters from them people were dying.

We had originally been scheduled to be at Everest Base Camp by then, but we were a few days behind, because months before a local priest — a Lama — had told us to start our expedition a few days later than we had planned. That's why we were still doing our altitude acclimatization climb on Lobuche before heading over to Everest.

I must say that we really had some strong helpers on our side that day.

~Siv Harstad

Loss and Found

Everyone entrusted with a mission is an angel.
~Moses Maimonides

"You'll need to care for Mom now, because I can't anymore," Dad told us from his hospital bed. His journey with esophageal cancer was nearing the end.

Being the only child of four living in the same town as my parents, I was the one who could care for them. After Dad's death, Mom and I were inseparable. Because she was legally blind with macular degeneration, she couldn't drive, read her mail or handle tasks that required visual acuity. I helped her as much as I could, but found it difficult because I was working full-time.

Thankfully my husband understood. He said I could quit my job and concentrate on caring for Mom. Throughout the next fourteen years I spent time with my beautiful mother nearly every day. We became very close. She was more than Mom; she was my best friend.

I thought Mom would enjoy a dog or cat but wasn't sure that was a good idea due to her limited eyesight. With this in mind, I bought her a stuffed animal for Christmas two years after Dad died. It came with batteries and would bark and wag its tail when petted. It was a perfect pet for Mom.

A few years ago, when Mom decided to move from her home to an assisted living facility, she had to leave many things behind. Her new apartment was small and would only accommodate a minimum amount of belongings. But there was no hesitation regarding the mechanical stuffed dog. It was making the move with Mom.

I adored my mom. She was a strong woman, full of grace. The last four days of her life I stayed with her. I watched her sleep and attended to her needs. On her last day, I woke the moment she took her last breath. It was 3:48 in the morning.

Mom was gone. After fourteen years of doctor visits, hospital stays, and sharing tears and fears, her trials were over. I brushed her hair for the last time and said goodbye.

The day following the funeral we were saying goodbye to my niece, Ann, as she was flying back to her family in Atlanta. She asked if she could have some of Mom's recipes. I immediately thought of the *Recipes from Home* recipe book.

Mom lived the last three and a half years of her life at an assisted living facility where the residents contributed favorite recipes for a professionally published recipe book. Many of Mom's recipes were included and she had purchased an extra copy to give as a gift — should the occasion arise. This was the time.

In the midst of funeral arrangements, we had moved Mom's belongings from her apartment and stacked them in our garage. A few pieces of furniture and numerous quickly-packed boxes took up half of our two-stall garage. Because my brother was one of the packers, I asked him to help find the recipe book. Five of us were standing in the garage and watched as he opened box after box. None of them produced the book.

In the interest of time, I told Ann that I would eventually find the book and ship it to her. As we were trudging toward the house we heard a dog bark. It was the mechanical bark from Mom's stuffed animal I had given her all those years before. The batteries had never been changed and were most likely the ones that allowed the dog to perform demo duties on the store shelf twelve Christmases earlier.

No one had touched the dog that day and none of the boxes we touched were close to the dog's box. We were surprised by the mechanical barking, but we kept on walking. And then, suddenly, my brother came to a halt. He remembered packing the recipe book in the same box as the dog. He walked over to the barking dog box and pulled out the book!

I truly believe Mom was helping us. She was always well organized, even in her later years with limited eyesight. She knew what was important and where to keep it for easy retrieval. I'm sure she wanted us to find the book so Ann could have it before going back to Atlanta. Everybody was comforted by Mom's unexpected message. We gave each other smiles and hugs.

Mom's death was a loss for my husband, too. Every Sunday it was Mike who insisted we spend time with her. He never wanted to miss a Sunday with Mom. We took lunch and sat around her table talking politics, religion, her life and anything else on her mind. He often said she was his Mom, too.

A few days after Mom and her dog helped us find the recipe book, Mike was leaving the garage and the dog barked at him, again without a touch or bump. He was surprised. He walked over to the dog and carefully turned it outward to face the garage door. When he looked back a few moments later, the mechanical tail was wagging.

Was this another message from Mom? A friendly hello? Maybe Mom was telling him, "You'll need to care for my daughter now, because I can't anymore."

Although the toy's unexplained barking may strike others as bizarre, it gives me hope and reassurance. It tells me that Mom is still with me and will be my angel whenever or wherever I need her.

~Carol Greenley Papenthien

Chapter 3

Angels and Miracles

Messages from Heaven

Mom Knows Best

Even as a small child, I understood that women had
secrets, and that some of these were only to be told to
daughters. In this way we were bound
together for eternity.
~Alice Hoffman, The Dovekeepers

I had been sitting by her bed for over an hour, just watching her sleep. In the last few days, even this was a gift. I was thankful for each extra moment she was with us, sleeping or not. I realized it was almost noon, so I got up quietly and headed toward the door to make lunch for my boys.

"Kimberly," she said.

Surprised, I turned around quickly. She was awake and looking right at me!

"Hey, Mom! How are you?"

She smiled at me lovingly and instead of answering my question, she said clearly, "I was thinking we need to have a sign."

My heart smiled and cried at the same time. My mom knew that I would continue to need her, but she also knew her time here was almost up. She was still thinking of me, boundlessly loving, even in her last days.

I replied, "Yes, Mom, we do."

I hoped that there was some truth to "signs," as I had always questioned things like that before. I figured there must be some kind of explanation. I knew that if a "sign" ever really did happen to me, it would need to be very obvious to break through my skepticism.

She continued on quickly, like she had already given this some thought. "Whenever you lose an earring, know that I am with you. Remember how much I love you. Think about what is going on in your life and what I am trying to tell you."

Hmm, I thought to myself… an earring? I rarely lose earrings. My mom and I always gave each other earrings for gifts, but I couldn't remember the last time I lost one. I remembered hearing people say they had experienced signs like birds or sunsets, so I was definitely thinking more along those lines than an earring! Anything that happened a little more regularly than losing an earring once every couple years would have been great! An earring seemed like such an unnatural, material thing—if a "sign" were real—how could it have anything to do with a worldly thing?

In just the few seconds it took me to think of other ideas though, she dozed back off to sleep. "Mom?" I said loudly… but she was out. Why in the world an earring? I decided that the next time she was awake and alert I would mention it so I could change the sign. I now had a list of them that I was sure would be much better.

The days went on however, and there was never another opportunity to bring it up. She passed away a week later. I thought about this "sign" conversation a couple times in those first few days without her, and was disappointed we never got to come up with something else.

On January 8th, two days after her funeral, my husband, our three boys, and I loaded into the minivan for the six-hour trip home to Pennsylvania. It was a hard ride home, filled with many tears. We had all been in New York for the last month, and the drive home now felt painfully final.

My husband and I talked about weird things we wished we didn't have to, like what kind of vessel we could use for my mom's ashes. Our family had decided on cremation, so my brothers and I needed to find something small for each of us to keep some. I was really quite unsettled about the whole ashes thing, and found it quite odd. Now, we were driving along, asking questions like "What in the world do we put them in?" and "What could I possibly find that would be special enough for her ashes?"

An hour or two from home, I remembered a little box that my mom had given me years ago. It was made from some kind of stone, and the top had a carving of a woman holding a flower. The more I thought about it, the more I realized it would be perfect for her ashes. It was from her, small, pretty, special… just right. Assuming I still had it, that is. It had been years since I even opened it, and I couldn't remember the last time I saw it.

Pulling into our driveway, the finality of her death suddenly became more real. I fought back tears as I thought about the fact that my mom would never again be coming to our house. She would no longer be opening her passenger door as the boys nearly tackled her with hugs. She would no longer be smiling at me as she walked up to our porch, ready with some compliment that instantly made me feel treasured.

As I opened the front door, I felt as if I just arrived home from a different world. A world I never wanted to be a part of, but a world that now seemed more normal than my quiet, foreign home. The trauma that my family and I had gone through in the last month suddenly became real. Even though the kids and my husband were there buzzing around, talking and unpacking, I felt completely alone.

I stood in our doorway fighting back tears, then remembered something that felt more normal than this house right now… finding the box for the ashes. Just hours ago it was weird, and now it was the only thing that felt right. Instead of unpacking or starting dinner for our hungry kids, I headed directly upstairs to my room on a mission.

I found the box quickly. It was sitting on our bathroom shelf, covered in a nice layer of dust.

"Perfect," I thought, as I grabbed it, relieved it was still around. I opened it to check what I would need to dump out to replace with her ashes.

Instant tears flooded my eyes. I fell to the ground as I held the open box in disbelief, now crying while simultaneously laughing hysterically.

There, in this box that hadn't been touched in years, were twelve missing earrings of mine from the last fifteen years or more! Earrings I had forgotten all about! Some of them had been missing so long that

I had already thrown out the single one left behind.

As I sat on our bathroom floor, I thought back to what she had said… "Remember that I love you, and know that I am with you." Holding those earrings, I realized that somehow in this new scary world, without my mom next to me, I was not alone. I felt hope knowing that somehow, however this crazy stuff works, she really is still with us.

~Kimberly R. Sokolofsky

Not Just a Rainbow Story

Even your past pain can be a blessing to someone.
Hopelifters are willing to reach back and pass hope on.
~Kathe Wunnenberg

The day after my friend Nancy's twenty-five-year-old son was accidently struck and killed by a train, her younger son was at our house, listening to music with my kids. We were all in shock and to make things even worse, it was Mother's Day.

It rained that day, but when the sun came out for a moment, I looked for a rainbow. From our deck we have a good view of the Vermont hills, and it's a perfect spot for sighting rainbows. I saw one that day.

"Guys," I yelled into the house. "Rainbow!" My family is used to this—I'm a big fan of rainbows and I want everyone to enjoy the miracle. "Get out here!"

It took a while for the teenagers to come down and onto the deck, and by the time they did the rainbow had grown, almost to a full arc. My son was quiet, taking his cues from his best friend who had just lost his big brother. We stood on the damp deck and as the colors brightened a second rainbow appeared above the first one.

David's pale and confused face began to take on the glow of the rainbow. "Maybe it's a message from Kevin," he said.

"Maybe," I said. "Why don't you call your mom? She should be able to see it from your house."

I brought him the phone and as he dialed I felt the weight of grief where he was calling: his house was filled with neighbors, family and friends, all sharing their overwhelming shock and grief. It was possible that Nancy wouldn't even hear the phone ring. But she did, and he said, "Mom, you should go outside. There's a rainbow." And then he was quiet. After a while he said, "I can hear her running down the driveway." And then he said, "She's crying."

Of course she's crying, I thought. He hung up and we watched the rainbow as it peaked and then slowly began to fade. I hoped Nancy might think the rainbow was a message from Kevin. Maybe it would bring her just a little shimmer of light during this unspeakably dark time. Maybe it was a visitation, a smile from Kevin who had been a sweet, happy, and extremely friendly young man. Perhaps it was his way of saying, "I'm okay! It's beautiful here on the other side. Don't worry about me." The miracle of a rainbow as a Mother's Day gift was perfect.

The rainbow had almost finished fading. But then something awful happened. As we watched the last of the colors disappear from the sky, we heard the unmistakable sound of a train whistle in the distance. I grimaced and shut my eyes, trying to picture the rainbow instead of the train, and wishing with all my might that I could have prevented David from hearing it.

We were all silent until I finally said, "Maybe don't mention that part to your mom. You know?"

He took a deep breath. None of us wanted to think about trains. "Of course I won't," he said.

"I'm sorry you had to hear that," I told him.

"I'll be okay," he said, and we all went back inside.

During the next few weeks, as I visited Nancy, I kept thinking about that train whistle. Maybe I should have told her about it. A little voice kept saying, "You have to tell Nancy about the train whistle." But why would I do that? She liked the rainbow. She posted a photo of it and said it brought her a bit of joy on a horrible day. Telling her that we heard a train whistle would ruin it, maybe even ruin rainbows forever. But the voice persisted.

I had many opportunities to tell her, as I saw her often, but it never seemed to be the right time. I mean, how does one say, "You know that beautiful rainbow that you saw on Mother's Day? The day after Kevin died? Well, I heard a train whistle the exact moment the rainbow disappeared." I didn't want to say anything about trains to her. And yet, I finally did, using those exact words.

Nancy was at my house and we were watching the kids play lawn games. I felt the timing was right so I told her. I expected her to cringe, maybe even look at me with confusion and say, "Why would you tell me that? Why would you go and ruin that for me?" Or worse, "How dare you mention a train whistle?"

I was totally unprepared for what happened next.

Nancy took my hands and her eyes grew shiny. "This is exactly what I was hoping for," she said. I must have looked confused because she squeezed my hands and continued, "Don't you see? The train whistle means the rainbow was definitely from Kevin. Now I know he's okay."

As she hugged me and thanked me again for telling her, I silently thanked the voice inside that made me say the words I didn't want to say. I was so sure my words would only bring more pain, and instead they ended up being a relief. As Nancy and her family continued on the long road of grief I offered my gratitude for this moment, for this little rainbow of grace.

~Lava Mueller

23

Hummingbirds from Heaven

*Quick as a humming bird is my love, dipping into
the hearts of flowers — she darts so eagerly, swiftly,
sweetly dipping into the flowers of my heart.*
~James Oppenheim

I plopped down on the bed in my stepson Ryan's room and leaned back on the pillows, listening to the humming of the fan he always kept running in the otherwise silent room. On the nightstand to my left, a dog-eared copy of *Beowulf* rested next to a half eaten bag of spicy Cheetos. I looked over to where two loaded bookshelves lined the wall, with various sizes of sketchpads piled on top. In the corner, two of his guitars jockeyed for position on a chair. The electric one sat plugged into the amp just waiting for him to walk in, pick it up and start playing. But Ryan was gone.

"He left us too soon, leaving brushstrokes on our hearts," those were the words that Scott, the minister, had spoken at his memorial service just hours before. The church was filled to overflowing with flowers, family, and friends and the outpouring of love was like salve for my husband Michael's wounded soul and mine.

Ryan had made quite an impression in his short life. But that's what artists do. They inspire and move you to feel something — and Ryan was truly gifted. Tears streamed down my cheeks as I was again struck by how someone with such big dreams and so much talent could be killed in an inexplicable gas-can explosion on a cloudless July day.

After the memorial service, time passed, people went back to their lives, and we were left with a hole in our hearts and an empty room in our home. For the next few weeks, I lived minute by minute, sometimes half expecting Ryan to come walking into the kitchen for afternoon coffee. But each morning brought the fresh realization that the nightmare of losing one of our children was now our reality.

July became August and one afternoon the final accident report landed in the mailbox. I laid the large manila envelope on the patio table and stared at it a long time before ripping open the seal. Holding my breath, I scanned the contents, then breathed a sigh of relief, which quickly turned to dread as I pushed the paper away and stood up. "How are we supposed to find peace when there are still so many unanswered questions?" I wondered aloud as I paced the deck waiting for Michael to come home from work. Suddenly, I stopped as it hit me. If I could just see some kind of sign from beyond about Ryan, maybe, just maybe, I'd be able to begin finding some peace. So, I sat down on the deck and prayed: "Dear God, could you please let me see a hummingbird as a sign Ryan is okay?"

I don't know why I asked for a hummingbird. Well, I mean, I do. I love hummingbirds. But despite the fact that we load our yard with red flowers and feeders to entice them to visit, seeing even one a year buzzing around our house is cause for celebration.

The next day, I was sitting at the patio table enjoying the cool morning, when out of the corner of my eye I saw something green flitting on the purple petunias spilling out of the flower boxes surrounding the deck—a hummingbird. Then, just as quickly as he'd shown up, he zoomed off. Our encounter had been brief, but hope shone in through the cracks in my heart. I had my sign.

That evening, as we were eating dinner, I told Michael about the sign I'd asked for and received. "That's so great, honey," he said, offering a small smile, but the joy didn't quite reach his eyes. I knew he wasn't doing any better than I was, so I prayed for another hummingbird.

The next Thursday we were enjoying a late start to the workday with coffee on the deck. I went inside and as I was refilling our mugs

I again saw the hummingbird flitting near the same flowerboxes. It was close enough for Michael to see, but had he? I had the urge to knock on the window and point to it but knew I would scare it away. "I saw it," I heard him say as I hurried back outside. He was leaning back in his chair with his legs stretched out. When I looked over at him and saw the relaxed grin overtaking his face I knew, he'd asked for his own hummingbird sign.

While working in the yard one September day my thoughts turned to Ryan. Over a month had passed since the hummingbird sightings and the hope and comfort that had sustained me due to those encounters were beginning to fade like my summer flowers. Doubts began to creep in like the cooler temperatures of the approaching autumn. Had it truly been a sign or had I been hoping so hard I convinced myself? The summer sun had made its way around to the back of the house and was heating up the deck where I was working. Sweat started to pool on my back where the sun was beating. "Time for a break," I whispered and stood up. As I headed toward the house, my mind was focused on a refreshing glass of sun tea.

I had just gotten to the edge of the deck when something flew up right in front of my face and stopped. I raised my hand, intending to shoo it away, until I noticed its size and bright green belly. I put my hand down and stood there as it hovered in front of me for what seemed like a full five seconds. Tears of joy filled my eyes as it zoomed away. The message had finally and fully been received.

"There's no question in my mind, the hummingbird visits were sent as a message that Ryan is okay," I told Michael that evening over dinner.

On a dreary day a few months ago I went into Ryan's room in search of a book I thought I'd left in there. While combing through one of his bookshelves I noticed a sketchpad sandwiched between two books. I pulled it out and as I leafed through the pages a small sketch popped out. As I touched the small drawing, a smile spread across my face. It was a hummingbird reaching into a flower with its long beak. I'd just discovered another one of Ryan's brushstrokes on my heart.

As I sit here writing this I'm still amazed that just when I needed it, hope flew in on a hummingbird, solidifying my faith in things unseen.

~Amy Catlin Wozniak

24

The Brown Glass Fish

While we are mourning the loss of our friend, others
are rejoicing to meet him behind the veil.
~John Taylor

My sister Judy and I stood by our father's bedside as he took his last breath. He passed away in the early evening surrounded by people who loved him.

He had fought the good fight for two months. Judy and I spent hours with him every day. Our conversations covered a lot of ground, not the least of which was his growing faith. He had one son who predeceased him and four living daughters. Dad was very close with Terry's widow, Laura. Each of us girls got to spend precious time with him except for Laura, who was struggling with a debilitating illness and was unable to travel to North Carolina from her home in New Jersey.

Remembering Gail and Joni's approaching birthdays, Dad was relieved when I offered to shop for him. I asked if he also wanted me to get something for Laura, whose birthday was a few weeks later.

He responded, "No, we have time to do that."

We didn't have time; we just didn't know it.

When Gail and Joni arrived from Pennsylvania, Dad presented each of them with a pair of lovely earrings and what we girls call a "lumpy" card—a greeting card that causes a lump in the throat. It was a tearful, tender moment.

He died two weeks later, on a Wednesday evening.

That Friday night, I lay in bed trying to fall asleep. My head was filled with thoughts of Dad. I thought, "Thank God my sisters Judy, Gail, Joni and I were able to spend time with him before he died. We will treasure those memories."

Laura's birthday was approaching and I asked the heavens, "Dad, what would you want me to get for her?"

Immediately, in that time between wakefulness and slumber, I heard my father's voice clearly; "The brown glass fish in the little brown box."

It was definitely Dad's voice.

Aloud, I said, "What?"

Again, he repeated, "The brown glass fish in the little brown box."

This was too much. I sat up and swung my legs over the side of the bed. I had heard it loud and clear, but what did it mean? I got out of bed and slid my feet into my slippers. I walked to the room where Dad had slept and stood in the doorway, sweeping the room with my eyes. I saw nothing resembling a little brown box. I backed out into the hall, turned and went into his bathroom. Again, nothing that looked like a little brown box. I walked into Dad's TV room, looking from one side of the room to the other. My eyes landed on three trunks stacked in the corner of the room.

The top trunk could look like a little brown box to someone with macular degeneration. To confirm that, I sat in Dad's recliner in front of the flat screen TV and looked to my right. With only peripheral vision, Dad would have seen that as a little brown box.

I stood up, walked to the stack and picked up the little trunk. I couldn't even remember what was kept in it.

Opening the trunk, I saw that the top trays were filled with small seashells and a variety of jewelry hardware. No sign of any brown glass fish. I removed the top tray and saw larger items in the bottom. Moving them around, my hand found an unopened package. Inside, I found a colorful enameled glass fish pendant. Of course! I vaguely remembered buying it several years ago. By then, it was 1 a.m. I closed up the small trunk and lay the package containing the glass fish on top of the sewing machine.

I told myself that I'd look at it more closely in the morning.

Suddenly, in spite of being very alert just minutes ago, I felt incredibly sleepy, like I could barely make it back to my own bed.

In the morning, I awoke feeling well rested. I got up and headed for Dad's TV room to get the glass fish. It was a glass fish, all right, but it wasn't brown as Dad had insisted.

I put the package in my bathrobe pocket, went to the kitchen, and poured a cup of coffee. While sitting in the breakfast nook sipping my morning jolt of caffeine, I opened the package and admired the workmanship of the enameled glass fish. The sun was streaming in the window, foretelling a gorgeous summer day. Impulsively, I held the fish pendant up to the light and couldn't believe my eyes. It looked totally brown, the colors of the enamel weren't apparent at all. It was simply a brown glass fish when held up to the light. This is what Dad wanted to give Laura for her birthday.

I created a lovely necklace with the glass fish pendant and sent it to Laura from Dad. When she received the package, she called me.

"Can I open it now?"

"Hey, it's not your birthday yet."

"I'm impatient."

"Okay. You can open it. I can't wait to hear your reaction. Dad wanted you to have this. After you open it, call me and I'll tell you the whole story."

Five minutes later, I received a text. Laura wrote, "I will call you as soon as I stop crying."

I knew then that it had a powerful message for her from Dad.

Ten minutes later, the phone rang.

"Tell me the story," she said.

I related the entire incident.

She replied. "When your brother was killed, your mom and dad literally and figuratively held me up and held me together. I had lost my husband, and they had lost their only son."

By this time we were both crying on the phone.

Laura continued. "Dad took me fishing every chance we got. It was just the two of us, sitting in a gently rocking boat in the warm sun.

As we fished, we reminisced about Terry and shared our grief. I know what Dad wanted to tell me with this gift. He and Terry are together."

~Nancy Emmick Panko

25

Heaven Sent

Love recognizes no barriers. It jumps hurdles, leaps
fences, penetrates walls to arrive at its
destination full of hope.
~Maya Angelou

Cuddled on the couch, I wrapped my arms tightly around my preteen daughter, Amber, as she sputtered through gasps and sobs about Grandma Grace. "I just want to see her again. I want her to cuddle me. I want to hear her say that she could just squeeze me to bits."

My teenage son, AJ, was observing with a numb look on his face. I guessed he needed to get away from the overwhelming sadness because he slowly walked upstairs.

My husband, Randy, sat near us, searching my face for signs of how to fix this. "Kleenex," was all I could whisper through the lump in my throat.

He jumped at the chance to help.

Colbie Caillat began singing "Brighter Than The Sun" on the TV in the background. Amber lifted her head and calmed to listen. "Grandma's favorite Colbie song," she said.

The TV turned itself off and back on. The overhead lights dimmed slowly down while the dishwasher droned on, uninterrupted in the next room. Amber turned to look at me, her red, puffy eyes wide. "Grandma?"

Mom had officially died at 11:11p.m. on 11-11-11. She had waited until the only day when all five of her children were home and by her side, to pass. Her timing was extraordinary, almost orchestrated.

Eleven became a phenomenon following her passing, showing up repeatedly in bizarre ways. My toddler niece removed batteries from a clock at 11:11, and it stayed stuck. My sister lent out my mom's ski jacket to a friend, and found an 11/11 lift ticket still attached.

Besides elevens, there had been several other oddities lately. Lights went on in the middle of the night, there were an abundance of butterflies everywhere, and random orbs appeared on home videos, darting sporadically in all directions.

I wanted to believe that Mom was around, but thought I was being silly. Perhaps I was so desperate to know she was okay that I mistook the hard-to-explain occurrences for spirit signs. My whole life I'd been taught that souls went to Heaven, never to be present with us until we passed ourselves.

Later that night, Randy and I discussed the possibility of an odd power surge at the very moment Amber had calmed... which only affected that room... and had never happened before. The theory seemed far-fetched, but so did an actual spirit sign.

The next morning, with the family off at work and school, my thoughts replayed the anomalies I'd encountered for months. One or two might be explained away, but there were literally dozens of peculiar instances. "Mom, it seems impossible that you're really here," I said out loud as I tidied up my house. "Please send something so obvious that I can't deny it."

I opened the dishwasher prematurely and steam rose, then disappeared. I knew water particles were still around me, just in a different form. I contemplated Mom's new existence, one I could recognize without seeing.

Cleaning off my nightstand I found *The Third Jesus*, a Deepak Chopra book. A friend had lent it to me before Mom died, and I had only read a few pages back then.

I felt strangely compelled to open it again. The subtitle of the bookmarked page where I'd left off read, "Live with Grace." My mother's name. I was intrigued.

The second paragraph said, "Therefore the best way to live at this very minute is with the knowledge that grace is real, even if that knowledge is not truly present without a shift in consciousness."

I reread the sentence three more times and put the book down, dumbfounded by its relevance. The key words replayed in my mind. Grace is real. Shift in consciousness.

I retrieved my cell phone from the kitchen to snap a picture of the sentence. The text message screen was up and words had been mysteriously typed in the box, "Kiss Kiss."

Although it felt like another incredible sign, I considered logical explanations. Something must have hit my phone and auto-correct changed the words. But, no, the phone had been face up on a counter and it would take several taps to type something even close to "Kiss Kiss." I hadn't touched the phone in hours, and no one else was around.

Still, "Kiss Kiss" was not something my mom often said. Possibly never. If she was going to type something in my text box, surely she'd write something more recognizable.

The microwave made an unusual beep, pulling me from my thoughts. I looked up to see its clock flashing 11:11. It blinked on and off.

Things were finally too outlandish to explain away. I didn't know what "Kiss Kiss" meant, but the flashing 11:11 told me I'd better pay attention.

I couldn't wait to share my stories with my family. But at after school pick-up, both of my middle schoolers were overflowing with news about their day. Amber spoke first. "We had to do a district test today and write about a time we overcame something. I wrote about losing Grandma."

AJ chimed in, "So did I."

"Really? Seventh and eighth grade had the same prompt?" I asked. "Has that ever happened before?"

The kids said that it hadn't.

"I cried when I was writing it," Amber whispered.

"I did too," AJ admitted., "I had to put my head down."

My heart broke on the drive home as the children paraphrased what they had written. I wondered if Grandma had seen them writing and struggled herself, helpless to console them.

At home, I got out of the car and stopped for a group hug with my kids. A monarch butterfly fluttered nearby.

We walked as one toward the house. Amber leaned in, clasping her arms around my waist. AJ tilted his head onto my shoulder. Squeezing my kids, I leaned left to kiss AJ's head and right to kiss Amber's, and then stopped in my tracks, remembering "Kiss Kiss."

"Did you take your tests at around eleven o'clock?"

"I think so — just before lunch." AJ said.

"Yeah, mine was third period," Amber added.

I closed my eyes and silently told Mom I finally believed.

I leaned left to kiss AJ again and then right to kiss Amber.

"Kiss. Kiss. Those are from Grandma."

~Jeannie Powell

26

Drop a Dime

*The tie which links mother and child is of such pure
and immaculate strength as to be never violated.*
~Washington Irving

My mother lay on her bed, silent, breathing quietly and peacefully in her morphine-induced coma. Lymphoma was ending her life. As I sat next to her, I took her hand.

The part of me that wanted this over, wanted her to leave our world and therefore her pain, wrestled mightily with the larger part that couldn't imagine life without my mom. Although it seems trite to say that we were best friends, it was nonetheless true. She and I had a bond beyond mother and daughter; throughout my life she had been my mentor, my shopping companion, my greatest fan and my support. There was no topic that was taboo between us, no conversation that we felt compelled to avoid. We laughed shamelessly when we were together, forgetting the politeness that normally checked our attitudes, and finding fun in the mundane. We simply enjoyed each other's company.

She had been suffering from a form of dementia for a couple of years; one that violated her short-term memory but allowed her personality and long-term memory to remain intact. And then she was diagnosed with a rare lymphoma. An intense, difficult chemotherapy was offered to possibly prolong her life and she was involved in the decision to decline the treatment. Mom shrugged, "We all have to die sometime; I want to live until I die."

I travelled to my parents' house the day before Mom's birthday. The plan was to stay the night and decorate the house for her party, which many of our extended family members were expected to attend. But that evening, when Mom labored to her feet, Dad and I exchanged glances as her once normal gait became a shuffle. I pulled him aside and shared my concern: "Either it's reached her brain or she's just had a stroke."

We helped her into her bedroom. It was the last time she would have to climb the short staircase.

I slept on their couch that night, with the intercom nearby should Dad need help. Mom had come down with a painful case of shingles and was on regular medication so I heard Dad shut off his alarm during the night and say, "Come on, baby, here's your pill." The love and affection was so clear in his tone. They had been together since Mom was fifteen and Dad was seventeen.

The next day, Mom's loved ones surrounded her bed in celebration of the seventy-five years she had graced the earth. With assistance, she enjoyed opening her gifts.

I had to return home that night, a ninety-minute drive away, since my husband had just set out for a long-ago-planned camping trip and we have many animals in our family. But the next day found me back and my husband returning home, as it had become apparent that Mom was dying.

I entered her bedroom, unable to hide my shock when I saw the sudden decline in her condition. "I love you, Mom," I managed to say through the knot that was now in my throat. She smiled, "I love you too, honey."

She looked at me in earnest, "I am not afraid," she whispered, clearly but with decided importance. With lips pressed between my teeth to quell the quivering, I nodded my reply.

The next couple of days were fraught with the difficulties of navigating the health care system. It seemed that the normal resources for the dying were not available to us. Even hospice had too many people to deal with. Mom's doctor was on vacation and his replacement was gone for the weekend. Our community nurse was also on vacation. Thankfully, before she left, she placed a standing order for morphine injections if needed. As it became more and more evident that Mom was becoming anxious and feeling a lot of pain, we called in that order.

Once the first dose of morphine was administered, Mom relaxed and slept. We became acutely aware of when the next dose was needed so that the pain and panic would not upset her again.

Early on the third day after her birthday, Mom took her last, peaceful breath, as her husband and many of her family were near. We all said our goodbyes, cried our sadness-filled relief, and then one by one, we went downstairs to make coffee and phone calls.

I returned, alone, and sat next to her. As is often the way with grief, it held itself at bay, allowing me to process all the other information and emotions. "Mom, say 'hi' to our twins for me. And Mom, when you come around to visit, drop coins, especially dimes, so we'll know it's you."

Shortly thereafter, the dimes began to appear. Our oldest son, Jordan, found them in hallways, at the bottom of the outside steps of a building in which he'd just applied for a job, which he got, and at a movie theater.

I was telling a dear friend about the experience, via telephone, when I looked over at Mom's old typewriter table. A lone dime was sitting there. Another dime presented itself on a table in a hotel in which I was hanging one of my photo-art pieces.

A few days later, on the birthday of our youngest son, Ben, I took him for lunch. Afterward he called: "Um, I just thought I'd tell you what happened. I went to Rucker's to play some DDR. I'd done a few dances and was getting pretty thirsty so I decided to play one more and then get a pop. I put in the token and nothing happened, so I pressed the release. Out came $1.75 in quarters, plus one dime."

My dad and I found two dimes at the funeral home as we were making arrangements.

On the morning of Mom's memorial service, my cousin, Rhonda, and I stopped at the drug store. I'd hoped to find a dime that day, but hadn't. As we waited for the cashier, there, on the counter, was a dime.

I pointed it out to Rhonda and the puzzled cashier said, "I just found it on the floor, right where you're standing, so I put it there." When I told her the story, she shivered, and said, "Take it."

I wore one of my mom's small purses to the service. It had room only for some much needed tissues, my driver's license and my keys. When I got home and emptied it, out dropped a dime. "Well done, Mom," I chuckled.

It's been nine years of living without Mom, and the dimes are found less frequently. But, when life throws struggles my way, a dime appears, the darkness lifts, and with deep gratitude to the soul who wove her essence into my own, I smile and say, "Hi, Mom. And thanks."

~Diane C. Nicholson

27

The Craigslist Vanity

Flowers grow out of dark moments.
~Corita Kent

The picture that accompanied the Craigslist ad showed a beat-up vanity in need of a major makeover. It was perfect! The seller, who lived nearly fifty miles away, even graciously offered to meet me halfway.

I found our meeting place, a local IHOP, and pulled in. I surveyed the parking lot. It didn't appear the lady I was meeting had arrived yet. I turned to check the back of my SUV and discovered I would need to do some major rearranging to accommodate my newest "Trash to Treasure" project. I opened all of the doors, and stacked some items to make room. Satisfied with the results I climbed back in my car. I took one last look in the rearview mirror and discovered I had not shut the back passenger door. I got out and walked around to close it.

There on the ground lay a single red silk rose that had fallen out of my car. I bent down to pick it up when I distinctly heard a voice in my head say the words, "Leave it there, it's going to mean something to someone." I stopped and looked around. I had come to trust that voice but I certainly didn't want someone to see me and think I was leaving my trash for someone else to clean up. I shrugged my shoulders, closed the door, and got back in my car, leaving the lonely rose in its place.

I couldn't see the far end of the parking lot from my vantage point. I decided I'd better make sure my fellow "Craigslister" wasn't waiting for me on the other side of the restaurant, so I put the car in reverse and pulled out of my space. No sooner had I started forward than a lady driving the truck I had been waiting for pulled in and waved at me. I took the spot next to her, only a few spaces down from where I had originally been parked.

She got out of her truck and introduced herself. She was a pleasant lady in her early sixties. As she helped me load the vanity into the back of my car I joked that my husband would be thrilled I was bringing him another project to complete. She laughed and shared that she had always done the same thing with her husband when he was alive. We got the vanity loaded and continued our small talk. She mentioned her husband several more times and the fact that she was a widow. She shared that she was having a hard time since her loss.

I understood about loss. My daughter had died in a car accident only a few years earlier. I asked her if she was familiar with the *Chicken Soup for the Soul* book series. She knew it well.

I told her about the book, *Chicken Soup for the Soul: Messages from Heaven*, explaining that after my own loss I found great comfort in its stories of people who had dreams and received signs from lost loved ones.

"Yes, I know exactly what you are talking about with signs!" she chimed in. She prepared to share her story when she stopped, suddenly transfixed on something behind me. She began pointing excitedly.

"Is that a rose?"

I turned around. She was pointing at the red rose that had fallen from my car.

She was excited and talked as if she couldn't get the words out fast enough. "I always tell my friends that the last time I received flowers was when my husband was alive. My husband was always bringing me bouquets of flowers and little coffee cups with floral arrangements in them. Anytime I see a flower lying somewhere I pick it up and I think of it as my sign from him that he's still near. I have an entire collection of flowers I've found since he died."

I looked at her in disbelief. I told her where the flower had come from and how I was going to pick it up but a voice told me to leave it because it was going to mean something to someone.

She got teary-eyed and asked if she could have the rose. I stepped to the side, making room for her to pass. "It's yours. I'm pretty sure it was meant for you," I told her.

She walked over and picked up the flower. When she faced me again, she was crying. We stood in the parking lot a while longer, two strangers sharing their hearts with one another. As we talked the woman twirled the red rose between her fingers while her hands shook with emotion.

I left the parking lot with more than a vanity that day. I left the encounter with a renewed sense of faith. Turns out that flower did just as much for me as it did for the lady for whom it was intended. And I just thought I was going to buy an old piece of furniture!

~Melissa Wootan

28

White Feathers

A guardian angel walks with us, sent from up above,
their loving wings surround us and enfold us with love.
~Author Unknown

As soon as I saw the small feather angel on the car floor, I knew it was a bad omen. It always hung from my mirror and even with the air conditioning on full blast, the angel had always stayed put.

My husband John had been in the hospital for almost three months, and even though the doctors stressed that his situation was severe, there had never been any doubt in my mind that he would make it home. Now I wasn't so sure.

This had been a month of deaths. My father's cousin had passed away unexpectedly and now my cousin Roy was dying of lung cancer. I was praying for him to make it, not only because he was my cousin, but because I am a highly superstitious person and I believe that things happen in threes. If my cousin died, I was sure John would be next. When I received the phone call that Roy had passed away I ran to the bathroom and threw up my breakfast.

Now I picked up the angel and tried to hang it on the mirror again, but it wouldn't stay put. It kept falling down, so I put it on the car seat. In a daze, I started the car and pulled out of the parking lot. I caught myself singing burial hymns on the way to the hospital. This really freaked me out and I almost hit the car in front of me as I stepped on the gas instead of the brakes. I was hoping it was not a sign, but deep down I was certain that John would not make it after all.

When I got to the hospital, I received bad news. My husband wasn't going to make it. Five days later he passed away and I fell to pieces.

After being cooped up in my apartment alone for an entire week, not wanting to talk to anyone, it felt like the walls were closing in on me. My son had gone back to his life and I realized that I needed to face the world again, too. I wasn't ready to return to work, but I needed to get out of my apartment before I lost my mind.

It was a beautiful summer day so I decided to take a long walk. I started on the walking trail behind the apartment building, my head down, afraid to run into someone I knew. I suddenly noticed white feathers scattered to my right. I didn't pay too much attention at first but every time I turned onto a new path, left or right, there were more white feathers, always scattered on my right. For the last fifteen years I had walked these paths almost daily and had never seen any white feathers, and now they were everywhere.

My spirits lifted immediately. I knew at that moment that somebody was looking out for me, and I hoped it was John. During the following weeks I saw feathers every time I went for a walk, even when I chose a different route. However, as the weeks passed they were more scattered. By now I was certain they were a sign from above.

After two weeks my boss called and encouraged me to come back to work. "You don't need to do anything," he said. "But I think you need to be around other people."

He was right, of course. Living on a military base in another country, I didn't have any family members close by. And talking to them on the phone wasn't the same as being with them. To my surprise, working actually helped dull my pain a bit.

One day, after an especially long and stressful day at work, I couldn't wait to get inside my apartment, lie down on my couch, and give in to the tears. I was filled with hopelessness, fear of the future, and a little panic over how I would manage on my own.

As I came up the stairs to my third floor apartment, I gasped. There, on my dark brown doormat, was a white feather.

How did the feather get inside the apartment building?

This was not a breezeway building, but an apartment building with a front door. My whole body shaking, I picked up the white feather and barely managed to open my front door. I still cried my heart out as I entered the apartment that evening, but the white feather confirmed that somebody was actually looking out for me and letting me know that I would be okay.

~Karin Krafft

29

Wonders of Nature

What we have once enjoyed deeply we can never lose.
All that we love deeply becomes a part of us.
~Helen Keller

I have always loved nature. And my husband, Tom, and I lived on a beautifully wooded, two-acre piece of property that was surrounded by it. Barred owls and various species of hawks and other birds were regulars in our trees. Hummingbirds and butterflies filled our gardens. Turtles and squirrels visited the property so often that we had named them. And on rare occasions, beautiful creatures such as foxes and bobcats could be seen wandering around the edges of our small forest.

Sharing the wonders of nature was a very special part of our relationship. Whether it was a delicate, intricate spider web, a colorful butterfly, or even new growth emerging on a tree, sharing the beautiful elements of the world was something that brought us closer together on a daily basis. We even made a game out of it. Whenever one of us saw something we wanted to share, we would say, "Wonder of nature! Wonder of nature!" No matter what we were doing at the time, we always went to see what the wonder of nature was that the other had found.

Not only was nature my passion, it was also my profession. For over fifteen years, I had been a wildlife writer and photographer, often using stories and photos from our own property.

I felt like a fairy-tale princess, living in my wooded wonderland with my wonderful prince.

The bobcats were some of my favorite animal visitors. Bobcats are beautiful and they are primarily nocturnal, so catching a glimpse of one of these magnificent creatures was always a rare treat. But one evening, around dusk, I looked out the window and caught sight of several cats that I was sure were bobcat babies. I rushed outside, but by the time I got there, they were gone. However, several of the neighbors reported sightings of a mother bobcat and three babies and I was excited about the prospect of seeing these beautiful creatures for myself.

Several weeks after I first saw the bobcat babies, my idyllic world came to a shattering end. My prince, my husband, the love of my life, died unexpectedly. And the beautiful woods that had once brought me so much solace and peace were suddenly nothing but a sad reminder of how the best thing that had ever happened to me was now gone.

From that point forward, every bird, ever bud, every bloom served only to remind me of what was missing from my life: the beautiful soul who always shared these treasures with me. What had once brought immense pleasure now brought only pain.

I fell into a deep depression that I couldn't seem to pull myself out of. The days and weeks passed. I stayed isolated in my home, listening to the radio rather than the birds outside my window; watching television rather than the wonders that were going on all around me on my property. My woods had once been like a quiet cathedral to me, bringing me inner peace whenever I needed it. But now, I couldn't bear to be outside.

Then, one night, I was awakened from a deep sleep by the alarm on my home security system. I cautiously walked out of my bedroom and checked inside the house. All of the windows and doors were secure and there was nothing obvious that could have set off the alarm. I reset the system and returned to bed to try to get back to sleep. In a few minutes, the alarm started sounding again.

This time, after resetting the alarm, I took a very powerful flashlight that I kept by the bed and started shining it out the windows, trying to see if there was a prowler outside. Instead of seeing a person, I saw four pairs of eyes reflecting in the beam of my flashlight. The beautiful mother bobcat and her babies were all staring back at me.

And in my mind I heard the words quite clearly: "Wonder of nature. Wonder of nature."

Tears began to well in my eyes. To me, there was no explanation other than the fact that my husband's spirit had wanted me to see those beautiful bobcats. I stood at the window, transfixed, watching the cats as they wandered along the edge of light from the flashlight and headed off into the woods.

And then I went back to bed, feeling a new sense of peace that I hadn't felt since Tom had passed away.

When the sun came up and I finally got out of bed, I immediately went outside. I took a deep breath and immersed myself in all of the sights and sounds and smells around me. Everything brought memories of my sweet husband and the life that we had lived together. But I was no longer afraid of the memories. I knew that he still wanted me to see all the beauty of the world, just as he had when he was here with me. I could feel his presence in the woods now as a peaceful, guiding spirit, pointing out all the beautiful sights and sounds just as he did in life.

When I lost Tom, it was so easy to think that my happiness had been dependent on him. I mourned so many losses, thinking that life would never be the same again. But that night when I saw the bobcats I was reminded that all of the beauty and joy and wonder that were a great part of our life together are still here, all around me. All I have to do to feel Tom with me again is step outside my door, open my eyes, open my heart, and listen. And as I look deeply into the beauty of the world around me, I can almost hear his words gently whispered in my ear "Wonder of nature. Wonder of nature. Wonder of nature."

~Betsy S. Franz

30

The Splendor of Spring

Where flowers bloom so does hope.
~Lady Bird Johnson

Is there anything more symbolic of spring, more emblematic of new life and renewal, than fruit trees bursting into blossom after a long Midwest winter? Sometimes, the only thought that sustains me through those dreaded months of shorter days and frigid temperatures is the certainty that the glory of spring will eventually return.

That's why, every fall, after the leaves have shriveled and the brilliant green of the garden has yielded to a dull, lifeless brown, I faithfully plant spring bulbs. Hope springs eternal, even in the Midwest. Thoughts of pastel blooms nodding in the gentle breeze enable me to overlook my chilled fingers and the lengthening shadows as I bury each bulb, wrapped in a winter "overcoat" of bone meal and rich soil. This climate definitely challenges my capacity for delayed gratification.

One fall, in addition to planting bulbs, my husband and I decided to add a pair of apricot trees to our yard. I could almost smell the sweetness of the blossoms and see the flower-laden branches reaching toward the sun. We weren't really concerned with harvesting a bountiful crop of apricots; it was the beauty of the blossoms that we anticipated.

That spring, while the apricot trees developed tiny, healthy-looking leaves, there were no blossoms, no heavenly aroma, no shower of petals as a brisk breeze suddenly stirred. We knew that it might take a few years for the blossoming to start. The rest of the garden was glorious, though, so we didn't mind waiting for nature to take its course with the apricot trees.

The second spring was a repeat of the previous one: still no flowering. The following year, the same thing. After nearly a dozen years, the trees became something of a joke: our "mock" apricot trees. In spite of fertilizing and pruning and treating them with the appropriate organic nutrients year after year, it seemed as though they had no intention of ever flowering.

And then one spring, in spite of the garden's pastel blues and pinks and purples, my world went dark. My husband died unexpectedly, shattering my world and everything in it. The brilliance of nature and the glory of spring seemed to mock me in my black cloud of grief.

Slowly, I realized that the blossoming, growing flowers and trees surrounding me might provide some consolation. I would try to appreciate the springtime that my husband and I had always treasured, as a tribute to him and the long hours he had invested in beautifying our surroundings.

A few mornings later, I took my coffee outside and watched the butterflies flit from tulip to tulip. Then I glanced to my right. Overnight, the apricot trees had burst into a riot of frothy blossoms. My heart skipped a beat. Clutching my coffee mug, I sat down on the garden bench before my knees buckled.

As the spring and summer progressed, tiny green buds of fruit began to form. The nurturing warmth of the sun developed them into ripened gold. When I picked each blushing apricot, I felt as though I was harvesting a tiny miracle. Day after day, I collected the fruit, and, before long, I had a refrigerator full of jam and a freezer loaded with preserves. For months to come, I savored the taste of summer each time I opened a jar.

The apricot trees never bloomed again. Somehow, I wasn't surprised. The blossoms were there when I needed them the most, to remind me of the promise of spring, of rebirth and eternal hope — and everlasting love.

~Joyce Styron Madsen

31

Are You All Right?

In the night of death, hope sees a star, and listening
love can hear the rustle of a wing.
~Robert Ingersoll

I lay on the sofa for three hours, unable to move. It felt like there were heavy chains holding me down. On top of that, I kept thinking about Jim, my oldest brother.

"Jim," I said aloud, and then prayed: "Lord, I don't know what's going on, but I can't get my brother off my mind."

Finally, I dragged myself off the sofa and into my studio. With quick brushstrokes, I painted a watercolor of a pink and yellow rose. "That's for you, Jim." My words startled me. What an odd thing to say. I shook my head and went to bed.

Jim lived in Arizona. He was a reserve deputy on the Maricopa County Sheriff's Posse. Reserves aided in search and rescue operations. Jim was a veteran of hundreds of searches who had spent thousands of hours combing deserts and byways for people in trouble during his nearly twenty years of loyal service.

Heavy rain coupled with thawing snow from the mountains caused flooding around Phoenix that spring. Dry creek beds suddenly turned into raging torrents that washed away everything in their path.

Usually the men of the Sheriff's department were teamed with partners for safety. On that particular day, my brother didn't have a partner. He went alone to check on conditions at a nearby crossing. At the site, he found two young women who had driven into the riverbed on their way home and were stuck.

A neighbor was already at the scene trying to help. Jim said he'd try. He walked into the stream carrying a chain to attach to their car while the women waited inside.

Suddenly an eight-foot wall of water rushed down the canyon. Jim was swept downstream. They searched three hours before they found his lifeless body.

I knew nothing about any of this, though, when I was weighed down on the couch and then felt compelled to paint that colorful picture.

At 1:00 a.m. another of my brothers phoned to give me the news. "Jim was held under. His jacket was caught on a tree branch. They finally found him when the floodwaters receded."

I called my husband at work. They allowed him to come home early from his twenty-four-hour shift as a paramedic. Later that morning we arranged to meet my mother and other siblings in Phoenix.

Most of my memories of the funeral have blurred over time. Except one.

I was shocked to see my brother lying in the coffin, but the bigger shock was to realize it wasn't him. Oh, it was his body all right, but he wasn't there. His body was like an empty suitcase with everything of value — everything that made my brother who he was — gone.

Back home after the funeral, I got a letter from Jim's thirteen-year-old daughter. It had been postmarked the day Jim died. He must have mailed it for his daughter just before he went to help those two women. He had written a PS at the end of the letter, saying, "It has been raining again the last couple days and is now getting to flood stage! ~Jim."

That night I sat alone in our living room with the television on — more for background noise than viewing. I flipped through a magazine without seeing any of it.

From my place on the sofa, I had the odd sense that someone was peeking through the diamond-shaped windows in our front door. Maybe the neighbor kids were playing a game. I opened the door and stood on the stoop. No one was there.

After locking the door, I returned to my magazine. Numb once again. Suddenly I felt Jim's presence in the room. He spoke into my mind, repeating, "Are you all right? Are you all right? Are you all right?" Just like a big brother to check on his little sister.

I finally said aloud, "It's okay, Jim. I'm all right."

Then I felt him in my mind, saying, "I'm going to check on everyone else." And he was gone.

We visited my mother a few weeks later. She related the following incident.

"I needed so desperately to know Jim was safe. I stood here in the dining room doorway and said out loud, 'Are you all right, Jim? I need to know!' At that moment, the words of a song on the radio caught my attention: 'It is well with my soul.' Those words seemed like a message from Jim to me. And the peace just washed over me."

So, yes, Jim is all right. And I am, too.

~SuZan Klassen

Chapter
4

Angels
and
Miracles

Miraculous Healing

32

God Comes Calling

Coincidence is God's way of remaining anonymous.
~Albert Einstein

We were sitting on the edge of our bed holding hands while Rick gathered his thoughts. It was early Saturday afternoon, but I couldn't help noticing how tired and discouraged he looked. "What do you mean?" I asked.

"It's just too hard. There have been too many surgeries, too much chemo. I can't try anymore and I want to give up," he sighed.

"Give up? For how long?" I asked shakily.

Stupid question. He just smiled sadly, squeezed my hand, and walked out into the living room. He gazed out the picture window at the view of Twin Sisters Peak across the meadow and then lowered himself to the carpet with his arms cradling his head and closed his eyes.

"What can he be thinking about?" I wondered as I stood in the bedroom doorway, watching him. As a ranger at Rocky Mountain National Park near Estes Park, Colorado, he had hiked to the top of that mountain many times.

Things were very different for him now. Diagnosed with stage 4 prostate cancer at age thirty-seven, he had quickly turned away from being a "Why me?" victim and turned toward finding a positive path toward remission and even recovery in the face of terrible odds. Our sons were ages ten and twelve at the time of the diagnosis, so with great determination Rick decided not to listen to the first three oncologists, each of whom had told him to get his affairs in order and spend the six months he had left with his family.

After intensive research he decided on MD Anderson Cancer Center in Houston, Texas. The doctors there came up with a very aggressive regimen to treat his cancer. They would collaborate with an oncologist in nearby Boulder, Colorado.

Three years later, Rick had been through half a dozen surgeries and several rounds of chemo and radiation treatments. Throughout it all he remained positive and focused on living his life as a husband, father, and ranger instead of a cancer patient. He refused to use words like "victim," "battling," "overcoming," and "fighting." He believed that continuing to *live* his life rather than *fight* his death was the way to deal with his situation.

So you can imagine how disturbing his comments were that afternoon when he went to lie down in the warm, sunny area in front of the window. I silently recited the 23rd psalm, my "go to" whenever I am frightened: "Surely goodness and mercy shall follow me all the days of my life." Every so often I would return to the living room to see if he had changed his mind about "giving up."

Late in the afternoon I heard a knock on the door. I was surprised because we live outside of town and most visitors call to make sure we are home before coming over. I opened the door to two young men holding religious literature. This was the first time we had been visited by missionaries in the four years we'd lived here.

"Hello, ma'am. Is there someone in your home filled with despair?" the first young man asked.

"Someone so discouraged he doesn't know where to turn?" asked the second.

I stood there staring at them. How did they know? After a few seconds the first one cleared his throat.

"Oh," I stammered. "Yes, yes, we do have someone here just like that!"

As their eyes lit up at the prospect of being invited in, I smiled and told them, "Thank you so much for coming by, but my husband isn't feeling well enough to have company right now."

Closing the door, I turned to Rick and said, "Get up! God has a great sense of humor, and he is telling you today is not the day for giving up!"

Over the next year and a half, Rick continued to find ways to keep cancer as small a part of our lives as possible. He attended Denver University and became certified in Alternative Dispute Resolution. He created his own position as an Ombudsman for Rocky Mountain National Park and volunteered as a mediator in the nearby town of Longmont. Then, one day, when the cancer had returned and the side effects of the chemo were getting hard to bear, it happened again.

"I can't keep doing this. It's too hard."

"Alright," I said. Rick turned, walked to the living room, and lay down in the sun to fall asleep.

As I let fear wash over me I turned again to the prayers that had sustained me. I was surprised when I heard a knock on the door and opened it to find two different young people on my doorstep holding religious literature.

"May we come in and give comfort to anyone in your home today who might need it?" the young woman asked.

"You already have," I replied, a big smile on my face.

As I closed the door, I asked, "Did you hear that?"

"Yes," Rick answered in a resigned tone as he got up to go about living again.

The next two years brought more cancer, more surgeries, and more chemo. Rick was missing work and began to feel that he shouldn't accept anymore of the donated sick leave that had poured in from our National Park Service family. He decided to retire.

On his last day at work his fellow employees gathered to say goodbye. After the cake was served and the speeches were made, Rick went to his office to gather the last of his boxes and go home. Later he would tell me that after he got home he changed out of his uniform and gave in to despair and sadness once again. He sought out his favorite place of comfort in front of the picture window and fell asleep.

He was woken up by a knock on the door. You guessed it — two earnest young people wanting to share hope and prayer.

During the course of the next year Rick continued to inspire the community we live in. He was nominated to carry the Olympic Torch for the Winter Games being held in Utah. By this time the cancer had spread to his bones and his lungs, but he was determined to carry that torch and, five months before he passed away, he was able to walk and run his portion of the Olympic Torch route to the cheers of onlookers.

One day in late March, two months before he left us, he was lying in his favorite sun-soaked spot when he heard a very clear voice say, "Live!" Not sure if he was dreaming, he sat up and looked out the window at Twin Sisters Peak.

He heard the voice again, very clearly and lovingly say, "Live!" He knew God wasn't telling him that he would live long, but that he should make sure to *live* his last few weeks. And so he did.

~Lynne Nichols

33

She Found Me

The most incredible thing about miracles
is that they happen.
~G. K. Chesterton

I didn't open an independent bookstore in a small Mississippi town for the money. I opened the store to save my sanity five months after my son Perry was killed in an automobile accident. An avid reader my entire life, I always found comfort in books.

One rainy Monday, however, I found peace in that bookstore — not from the books — but from a source far beyond my wildest imagination. I spotted an elderly woman standing in the rain right outside the water department office across the street from my store. I assumed she had gone in to pay her bill and was waiting for someone to circle the block and pick her up.

But I was perplexed as to why she didn't take a couple of steps back and wait under the awning of the building rather than stand there in the rain. After several minutes the rain was literally dripping off the end of her nose and I couldn't stand it any longer. I feared she was senile or suffered some form of dementia and had wandered away from home. I grabbed my umbrella and hurried across the street.

As I approached her she gave me the sweetest smile. "Ma'am, are you waiting for someone?" I asked.

"No," she said simply. That was even more disturbing. She was just standing there in the rain on a city sidewalk?

"Would you like to come with me to my shop and maybe I could call someone to come pick you up?" She agreed without hesitation and, sharing my umbrella, we darted back across the street.

As soon as we entered the shop she said, "Oh! This is nice. There's a book I've been looking for." She seemed unconcerned that she was practically drenched, and though she seemed perfectly lucid I doubted very much that she had been looking for a particular book or, if she had, that I would happen to have it on my shelf.

She went straight to the religion section. The gray in her hair had fooled me but now I realized she wasn't nearly as old as I had thought. To my surprise she quickly made her selection and came to the counter to purchase the book. I remember it was a very thin volume on prayer.

I had meant to ask her if she needed me to call someone for her but I suddenly felt foolish. She was trim, her posture erect, her speech clear and precise, and her gaze seemed to see into my very soul. This woman didn't need anything from me.

As if we were discussing the weather she began to tell me about her daughter who had died. I struggled to offer my sincere sympathy but all I could think was *Please — not now. Not today.* This was one of those days I was weary of the pain and just wanted to wall myself away from it. I didn't want to share my own story and relive the trauma.

Her daughter had died of a brain tumor. She told me in great detail about the final twenty-four hours of her life. Perry's cause of death from the accident was a severe head injury. They had kept him on life support for about twenty-four hours. The account of her daughter's last twenty-four hours was almost identical to what I had experienced with Perry. How could this be!? I began to tremble with emotion yet she continued with her story relentlessly, her words slowly loosening the iron grip I had on my emotions. At this point I just wanted her to leave. I did not feel like reliving this right now and, quite honestly, I felt angry with her. Suddenly I burst into tears.

There was not one flicker of surprise on the woman's face. As she reached and took both my hands in her own, her exact words were, "Ah. So I have found you." To this day I cannot think of her saying those words without goose bumps rising on my arms. A warm rush of energy seemed to course through my body.

Without hesitation I surrendered to the wonder of her otherworldly presence. I laid my head down on the counter between us and sobbed as she gently stroked my hair. I remember being acutely aware of every drop of rain that fell outside my window and I was sure that heaven was weeping for me. It was no time for questions; all I could do was bask in the amazing feeling of love and peace that enveloped me. When I finally composed myself she asked if she could pray with me. Her prayer was brief and profound. After she left I could not remember a single word of that prayer but I will never forget its power. I only remember that her words were simple and seemed a little strange compared to all the prayers I had ever heard. It was not a prayer for comfort for my loss but a prayer for guidance in my spiritual journey.

She left, walking right back out into the rain as if it did not matter at all. I don't know how long I sat there. The shattering pain I had felt for months was lifted as I seemed to float in a space where I felt nothing but a powerful healing peace. Slowly I became aware of my surroundings and considered my encounter with this amazing woman. It was only then I realized I had never spoken a word to her from the moment I began to cry — never even told her why I was crying. She never asked because she didn't need to ask. "Ah," she had said. "So I have found you."

~Carolyn C. O'Brien

The Gift of Hope

*Do not pray for an easy life, pray for the strength
to endure a difficult one.*
~Bruce Lee

I left my Brooklyn apartment for a bike ride at about 6 a.m. on October 2, 2007, and it was an unbelievably beautiful day. There was the smell of fall in the air, the sky was a deep blue, and there was no one on the streets. The morning felt like a secret; it was so dark and quiet it gave me shivers. The leaves that remained on the trees on my block were starting to turn a golden yellow.

On this particular morning I rode past the apartment buildings in my neighborhood and then into the more commercial area: the furniture outlets and the mattress factories, the abandoned brick buildings with the painted names of past tenants chipping off their brick façades. I wanted to take it all in. I was feeling good. The world felt big and I felt wonderfully small.

About a half hour into my ride, the sun was starting to rise over the low buildings in the industrial area by my place and I decided that watching the sunrise as I rode out the last fifteen minutes would be a perfect conclusion to my morning workout. I wanted to see something beautiful that would stay with me all day, like a secret that I would carry with me.

Stopping at the light at the corner, I signaled to the car that was behind me, and to the truck that was in front of me that I was turning right. Neither of the vehicles had indicated that they were turning right, so when the light turned green, I took my right turn wide and easy, without a thought about the eighteen-wheeler to my left — because it wasn't turning, and for that matter the car behind it wasn't either. I thought I had tons of room.

I didn't.

The truck driver hadn't seen my indication that I was going to turn right. He hadn't seen me at all. All he saw was a green light, and he turned.

The last thing I remember before actually being run over was the hollow sound of my fist banging the side of the truck, and then I felt as though I was tumbling. I don't know where my bike went. I knew I was on the road, and there was this moment when I thought, "Am I in an action movie? This is the kind of stuff that happens in action movies. What can I do to stop this?"

The answer was nothing. There was nothing I could do.

Before I even really realized what was happening, I felt pressure and then heard a cracking sound. The realization that the cracking was my bones shocked me. I squeezed my eyes shut, and I felt the first four wheels of the truck run over my body. I didn't have time to process the pain. All I could think was, "Sweet Jesus, please let this man stop before the second set of wheels comes for me."

"No, no, no, please God no," I shrieked before the second set of wheels rolled over my already crushed middle.

This time I kept my eyes open. I watched those giant wheels run over my body. I heard more cracking and felt the grooves in the tires on my skin. I heard the mud flaps thwack over me. I felt gravel in my back.

I lay there waiting for something to change, to get better or worse. I waited for a break in the silence that kept ringing in my ears. I remember looking up as the early morning sky went from that deep blue to a sunlight-pale, pale blue — the clouds looked as if they were whipped out of cotton candy.

As the initial shock of impact began to wear off, my body reacted with crushing pain. It was unlike anything I could have imagined.

This excruciating pain was doing relay races up and down the length of my body. I didn't know what to do. I didn't know how to stop it. I couldn't shake it off, or massage it, or walk to a place that I thought would somehow give me relief. I had no choice but to just lie there, trying not to drown in it. I began to pray every prayer that I had ever learned. I begged God to help me, to save me, to not abandon me.

Moments later, as if summoned, a middle-aged man in khaki cargo shorts, a plaid short-sleeve shirt, and a New York Yankees hat stepped out of his Toyota Camry and walked toward my spot on the asphalt.

With no hesitation he slipped his rough hand into mine, looked into my eyes, and with a Spanish accent and a confident tone said, "Listen to me, I am a pastor — I have spoken to God, and he has told me you are not going to die today. Okay?"

I needed for him to be right. "Do you promise?" I asked, with the sincerity of a six-year-old.

"Yes," he promised. If I could have lifted my hand, I would have made him pinky swear.

He took my other hand and said, "Let us say the Lord's Prayer," and as I held his hand and said the prayer that I had been saying since I was four years old, I suddenly felt less alone, less afraid and I was filled with a feeling that surprised me. I felt hope. I knew this person had come to give me strength when I was at my weakest.

Because of that hope, I began to fight for my life. I was backed into the corner, but I had to keep punching. I had to have faith that I was going make it through this. Even as the emergency room doctor told me that I probably wouldn't make it through the surgery, I still held tight to that hope.

After five hours of emergency surgery, the doctors told my parents my blood wasn't clotting and they were going to give me one more hour of blood transfusions before they gave up and let me go. With only fifteen minutes until my deadline, my blood miraculously began to clot.

I later found out that October 2nd is the Feast Day of the Guardian Angels. Every year on that date I go to the corner where I almost lost my life. I bring a glass of champagne for myself, and one for my angel, to celebrate the gift that I was given that day. I raise my glass, say the "Our Father" and count my blessings that my angel kept his promise, and gave me the greatest gift I have ever received: hope.

~Katie McKenna

35

Visiting Nurse

*Faith is courage; it is creative while despair
is always destructive.*
~David S. Muzzey

My brother Juan was barely eight years old when he contracted polio. I was five and remember the day so well. The year was 1949 and there was no cure for the crippling disease. Mother noticed Juan's flushed face and felt his forehead. He was burning up with fever. She repeatedly applied cold compresses and tried home remedies that usually worked, but not this time. Dysentery and vomiting soon followed and Juan complained that he could not feel his legs.

Mother quickly picked him up in her arms and hollered, "Let's go, Maria. I'm taking your brother to the doctor!"

As we hurried to the bus stop, Mother struggled with Juan's weight. He was tall and his legs motionless.

Once we arrived at the clinic, doctors examined Juan and gave Mother the bad news: "Your son has polio."

Mother walked out of the clinic with tears streaming down her face. I cried with her.

"Why Juan, dear God? Why Juan!" she repeated over and over.

Father worked long hours at a brewery and Mother had no one else to turn to.

Two weeks later, Juan had an appointment with a specialist at a distant clinic. With Juan in her arms and me holding onto her dress, we boarded an old bus that would take us to our destination. Mother truly hoped for better news.

During the examination, the specialist extracted fluid from one of Juan's legs and gave Mother the gloomy diagnosis: "Your son will be a cripple for life. He will eventually lose every bit of strength in his legs and he will never walk again."

Instead of going straight home, we walked into a cathedral next to the clinic. Mother headed to the altar and placed Juan at the foot of Jesus on the Cross. I knelt next to Mother and watched as she prayed with all her heart and soul.

"Oh dear Jesus," she said looking up at the cross. "Please heal my son. Help him walk again. Make him well. If not, take him with you. While I'm here on earth, I can take care of him, but what is going to happen when I am no longer here?"

With despair in her voice, she ended her prayer with the words, "Just give me a sign. I'll do anything to heal him."

Three days later, Mother stood in front of the house, watering her small garden. Although she had forgotten to water her plants, they still had fresh blooms.

While I played on the front porch with my favorite doll, Juan rocked back and forth in a small rocking chair next to the front door. Mother had wrapped a wide belt around his waist to keep him from falling forward. As Juan rocked, he watched three tiny birds chirping noisily in a nest above us.

Suddenly, from out of nowhere, an elderly woman appeared at the front gate. Mother had not seen her because she had her back turned.

"Good morning. How are you today?" the lady greeted her.

The lady wore a long, black skirt and a white blouse, and she had a black shawl draped over her shoulders. Her hair was rolled into a ball in the back.

"Oh my, you have such beautiful flowers!" the lady remarked in a sweet, angelic voice.

"Thank you," said Mother. "Would you like some plant cuttings?"

The lady accepted the cuttings and when she turned her head, she spotted Juan in the rocker, swaying back and forth. She smiled at him and he smiled back.

"What's wrong with your little boy?" she asked.

Mother explained that Juan had contracted polio and doctors had given no hope for a cure.

"May I come in to see your little boy?" the lady asked.

"Of course," said Mother, quickly unfastening the latch on the gate to let her in.

The lady got on her knees and gently removed the blanket wrapped around Juan's legs. Mother kept his legs covered because they always felt cold.

While she examined Juan's legs, she looked up at him with love. Then she proceeded to rub her hands up and down, from his hips to his toes. Afterward, she wrapped him up again.

"Your son will regain the movement of his legs," she told Mother, "but you must do what I tell you, and you have to do it hour after hour, day after day without fail."

"I'll do anything, no matter what it is, to heal him," said Mother.

The lady then gave her instructions: "First, you get some flannel cloth and cut it into small pieces. Next, you place it into a bucket with warm water. With a soft brush, you massage him from the waist down to his toes. Then, you wrap his legs from his hips to his toes using the wet, flannel cloth."

"Remember, the water must be kept as warm as possible," she repeated twice. "If you do exactly as I tell you, your son will get well."

Mother did not know how to thank the lady. She quickly bent down to pick up the plant cuttings the lady had placed on the ground and when she turned around, the lady had disappeared.

"Do you see her, Maria?" Mother asked me.

"No," I said, looking down the street. "I don't see her anywhere."

Mother inquired with neighbors about the lady, but no one seemed to know her. We never saw her again.

Day after day and night after night, Mother followed the lady's instructions. She repeatedly rubbed Juan's legs with a soft brush and then followed up with the soaked flannel cloths.

As a result of continuously soaking her hands in hot water, she developed large sores on her hands and her skin peeled. But she would not give up.

Mother encouraged the mothers of other children who had contracted polio to do as she did but they only criticized her.

"There is no cure for the disease. You're killing yourself and nothing will be accomplished," they said.

Mother ignored their remarks and soon proved them wrong. After two months of non-stop therapy, Juan moved one of his big toes. Mother cried tears of happiness. Juan's progress only gave her more reason to continue the treatment, even if it meant a sacrifice on her part. She barely slept and lost a lot of weight because she skipped meals. Her only goal was to heal my brother.

Two more months passed and Juan began to move his legs by himself. Within three months, he crawled like a baby and by the time school started, he was ready to walk to school with his friends.

Mother and I strolled into church one morning with Juan at our side. We headed to the altar and Juan knelt before Jesus on the Cross.

"Thank you, Jesus, for healing me," he said.

I truly believe that Mother's love, faith and persistence played a major role in my brother's healing. Juan became Mother's "little miracle." In high school, he played baseball and football, and after he graduated from college, he became a law enforcement officer.

~Mary Vela

36

A Close Call

*The miracle of self-healing occurs when the inner
patient yields to the inner physician.*
~Vernon Howard

I was visiting friends near Orangeville, Ontario one summer weekend. They had a trampoline set up in their back yard on a grassy knoll. I loved the feeling of freedom as I bounced leisurely on the trampoline under the open blue sky. One of my friends, a tall young man joined me. We laughed as we alternated launching off the springy surface, like two kids on a seesaw.

We didn't know that two adults aren't supposed to jump together on a trampoline, and I began to go off to the side, being no match for his weight. I lost control and flipped over the edge of the metal frame and landed hard on the back of my head. The sound of my neck cracking was like dominoes falling on a hard surface. I lay on the ground without moving.

Several people came running. A woman tried to help me up but I felt a sharp pain shoot up my neck. I recalled from a first aid course that it is not recommended to move a person with a spinal injury. I asked her to call an ambulance.

When the paramedics arrived they placed a cervical collar around my neck and shifted me onto a transfer board. I was rushed to the hospital in Orangeville. The X-ray revealed subluxations of the C2 and C3 vertebrae. The bones were dislocated and essentially nothing was supporting my head. The doctor was concerned that one of the vertebra would nick or sever my spinal cord.

I remember looking at the film, thinking how odd it was to see my own skeleton. The technician had not removed my silver rabbit earrings before taking the X-rays, so I could see small rabbit-shaped shadows dangling from each side of my skull.

The doctor in Orangeville sent me to Sunnybrook Hospital in Toronto because it specializes in spinal injuries. A few hours after the fall from the trampoline, I was in a second hospital getting a second set of X-rays. It was not comfortable being strapped to a board with the ability only to move my arms. The pressure from the hard surface on the back of my skull was painful. It all seemed surreal.

It was a Sunday evening and only one surgeon was on staff who could handle spinal injuries. He would perform a procedure to stabilize my neck and protect my spinal cord. That required drilling into my skull and screwing in a metal halo. It would be attached to a vest with a frame to brace my spine. I would be in a wheelchair for a few months until it healed. I would have to stay in that hospital for several weeks.

I wanted to talk to my family before consenting to surgery. I hoped I could be airlifted to a hospital in Ottawa closer to home. An orderly wheeled me on the gurney to a phone. I called my mother and she agreed to look into having me flown back.

Then I called my grandmother, a Cherokee Elder, visionary and healer. She brought something important to my attention; that for some time my body had been trying to communicate with me but I had not listened. The injury to my neck was symbolic of a conflict between my body and mind. She asked for my thoughts on having the doctor do the procedure or considering alternatives. I told her I wanted the alternatives. She offered to do a healing ceremony, but I had to do my part by taking a Medicine Journey and facing what I saw there. I agreed to do it, just before the orderly showed up to take me back to the room.

The doctor returned with news. Situations had arisen due to a huge storm rolling into the city. Extreme high winds had shut down the airport and I could not be airlifted. He intended to perform the surgery himself, but I would have to wait. A golfer had been flipped over in his golf cart by the wind and his skull was crushed. He was in critical condition, so his surgery came first.

I fell asleep while waiting. The next time I saw the doctor, it was 3 a.m. He was too exhausted to begin another surgery. He sent me to the intensive care unit (ICU) to wait for the doctor on the next shift. I lay there, remembering the instructions from my grandmother. I had no idea what a Medicine Journey was, and regretted not asking. I decided to do my best. Closing my eyes, I began.

In my mind's eye I was standing on a narrow path in a forest of tall pine trees. Far down the path I could see a glowing light and began to walk toward it. As I got closer, a figure appeared in the light and soon I could make out the features of a beautiful yellow hound dog. I walked right up to her and looked into her soft brown eyes. She turned her head and to my horror the entire side of her face was mutilated.

Instantly I had the thought that the beautiful dog was me. During my childhood I had experienced multiple traumas and she represented my self-image. Over a two-year period, this was the third time I had ended up in the hospital with a serious condition. Even though I had moved away from the people and the environment that had been harmful to me as a child, I had continued to find ways to hurt myself.

I understood the message my body had been trying to send me. By my own choices I was on a course of destruction. Something even more drastic than my current condition would result if I didn't make a change. I had to get on track with my purpose in life.

I touched the dog where she was maimed, and then I said, "This is where it stops. This ends now." I fell into a deep sleep and didn't awaken until daylight when I was being wheeled into the X-ray room for another set of images. Back in the ICU, I slept again until I became aware of being watched. Opening my eyes, I saw several white coats surrounding the bed. I couldn't turn my head to see who was speaking but one of them said the surgery would not be necessary. The dislodged vertebrae had shifted back into place. The doctor had no logical explanation.

Sunnybrook Hospital kept me three more days for testing. On the second day I was able to stand up and walk. On the third day, I was released with my spine intact. I received a follow-up visit with a doctor two weeks later, and he found no signs of damage. None of the doctors was ever able to offer an explanation.

I had read about miraculous healing, but this was the first time I had experienced anything like it. I could have been in a wheelchair wearing a cervical brace, but divine intervention through my grandmother's healing ceremony allowed me to walk again.

~Robbi Ann Gunter

37

The Proof Is in the Cheeseburger

A good man's prayers will from the deepest dungeon
climb heavens' height, and bring a blessing down.
~Joanna Baillie

My eighteen-year-old son Caleb lay in the ICU of Deaconess Hospital in Billings, Montana. The sunshine could not be seen in the windowless room. Even before Caleb had been transferred to the ICU, the days had seemed dark and filled with uncertainties — starting two weeks prior when he came home with a severe, throbbing headache unlike anything he had ever had before. He isolated himself beneath the covers of his bed. A few days later, with the help of a young muscular friend, we forced a disoriented Caleb into the car and headed to the emergency room.

After lumbar punctures, multiple lab sticks, a life flight, and prods and probes from half a dozen physicians, Caleb was fighting for his life. A couple of days after his admission to the medical floor, the pulmonologist was making rounds over the noon hour. While examining Caleb, he gave the order to transfer him to ICU.

"Look at his breathing," he pointed out to me. "That's what we call paradoxical breathing. He is no longer able to protect his own airway. We need to get him on a ventilator where he doesn't have to fight for each breath. If we can help him save energy by breathing for him, then our hope is that he can use what energy he has to fight the meningitis." I nodded and put the spoon down. I had been trying to feed my son — something I hadn't done since he was a toddler, but with every bite it was necessary to remind him to swallow. It wasn't that way the day before. He was holding his own utensils then. As a nurse, I understood the implications of all this, and it wasn't good.

As his pale, limp body lay supine on the ICU bed, it was hard to believe this was my son — the one who two weeks ago was laughing and playing Hacky Sack with his friends in the front yard. Now he had tubes emerging from almost every orifice, including a feeding tube that fed him liquid nourishment since he was no longer capable of chewing and swallowing food. I tried to keep my mind off the dismal situation by busying myself with nursing tasks. I watched the urine that gathered in the measuring device attached to the catheter bag on the bedrail. I rubbed Caleb's feet with lotion although I think he was too sick to care. I combed through his stringy black hair while telling him things we would do when he got better. He was still capable of saying short sentences and occasionally I would see a smile.

As the week passed, he became more disoriented. He continued to know who I was, but no one else. The worst morning of that week, Dr. Peterson, Caleb's neurologist and primary doctor, came to seek me out in the waiting room. (Family could not stay in the rooms when report was being given to the next shift.) He asked me to follow him around the corner to a vacant hallway. "No! No," I screamed inside. I didn't want to do this. I had been on the other side of this too many times — when doctors took family members to quiet hallways.

"We have tried and done everything we know to do for your son, but today he is not only physically deteriorating, but mentally as well. That is always a grim sign. I had hoped I would never have to have this conversation with you." The lump in my throat continued to expand as if it was a marble transforming into a tennis ball. Dr. Peterson didn't stop there. "I feel you need to prepare yourself for the worst. We won't stop doing what we are doing, but if Caleb gets better, it will not be because of anything we have done."

A good friend from my hometown three hours away came to visit us after lunch. I told her what was going on, and she excused herself for a few minutes and made a phone call.

Later that afternoon, the youth pastor where we both attended church back in Wyoming came to see Caleb. He laid his hands on Caleb, anointed him with oil, and said a prayer over him. Before leaving, he encouraged me with words from the Bible, but I could not tell you what they were. I was in a daze.

The ICU did not permit family to stay at the bedside through the night. I spent a restless night at the Ronald McDonald House, one ear tuned to the phone in the hallway. A call never came and I released a sigh of relief upon rising that morning. I hurried and showered and opted not to eat breakfast. I wanted to get to the hospital as soon as visitors were allowed into the ICU. When I got to the doors of the unit, I couldn't help but wonder if this might be the last time I would go through these doors.

As I hurried past the nurse's desk, I saw Dr. Peterson with his head down, peering through charts at one of the tables. I didn't stop to interrupt him, but hurried into Caleb's room.

A surprise awaited me. Caleb was sitting up in bed. His brown eyes were open and bright, and he even had a bit of a smile. To my ears, his slow, slurred words put the most beautiful music to shame: "Mom, suppose I could have a cheeseburger?"

I had not shed a tear before this, but it was as if Old Faithful was erupting through my eyes now.

I had thought that Dr. Peterson was studying charts, but it turned out he was finished with all of that and had been waiting for me to arrive. The entire nursing staff and Dr. Peterson stood and watched me walk into Caleb's room. They weren't about to miss out on my reaction to a miracle — the one that Dr. Peterson said would have nothing to do with what they had done. I had no doubt that Caleb was on his way to recovery — the proof was in the cheeseburger!

~DeLila R. Lumbardy

38

Every Move I Make

Hope is putting faith to work when
doubting would be easier.
~Author Unknown

"Look! All of the supervillains are over there!" my six-year-old shouts, her ponytail swinging as she points dramatically down the hallway.

"Let's capture them!" her older brother declares.

"Superheroes to the rescue!" crows my four-year-old, his short legs pumping as we thunder across the house, doing our best impression of a heroic charge.

Having reached the imaginary foes, the older kids shout instructions.

"Use your superpowers to trap them!" the oldest orders, furrowing his brow and determinedly holding his palms before him, exerting imaginary effort.

"Go like this!" My daughter balances on one leg, flailing her arms comically as she informs me, "This is Stun!"

Obediently, the youngest and I begin balancing on one leg and flailing our arms until our superhero leader declares, "We've defeated them! Hooray!" We cheer wildly, jumping up and down and exchanging high-fives.

Though moments like this are precious in and of themselves, they are especially meaningful if you once believed them to be impossible.

Nearly fifteen years ago, my eighteen-year-old self was lying in a hospital bed restlessly awaiting my first chemotherapy treatment when I began to lose feeling in my legs. At first they merely tingled and felt heavy, as if they were on the verge of falling asleep, but as the tingling turned to stabbing pain and the heavy feeling became an inability to move, my parents and I grew increasingly frantic.

After numerous attempts to page my doctor over the course of the day, my room was finally invaded by a flock of white-coated physicians.

"Can you feel this?" asked one, squeezing my toe.

"Press your foot against my hand!" demanded another.

"Roll on your side," commanded a third.

I could do nothing.

The doctors whisked my bed from the room, and my parents and I were herded down the hall, crammed into the elevator and rushed through a maze of hallways to the MRI machine. After an eternity spent sweltering within the clanking coffin, I emerged to be hoisted back onto my bed for another journey.

In the hallway, we hesitated just long enough for them to inform my parents that the tumor was strangling my spine. "I want you to prepare yourselves for the fact that she will probably never walk again," intoned a voice from the head of my bed. "Even if she does regain some mobility, she will never be able to move normally. I suggest that you start looking into ways to make your home wheelchair-accessible."

It seemed so unreal. I tried to picture myself in one of those low, sporty wheelchairs that I'd seen disabled people using to scoot around, but my brain rejected the image as ridiculous. Instead of dexterously wheeling myself around, my mental image had me hopping out of the wheelchair and walking off with my friends.

My parents followed silently as the doctors whisked my gurney through the halls for the agonizing wait until the neurosurgeon finished his last surgery of the day and could be informed of my emergency.

I awoke the following morning to find my body hooked to tubes and wires, evidence of my midnight surgery and the beginning of my first chemo treatment. As soon as I was coherent, the white coats gathered around the foot of my bed, tense with anticipation. "Can you move your toes at all?"

I stared at my feet, my entire body taut with the message I was trying to send: MOVE! On my right foot, one toe twitched.

A collective sigh of relief came from the doctors, who immediately demanded that I repeat the feat.

Again, that big toe obediently jerked ever so slightly.

Within days, an occupational therapist hauled me to my feet and began teaching me to walk again. Against all odds, I would be mobile — but my parents were encouraged to install railings in our home and invest in an electric scooter to allow me greater mobility in public. As I endured six weeks of radiation and returned to the hospital time and again for chemo, I very slowly continued to regain more movement.

At my six-month follow-up with my neurosurgeon, I obligingly walked across the room, limping only slightly. Reaching the far wall of the little examination room, I turned to my doctor, awaiting his next instructions.

"Walk across the room one more time," he said eagerly.

I complied, then looked at him again.

"That's amazing!" he said. "How much mobility did you have when you went into surgery?"

"I couldn't move anything below my armpits."

The young doctor shook his head in wonderment, checking his charts for confirmation.

"When do you think I'll be able to run again?" I asked. I had gotten somewhat used to walking again, but my legs did not seem to work for anything else: my run was no more than a clumsy, high-kneed walk.

"Run?" the doctor said with a chuckle. "With neurosurgery, any mobility you gain back comes within the first six months. You've already regained all you will...." He shook his head again. "Walk across the room again."

Despite my neurosurgeon's prognosis, I remained undaunted. If my walking was itself a miracle, there was no reason God could not do more; He was not bound by a neurologist's timeline. So I continued to progress.

After eleven months of chemo treatments, I was finally free to rejoin the world. Weeks later, I moved away to college and found that, though I still had to concentrate to walk without tripping over my toes, I could make my way across campus to my classes without the need of my scooter. I continued to attempt to run, my legs clumsy and unable to match my upper body's intended pace. But with practice, I managed a lumbering plod that slowly grew less cumbersome. And one glorious day, I bent my knees and propelled myself upward and to my delight, my heels lifted almost imperceptibly off the ground. I had jumped!

Not every miracle is over in an instant. My "impossible" recovery took much longer than the brief, six-month window my neurologist was willing to grant — but each new ability I regained was a joyful victory.

Today, if it were not for the scar on my spine, no one looking at me would know that I had undergone a surgery to reverse paralysis. I ride my bike with my family, race my children across the yard, engage in wild soccer matches with them, teach them to cartwheel, and demonstrate my childhood jump-roping tricks for them to admire. And with every step I run, with every jump I take, with each new skill that tests my balance or calls for the dexterity of my legs — with each of these I rejoice, for each of them is a move I was told I would never make.

~Shereen Vinke

Picking Up the Pieces

However long the night, the dawn will break.
~African Proverb

The first year after my husband John died, I felt as though I had plunged down some enormous black hole. John had died suddenly — violently — in a plane crash. I was unprepared. What wife at thirty, mother of three small children, thinks of becoming a widow?

I missed little things the most. The way John and I touched toes at night as we slept. Our Saturday ritual of shopping together, always winding up at the ice cream store. Silly games he played with our kids who were nine, seven, and five.

Sometimes, as I folded clothes or brought in groceries, I felt like a vase I remembered from my grandmother's house. Something had struck it, shooting hairline cracks all through. From a distance it still looked whole, but one day, before our eyes, it simply collapsed and fell into pieces.

Would that happen to me? It seemed so hard to hold myself together.

My parents worried about me. One day, six months after John died, my mother suggested, "Why don't you go back to school? I'll help with the kids."

I had married after only two years of college. Now that I was the head of household, I would soon need a job. A college degree would help, I agreed. So I signed up for an English Lit class at San Diego

State. Alan Richards, the young professor, was a stimulating teacher.

One October morning, between classes, I bumped into him in the student union.

"Join me for coffee," he invited.

I was delighted and followed him eagerly through the crush of students. He wasn't a tall man but he had a freewheeling, sure-of-himself air. "You turned in a good paper last week," he said, as we found a table. I blushed like a teenager. Soon, I was telling him about John and how I hoped to earn my bachelor's degree.

I learned that Dr. Richards was a never married bachelor of thirty-five. He liked classical music, as did I, and theatre. And sailing. A few weeks later, he invited me to the symphony. The next weekend he invited me to go sailing.

The rest of that fall we saw each other. He seemed to like my kids, although they didn't pay much attention to him. By the New Year, I began to have thoughts I never expected. I had deeply loved my husband, but I missed being part of a couple — part of a family. Could it be that I had met someone else I could love?

But as the semester ended, Alan seemed — well, agitated. As if something bothered him.

"Is everything okay?" I asked softly, when he picked me up one Friday evening.

He drove for a few blocks without speaking and then pulled off into a parking lot near a neighborhood park. He swallowed hard and said, "Barbara, I'm so sorry. You're a wonderful woman but — I've come to realize I can't handle a ready-made family and — well, I think it's best if we stop seeing each other."

My ears buzzed. Something inside me seemed to crack, like my grandmother's vase. "I hope you can understand," he said, as he drove me back home. But all I understood was the dreadful emptiness of another loss. In the weeks that followed I felt nearly as bereft as I had in the first weeks after John died. And something more. I was angry.

One morning, as I reached for a juice glass, something inside me exploded. "It's not fair!" I screamed as I threw the glass to the floor. It shattered noisily and as I looked down I felt as if my life was as shattered as the bits of jagged glass.

I didn't want to sign up for another class the next semester, but my mother persuaded me. "It's a big campus," she said. "You won't have to see him. And you need to earn your degree."

Reluctantly, I agreed. But as I headed toward the registration building, I suddenly saw Alan striding across campus in his self-confident way. I couldn't face him. It still hurt too much. In a panic, I darted into the first doorway I saw, and found myself inside the college chapel.

I had probably passed the small stone chapel hundreds of times but had never gone inside. It was empty. Thick walls muffled the college clamor outside. Wooden pews faced a bare altar. Behind the altar was a stained glass window through which light flooded the chapel. I slid into one of the pews.

To some, the chapel might have held a quiet peace. All I felt was an unpleasant queasiness, as if I were in an elevator that had dropped too suddenly.

My throat clogged as I began to cry. "I'm not going to make it," I said to the empty air. But then something made me lift my head — and look directly at the stained glass window. It dominated the little chapel and showed God's finger reaching toward man's in a depiction of Michelangelo's famed painting. A mosaic of colored glass chips formed a rose-and-lavender border.

I suddenly felt as if God were reaching down to touch me at that very moment. Slowly, it dawned on me. This window — this beautiful whole window — was formed from hundreds of tiny pieces of broken, shattered glass. If those fragments could be shaped into a beautiful whole pattern, perhaps God could do the same with the pieces of my life. I could be whole again.

As clearly as if I heard the words aloud, a voice spoke inside me: Pick up the pieces, Barbara. Make something of them. Something beautiful.

For one brief, luminous instant, I saw in my future a kaleidoscope of possibilities: Mother! College graduate! Working woman! And yes, perhaps even wife again. Successful! Happy!

The moment passed. But something changed in me after that day.

I saw that Alan was not the only way to rebuild my life. Depression gave way to a sense of acceptance, and eventually to an eagerness to go on. I would always love John, but life beckoned like an unfinished picture. It would be different from what I had once imagined, but now I knew it could still be beautiful.

~Barbara Bartocci

Dreamy Eyes

A soul mate is not the person who makes you the
happiest, but the one who makes you feel the most.
~Sierra DeMulder

The first night I saw Jordan I didn't actually speak to him or learn his name; rather I saw him from across a crowded room and noticed his deep blue eyes staring at me. It could not have been more cheesy and my friends teased me incessantly for falling for "dreamy eyes."

As most love stories go, ours was far from perfect. It was messy, passionate, and at times downright unhealthy but one thing stayed the same for the next five years: we always ended up together. We were that annoying couple that breaks up all the time, and after years of the vicious cycle, I was at the end of my rope.

Our last breakup was different. There was no fighting or name calling, but it was still heartbreaking. That night I looked deep into those dreamy blue eyes and confessed that I loved him too much to stand by his side while I watched him die of a nasty drug addiction. It was the first time in five years that he wasn't able to muster any promises or lies; he simply kissed me and walked out of my apartment for the last time.

The months that followed were difficult but I was determined to make things different this time. On a mission to completely "de-Jordan" my life and move on, I got rid of anything and everything that had ties to him. This included photos, gifts, social media posts, and even some of my own items that simply reminded me of him. It was a long and emotional process and at the end I was left with two items of jewelry. I was conflicted on discarding these items simply because I didn't know how. Could I really throw away expensive jewelry? The Pandora bracelet could have been thrifted but the other item was engraved with our initials. Not exactly something to donate to your local Goodwill.

I did what any good daughter would do and consulted my resident expert on matters of the heart: I called my mother. She suggested I hold onto those two items for a year, in case Mr. Dreamy Eyes should request his valuable items back for some reason. I stowed them away inside a bag in the corner of a jewelry box and metaphorically wiped my hands clean of the entire five-year relationship. I had moved on for good.

As most life stories go, mine is also far from perfect. I am messy, passionate, and at times downright unhealthy. About six months later and after many ignored phone calls and texts from my ex-beau, I caved and dug down deep in my jewelry box for the items. I wasn't interested in the bracelet, but I wanted that necklace. It just hit me one day that I had to have it. I didn't care that I was dating someone new or that I had made so many dramatic I'm-done-forever statements. I took that engraved necklace and hung it over the rear view mirror in my car.

The necklace stayed there for months. I didn't touch it. No one noticed it among the other items hanging from my mirror. In the months that it hung in my car Jordan and I teetered on the edge of our dangerous pattern once again, spending way too much time together being "just friends." By the end of the summer we were spending most of our lunch breaks together (we worked in the same part of town) and were talking and texting nearly every day. I still didn't touch the necklace.

Jordan and I were never good at being "just friends" and as we'd proved many times before it always ended badly. This time there was a nasty fight, jam-packed with all the name-calling and low blows we could think of, most likely saved up from the extremely anti-climactic breakup earlier in the year. When the dust settled I was right back where I started — devastated. Despite all of my hard work and efforts,

I hadn't stopped loving him and I couldn't shake the feeling that he was headed for disaster.

I spent the next two months talking myself out of calling him every day and forcing myself to ignore his calls and texts. Through all this, the necklace hung in my car and no one noticed it but me.

On Christmas Eve I woke up anxious. I went about my business but nothing I did eased the anxiety; I just felt "off." As I was driving out to my parents' house that afternoon something hit me. I needed the necklace in my hands. I couldn't describe why, but I was certain that the necklace needed to be on me. As soon as I had the necklace wrapped around my fingers my anxiety completely vanished. I felt peace and contentment, something I hadn't felt for months.

When I pulled into my parents' driveway I stuffed the necklace into my pocket. I didn't want my mother to see me wearing it and question me about it with her weary are-you-seriously-back-with-that-boy tone but I knew for some reason that I needed it with me.

Jordan died a few hours later of an accidental drug overdose. The necklace with our initials, LH & JD, was in my pocket as I sat on the floor of my childhood bedroom sobbing. After almost a year, I put the necklace back on. I haven't felt that peace and contentment again since Jordan's death, but I know that it was one of his final gifts to me, a little nudge to tell me, "I'm leaving, but I'm not going far, just somewhere different."

~Lane Elizabeth Hall

Chapter 5

Angels and Miracles

Divine Intervention

41

My Interstate Navigator

Not everything we experience can be
explained by logic or science.
~Linda Westphal

I was zooming down Interstate 80, heading east in Pennsylvania. The beautiful mountains covered with lush greenery loomed above both sides of the highway. Every few miles a farm appeared nestled among the rolling hills. It was a beautiful day with no weather issues and very little traffic.

But I couldn't really enjoy it. I was rushing to Lehigh Valley Hospital, where my mom had suffered a setback. She had called me at work just two hours before, crying that she needed me. As her daughter and a nurse, I couldn't ignore her plea. I left work and drove home to throw some clothes into a suitcase and let my husband know where I was going and why.

In an effort to calm my mother, I had promised her, "I'll be right there." What was I thinking? It was a three-hour trip.

Ahead I saw a large tractor-trailer laden with lumber. The load was held in place with multiple straps. As I looked at the trailer, I started to feel uneasy.

A voice said clearly, "Those straps are going to break."

"What?" I asked incredulously.

The voice elaborated. "The straps are going to break and that lumber is going to spill onto the road."

"Holy Mother of God!" I thought, panicked at what the voice was telling me. I was a few car lengths behind the truck and we were both moving at about seventy miles per hour.

The voice urged, "Pass him. Get away from him. Do it now!"

I obeyed, but when I pulled into the passing lane, the truck accelerated. This was creepy. I increased my speed enough to overtake the truck and kept an eye on the hazardous load.

Horrified, I watched as the straps holding the stacks of lumber in place started snapping, one by one, and twirling around uselessly in the air. Everything seemed to be happening in slow motion. When the third strap broke, the lumber started to shift.

The voice said authoritatively, "Pedal to the metal; get away from him as fast as you can."

I didn't question the voice. I floored it.

As my small sedan pulled away from that big truck, I watched the scene unfold in my rearview and side view mirrors. The stacks of wood rotated sideways and cascaded onto the road. The first pieces missed the back of my car by a few feet. I saw the truck slow down and could see the look of horror on the driver's face as he realized what was happening. He could clearly see the lumber slide off his truck onto both eastbound lanes of Route 80.

I safely pulled away and my speed returned to normal as I viewed the spectacle in the rearview mirror. I watched as the trucker brought his vehicle to a stop.

I offered up a prayer of thanks for having heard the voice. There was no doubt in my mind that God was my navigator on the interstate that day.

~Nancy Emmick Panko

42

A Gentle Warning

Music is well said to be the speech of angels.
~Thomas Carlyle

My husband Kurt put down the car magazine he was reading. "Sue, where's that loud music coming from?"

Glancing up from my laptop, I replied, "I don't hear anything."

Kurt continued, "Are the neighbors blaring a radio outside? Maybe a car is blasting music."

I strained my ears. No, there definitely was no music. I stood up from my recliner and walked over to the window. No neighbors were outside, and no cars were parked on our quiet cul-de-sac. Our living room was serenely quiet.

"Are you sure you don't hear the music?" Kurt asked.

I once again affirmed that I heard nothing.

"Hmm… it's gone now," Kurt said, and he resumed reading.

I thought the incident was strange but Kurt wasn't overly alarmed so I didn't give it much thought.

Over the next two weeks, Kurt continued to hear music that wasn't actually playing. He said it only lasted a minute, then stopped. This occurred several times throughout each day. He joked that it was from paint fumes, as he was a custom motorcycle painter. Then I noticed he was having trouble with his speech — mispronouncing words or not being able to find the right word. Kurt attributed it to growing older, but I knew something was wrong.

"I think you either had a stroke or have a brain tumor," I said. I convinced Kurt to see his doctor, who immediately ordered a brain MRI. A tumor was discovered in his left temporal lobe and surgery was scheduled.

After receiving the diagnosis, the music disappeared! When I quizzed Kurt about the music he had been hearing, he recalled it was Christian in nature but not a particular song. It sounded like a combination of songs he'd heard at church that blended together into one beautiful, melodious song.

The neurosurgeon concluded the music had been produced by auditory seizures, but Kurt and I are certain it was the songs of angels, gently guiding him with an early warning to seek treatment before the tumor was too large to remove.

~Sue Carloni

43

The Desk

*Accept the things to which fate binds you and love the
people with whom fate brings you together, and
do so with all your heart.*
~Marcus Aurelius

I got the mahogany desk in my early twenties, after my grandfather passed away and my grandmother gave away most of
their possessions in order to move in with my aunt. I felt my
grandparents' presence when I stroked the desk's deep cherry
serpentine molding or tugged on its worn but sturdy brass handles to
open its dovetailed drawers.

When I sat at the desk to write a letter, I'd picture Grandma doing
the same. At times, I smelled her scent in the room, a faint hint of
sweet rose petals and delicate honeysuckle. Often, I'd daydream about
the energy captured in the desk, the decades it had traveled with my
grandparents, the thousands of times they laid their hands upon it.

That desk was full of the spirit of Grandma and Grandpa — two
people who were the most loving and happy couple I'd ever known.
They were the best example of the kind of relationship I hoped to
have someday.

For the next thirty years, the desk traveled with me — through a
short-lived marriage and through multiple relationships. When Grandma
passed away, the desk became even more important to me.

When I married again at age forty-two, the desk accompanied me
through eight years of significant emotional hardships that ended in a

painful divorce. I lost most of my material possessions, but I insisted on keeping the desk, and it went into storage while I traveled around figuring out the next phase of my life. When I settled down again, in a rented room, the desk seemed an impractical luxury, so I gave it to my sister.

A year later, my life had turned around. I moved across the country to be with a man who would become as wonderful a partner for me as Grandpa was for Grandma. He'd also been through a recent divorce. Together, we had very little furniture, which was fortunate because we could only afford to live in a tiny, overpriced cottage. We appreciated our forced downsizing. We worked side-by-side in our combo office-bedroom and played music together in our combo kitchen-living room, filling the rooms with love and laughter. Life was simple. I'd never been happier.

Two years later, we moved to Arizona and rented a house three times the size of the California cottage for several hundred dollars less per month. To fill what felt like cavernous spaces in the house, I perused online ads for used furniture and stumbled upon a listing that took my breath away. It looked just like my grandparents' desk.

Courtney, the seller, drove forty-five minutes to show us the desk. She had bought it for her daughter because it reminded her of her own grandmother's desk. She lamented having to sell it, but she was moving and couldn't justify lugging it around. When I explained what the desk meant to me, the energy in and around the exchange felt right. There, in a convenience store parking lot, we sealed the deal.

My car was too small to accommodate the desk, so I asked Courtney if she would mind delivering the desk to our house. She agreed, especially after I mentioned the cross streets to her.

"Oh, I know where that is," she said. "My sister used to live around there."

When Courtney pulled up to our home, she stepped out of her SUV, and exclaimed, "Yep, this is it. My sister lived in this house for four years. She moved out a couple of months ago."

I shook my head in disbelief at the coincidence and then smiled. It was all coming together. It almost felt like Grandma and Grandpa were giving their approval for my new life, having conspired to deliver us the perfect housewarming gift—a used, sentimental desk with serpentine molding.

~Susan Maddy Jones

A Voice in the Desert

Angels deliver Fate to our doorstep — and
anywhere else it is needed.
~Jessi Lane Adams

I was jogging around our base in Tikrit, Iraq. As I rounded the corner I could see the front gate and was glad the run was almost over. Then, as I headed for the final stretch, a voice in my head said, "Take cover behind the wall."

I looked up and did not see any imminent danger. There were no missiles in the sky, the alarm bell was not sounding, and everything was relatively quiet. I kept jogging, assuming that the paranoia of being on a battlefield had begun to take its toll on me. Then I paused for a moment as I got closer to the wall because my brain was screaming, "Take cover!"

Suddenly, I heard a bloodcurdling scream coming from the front gate. As I whipped my head around I saw a huge ball of flames, and then everything went black. When I woke up I was at the medical station with the medic staring down at me. I was confused about what was going on. The medic told me to hang on a minute and went off. He brought back one of the other medics with whom I had done a great deal of work during my deployment. Jim put his hand on my shoulder and said, "Ma'am, you were the only survivor. Do you remember anything that happened?"

I was stunned and couldn't speak. Jim told the others that I might be in shock. I looked at him puzzled and said, "All I remember is screaming, a large bang, and then a fire ball. The fire ball was about a mile across." Jim nodded and said that would make sense because it was a tanker full of explosives that detonated at the gate. I instantly felt sick. I knew there were always six guards stationed at the gate. I asked about them and Jim repeated quietly, "You are the only survivor."

And with that I became consumed with "survivor guilt."

Once released, I went back to my bunk, where I found glass had shattered all over my bed and belongings. My roommates greeted me enthusiastically and asked how I survived. I explained that I had heard a voice telling me to stay behind the wall and so I did though I did not know why. My closest friend, Kathy, said quite simply, "Well, you have a divine purpose; that much is for sure." I doubted her. After all I was a single person with no real purpose in life, so that could not be the case.

A few weeks later, I received an e-mail from Robin, the mother of a girl named Erica who I had been a "big sister" to for the past six years. Its message was simple:

"Linda, Child Protective Services took Marissa. Can you please get her back when you come home?"

Marissa was Robin's grandchild and Erica's niece. I knew her and had taken care of her on many occasions prior to my deployment. I was confused, though. I was a "big sister," a volunteer, not an official foster parent. When I went back to my bunk I sat staring off into space. Kathy came over to me and said, "What's up you?"

I told her about the e-mail I had received. Kathy and I had been friends for years, so she had met Erica and Marissa. She gripped my shoulder and stared at me intently. "Linda, don't you see? You survived the explosion to be a mother!" I shook my head in disagreement; after all foster care is temporary. But Kathy shook her head firmly and said, "No your purpose is to be Marissa's mother."

When I returned home I did in fact go through the steps to gain custody of Marissa. I learned she had a sister, Mary, who no one had mentioned, so I took her, too. After fostering them for two years, I adopted Marissa and Mary.

Kathy was right. That voice saved me for a very special purpose, to be a mom to two wonderful young girls.

~L. Thorburn

45

Shaken

*Miracles, in the sense of phenomena we cannot
explain, surround us on every hand: life itself
is the miracle of miracles.*
~George Bernard Shaw

I was a nuts and bolts, black and white, no-nonsense kind of person. But that changed one spring day a few years ago.

It started with the weather, which can shift fast in South Dakota. I'd left for a gathering an hour and a half away under a sunny, blue sky. And now it was time to return home and an unexpected ground blizzard was brewing. Ground blizzards, for the uninitiated, occur when there is no storm, but loose snow and ice already on road surfaces are violently whipped about by very strong winds.

A lengthy drive north on an isolated secondary road was the only route home. So I stopped at a gas station to fill up and grab a snack — I knew the trip would take longer than usual because of the weather.

I was so preoccupied with the deteriorating weather that I forgot to put on my seatbelt when I resumed driving. Suddenly, I heard an extremely loud, commanding voice bellow, "PUT YOUR SEATBELT ON."

I was totally alone in the car and a voice was yelling at me. Despite my confusion, I obeyed and strapped myself in. Of course, now, in addition to the poor driving conditions I had to wonder about my sanity.

Ten minutes later I hit black ice. I held my breath as I slid out of my lane into the empty oncoming lane, and was just about to relax as I glided the car back when I glanced up. There, barreling down at me over a hill, also out of control on the enormous ice slick, was an eighteen-wheel double tractor-trailer hauling coal.

The truck jackknifed, and I knew a collision was unavoidable. There was nothing I could do and nowhere I could go. Though not a believer, I remember shouting, "God, this is in your hands!"

After impact there was nothing at first, and then an image appeared. I was looking at myself, a traveler ready to embark on a journey into a dark, hazy space. Then I suddenly realized how much I'd miss my two children. Instantly, I was catapulted back to reality— to find myself miraculously in one piece in my smashed, upside-down, windowless car. I was hanging mid-air, facing the rear, secured by my seatbelt.

Incredibly, my only injuries were a broken bone in my left foot that didn't even need to be set, and a messy four-inch gash on the left side of my head. It was nothing short of miraculous.

But about that head gash...

Savvy South Dakotans keep emergency kits in their cars due to the weather's vagaries. My kit, stashed in my car's rear hatchback area, consisted of a plastic bag stuffed with a blanket; some pull-tab cans of sardines and peaches; a plastic fork; a chocolate bar; a bottle of water; batteries; a tall, thick, long-burning, glass-enclosed candle; and matches.

Immediately after the accident, facing the rear as I hung from my seatbelt, I saw the bag within reach and gratefully snatched the blanket to staunch my bleeding head wound. As I hung there suspended above piles of shattered glass waiting to be rescued, frigid winds started raging through the blown-out windows of the car. Between shock and the cold, I started to shake violently. I reached down again into my emergency bag for the candle and matches to create a bit of warmth. They were nowhere to be found. I searched again. Though every other item was in place the candle and matches were missing.

✳✳✳

A few weeks later, I went to sign a release to have my car scrapped. I was handed a plastic bag with personal items from my car. There, right on top, sat the missing candle and matches. I asked the scrap dealer where he'd found the two items, explaining how I'd needed them after the accident but couldn't find them.

He looked at me strangely. "These two? They were wedged so tight under the glove compartment I had to use a screwdriver to pry them out."

He paused, and then he said, "Y'know, you're one lucky lady. That truck hit you where your gas tank sits. There was gas everywhere. Had you lit one of those matches for the candle you would have gone up in flames — big time. You'd have been a goner."

I stood there — shocked, grateful, shaken to the core. How had the candle and matches become wedged in the front of the car, under the glove compartment, when the emergency kit and the rest of its contents were seven feet away in the rear? Why had the blanket still been exactly where I could reach it to stop my bleeding? What was that voice I heard?

The accident became a pivotal point in my life — it shook up far more than my physical being. It totally shook my long held belief that what you see is what you get. I know now, without a doubt, that we're never truly alone; that help is always available. That some kind of benevolent presences we can't see or interact with, and that aren't tangible in this dimension, are nevertheless capable of interacting with those of us who inhabit this dimension.

And they must really care and love us to go to such trouble....

~Marsha Warren Mittman

46

The Yahrzeit Miracle

Angels are never too distant to hear you.
~Author Unknown

I turned the calendar page to the month of April. This month it would be a whole year. I shuddered, still reeling from the entire experience. It seemed like it just happened. How could it be a whole year since my brother Louis died?

Louis, my only sibling, was born with Down syndrome. Despite this, or perhaps because of it, I took my role as big sister very seriously. I helped my brother learn to tie his shoelaces, taught him the alphabet and sat in front of the clock with him for endless hours until he could tell time. Often, too, I would chaperone his play dates with schoolmates, keeping score at dominoes or calling out numbers for a game of Bingo. One year, I even hosted a Christmas carol sing-along for my brother and a few of his friends where I accompanied their sincere voices on the piano. I still remembered it so well. It was a night of pure enthusiasm all the way around.

The connection my brother and I shared never wavered throughout the years and became even stronger after our mother's passing when I became his legal guardian. Though I had since married and moved out of the family home and Louis had moved into a community residence that he shared with five other special-needs adults, I would take my brother out for lunch and on the errand or activity of his choice every week. In return, Louis was sure to phone me each day. I also accompanied him on his numerous doctors' appointments. We had been through a lot of health crises together, Lou and I — a broken elbow, his hernia surgery, and pacemaker surgery, to name a few.

That was why his passing cut so deeply at my heart. I knew for several months that my brother had not been feeling well. His hearty appetite waned. He became pale and thin. When I took him to the beach that summer, he refused to swim in the ocean — something he looked forward to each year — napping instead on a lounge chair and asking to go home early. I took him from one medical specialist to another. The closest I got to a definitive diagnosis was anemia. The rest of the symptoms were written off to aging. He was, after all, close to fifty years old.

Then one day, he stopped eating altogether. When questioned by his aide at the residence, he told her matter-of-factly, "I'm dying." She called me that night and the next morning we took him back to his doctor again. He took one look at my brother, phoned some associates at the local hospital and arranged for Louis to be admitted immediately. By the end of the week Louis was gone — a week before his fiftieth birthday and two days before the big party I had planned for him. The cause — a very rare, difficult to detect, aggressive form of lymphoma.

I put on a brave face for those around me, yet inside I was torn apart. Decisions about his care had been entrusted to me and I had failed him. I knew he hadn't been well and scolded myself for not doing enough to ensure a proper diagnosis had been secured while treatment could have still been an option. Some days, I tried to find comfort in the fact that, despite his disability, Louis had had a good life and had accomplished everything we all hope for on this earth. He had a small job in which he took pride, had won sports trophies, lived in a lovely home, became an artist who crafted beautiful paintings and collages, and had friends. In the last few years he had even found love when he met his girlfriend, a delightful young lady, at his art program. Together, they would sit side-by-side searching magazines for just the right photos to add to Louis's collages. I believe those were the happiest times of his life.

Well, I thought, as I looked at the calendar, a life like that needs to be honored. I decided that his anniversary needed to be commemorated in some way. But how? The grief and guilt were still too raw for me to include anyone else in my plans. Whatever I decided to do in his honor needed to be done privately, just between Louis and me. I turned the idea around in my head for several days. Then the answer came.

I had often heard my Jewish friends speak of the Yahrzeit tradition used to honor loved ones on the anniversary of their passing. Although a Christian, I've always had a respect and interest in Jewish tradition. It is, after all, the root of my own religion. So I did some Internet research. I discovered that Yahrzeit, from the Yiddish word meaning "year time," involved lighting a special twenty-four-hour candle on the anniversary of a person's passing along with recitation of certain prayers. One website even suggested that the spirit of the deceased comes back to its loved ones for that twenty-four-hour period. Oh how I wished my brother's spirit could come back to me, if only for a moment, to let me know that he was well and happy wherever he was.

Fueled with enthusiasm, I set out to purchase a Yahrzeit candle, which all websites indicated could be easily found in any supermarket. Once there, I surveyed the aisles, grabbing a few groceries. Suddenly, from the other side of the shelves, I heard a familiar voice. I recognized it immediately — my brother's girlfriend. I turned the corner quickly, excited to see Louis's dear friend. I just had to say "hi" to her. Yet as I approached her, I became so overcome with emotion that I dropped my groceries and left the store empty-handed. I drove home, sobbing.

Now I had even more reason to scold myself. I had failed my brother again, I thought as I turned the key in my front door. I couldn't even buy a candle in his honor. I stepped into the warmth of my sun porch with my head low. There, I saw something amazing. The peace lily that had been the centerpiece at my brother's memorial service was in full bloom, with not one but several white lilies standing at attention. It was the first time the plant had flowered. I was still shaking my head as I walked into the kitchen. And there, I saw something even more amazing. On the shelf where I kept my brother's prized basketball trophy stood a white candle. On its label was printed "Yahrzeit."

I couldn't logically explain these happenings. Yet, seeing my brother's girlfriend, the lily plant in full bloom and the mysteriously appearing candle all pointed to one thing as far as I was concerned. My brother's spirit did not require a special candle to be lit or prayer to be said in order to be with me. It was with me always, as I had been with him. Louis was fine, wherever he was. And so was I.

~Monica A. Andermann

The Blessing of Fear

If you are brave enough to say goodbye, life will
reward you with a new hello.
~Paulo Coelho

s it possible that a miracle could lie hidden, dormant for years, like a frightened wildflower seed — waiting and waiting for the right time to grow and make itself known? Its path, blown by the winds, burying it beneath the soil until the day that God says, "It's time." Finally, it sprouts and pushes through, reaching, no longer encumbered by its earthly bounds, only to bless the world with its colors and scent.

Fears are like seeds, too, mere shells or wrappings to break out of if you view them with the right perspective, waiting to transform into miracles if you really look at them.

It was a long time coming for me, but that's what I did. I faced a fear and visited the Metropolitan State Mental Hospital in Norwalk, California, the place where my mom had been a patient back in the mid 1970's. I was fourteen at the time and visited her there only once, but I remember it well. As though it were yesterday.

Soon after ending her stay there…. she ended her own life. I never got to say goodbye. Years later the aforementioned became "the seed" for my art, my writing, my passion for helping others. But, much like the wildflower seed, I needed to push past my earthly boundaries. Hence, my visit there that day.

During my visit I was drawn to a particular set of dilapidated old buildings, which were built over 100 years ago. Some say they are haunted, and from the looks of them I would be inclined to agree. On the other side of the mile-square property are several other buildings, still used today. These house the criminally insane, among others. Many sheriff deputies were on high alert and, of course, wondering why I was there when I appeared one day. But I explained my mission and with raised eyebrows they sent me on my way.

Soon I discovered the abandoned building my mom once resided in. It seemed to be calling me as it sat stoic, even in disrepair, covered in vines. Its broken windows peered back with a blank stare that I am sure many of its long ago patients also shared. In spite of my reluctance I entered the building. The eerie ambiance was straight out of the movies. Long pitch-black hallways, old brick arches and well-worn linoleum floors spread throughout. The giant catacomb of rooms was dark, dreary, dusty and trashed. A wild cat or two scurried about, as did my heart.

Soon I found the very same room that my mother once called home for a while, with the same teal colored paint I remembered so well, now cracked and peeling. Brighter unblemished patches of paint shone where pictures once hung like windows to the past. Oh what these walls must have seen.

And then it hit me — many things I had put to rest came flooding back in an avalanche of emotion. Cascading memories flickered by so fast that it made it hard to focus. Were these windows to the past really working?

I reflected for a moment, letting everything sink in. I thought of forgiveness. I thought of the good and the bad, the memories. And, I thought of my mom's fondness for horses — a result perhaps of her having grown up very close to Santa Anita racetrack.

I looked into the shadows and saw something. A small plastic horse lying in a corner covered in dust, a symbolic reminder of why I was there. A gift, if you will, for facing my fears. I can't put into words all the emotions I was feeling, other than to say that my visit there felt like an atomic bomb of emotional confetti going off. A bomb of closure, healing, sadness, and yes, strangely enough… joy… all at once. I finally got to say goodbye.

One of the hardest things I have ever done was to visit there that day. Yet I needed to do it. And thus, I received the miracle of closure — in a brief instant… an instant that took forty years.

When you face your fears, they become your strength to receive the miracles laid out before you. And this is when God says, "It's time."

~Stan Holden

48

Mike's Calf

*Symptoms, then, are in reality nothing but
the cry from suffering organs.*
~Jean-Martin Charcot

One often hears people say that God works in mysterious ways. Well, my husband is proof that God's ways are not only mysterious; they are often veiled in circumstances that seem less than ideal.

It was a weird injury, one that bordered on unbelievable because of the way it occurred, and one that would ultimately save my husband's life.

"You did what to your calf muscle?" I asked in late 2008, needing him to repeat what he had just said because I was sure I had misheard.

"I exploded it," he said slowly, shrugging his shoulders.

"Like, *exploded it* exploded it? What were you doing?"

"I was on the elliptical at the gym and it just… exploded. Blew up. Like, the muscle part."

"The elliptical?" I asked. "You mean, the machine you use so that you don't injure your body actually running?"

"I know," he said, looking sheepish.

"How fast were you going?"

"Just my usual speed. I don't know why it happened. One minute I was fine and the next my calf felt like it exploded with pain."

It was just another inexplicable event in the saga of unusual physical ailments he had been going through in the past few weeks.

Each new ailment added to the confusion because they didn't seem to be connected in any way. His palm had developed a lump. His fingernails had weird black lines in them. His sleep was interrupted by alarming hot flashes followed by chills. The calf was the strangest injury of them all.

In spite of all the ailments, he had stubbornly maintained a strict running schedule. He was training for a half marathon and every week he would kiss me goodbye and disappear on the back country roads next to our home for hours at a time, only to reappear sweaty and happy. But now that was definitely over.

I called the physical therapist to set up an appointment and in the meantime it took all of my powers of persuasion to keep Mike off his feet. When he went to work, his calf wrapped in an ACE bandage, he hobbled around, sometimes hopping instead of walking. He was frustrated to not be able to walk and even more frustrated because all of the progress he had made with running seemed to be slipping away. He grew discouraged and I felt helpless.

"Lord, why did you allow this to happen?" I prayed in frustration. "He was loving running and now he can barely walk, let alone do his job. Hasn't he endured enough recently with all these weird health things? Please heal his leg so that he can walk again. And quickly? Amen."

Mike's physical therapist was kind, but also a bit bewildered by how his injury had occurred.

"I've never heard of someone exploding his calf on an elliptical machine," she told Mike after he explained his injury.

"I'm special," Mike said, with a grin that masked how disheartened he felt. The physical therapist stretched his muscle and used an intimidating looking machine to shock his calf with electricity, a process that looked incredibly painful from my perch in the corner of her office.

"Stay off it as much as you can. I'll see you next week," she instructed as she walked us to the door. Mike didn't look at me. We both knew he wouldn't stay off his feet; he couldn't if he were going to continue to work. And he needed to work. Since I was in graduate school full-time, he was the only one making any money and we couldn't afford for him to take the three to four weeks off they had suggested for a full recovery. This injury was not only a nuisance, it was also becoming a financial burden.

"Lord," I silently prayed as we drove home. "This timing is awful. What are we going to do? He can't stop working. Please heal his calf, like, tomorrow? We can't take much more of these health issues."

Mike's ten-mile runs were becoming a distant memory and when his strange string of ailments landed him in the hospital, the doctors asked about his exercise regimen along with several other questions.

"I run. A lot. At least, I used to," Mike said, and I could hear the sadness in his voice.

"Well, I have good news and bad news," one of the doctors said after they finished their initial examination and ordered several tests. I grabbed Mike's hand and held on tightly.

"The good news is that we know what's wrong with you."

I saw Mike sigh and then steel himself for what came next.

"The bad news is that your heart has problems, problems that require surgery to fix."

The room seemed to spin and I could feel both Mike and I struggle for words. We came up empty and so the doctor continued.

"You were born with a heart defect and somewhere in the recent months you developed an infection in your heart. We need to replace your aortic valve because the infection has destroyed it. Every time your heart beats, it is flicking off little bits of infection into your body. That's probably why you have had these weird injuries. Like with your calf. Although, that injury was pretty lucky," she said.

I felt myself balk. Lucky? How was my husband, who had just been told he needed open-heart surgery, lucky? How was an injury that left him hobbling around barely able to do his job lucky?

Sensing my doubt, the doctor continued.

"The truth is, with this type of heart problem and how much you were running, you probably would have just fallen over dead during one of your runs. Your heart couldn't sustain such intense cardio in its current state. Your injured calf most likely saved your life."

Mike and I stared at each other in stunned silence. His hand began to shake in mine. My thoughts jumped to the long stretches of lonely dirt roads that Mike liked to run on, with no one but a herd of goats to keep him company. I knew the gist of where he ran, but not the specific roads and the realization of what could have been nearly floored me. He could have died, alone and scared, on a backcountry road and I wouldn't have known where to find him until it was too late.

In the light of this new revelation the calf injury that had seemed like such an inconvenience began to look like a divine warning. I had been angry at God for allowing Mike's calf to be injured and yet, in his infinite wisdom, he had allowed it in order to spare Mike's life.

"Thank you, God. Thank you for allowing this injury and saving my husband," I whispered.

Mike's heart surgery was a success and strangely, after the surgery, his calf seemed completely healed as well. It hasn't bothered him since.

Whenever life becomes difficult or circumstances seem dire, Mike and I look at each other and say, "Exploded calf." It reminds us that circumstances that seem pointless or discouraging might just be divine intervention in disguise.

~Jessie M. Santala

49

Touring Paris with Jim Morrison

*There are things known and things unknown
and in between are the doors.*
~Jim Morrison

When I was twenty-seven years old, I traveled to Paris alone. Shortly after my arrival, I met a local woman named Lauren who offered to show me around the city. I asked her to take me to Père Lachaise Cemetery. She thought it was strange that, of all the tourist sites in Paris, I wanted to see a graveyard first.

At that time in my life, I was obsessed with finding out what happens when people die, mainly because I had lost a good friend to a car accident several years earlier. After she died, I started reading everything I could about near-death experiences and accounts of the afterlife. I also became drawn to old cemeteries, and even conducted a séance in one. I didn't expect to communicate with my friend, and had been warned by more faithful friends that I might attract malevolent spirits, but I did it anyway because even if something bad happened, I would at least know that there was something beyond life, and that my friend might still be alive in some way.

Père Lachaise Cemetery is a tourist attraction because many notable artists and luminaries are buried there, including Oscar Wilde, Marcel Proust, and Frederic Chopin. However, the grave I was most interested in seeing was that of Jim Morrison, the lead singer of The Doors, because I had been exploring his music and writings for months before this trip.

Jim Morrison shared my obsession with death and the afterlife, perhaps because of a similar experience — he had witnessed the aftermath of a terrible car accident as a child. His poetry and raging vocals gave a voice to the darkness in me. He wrote and sang like an animal crying out in pain. There was no self-consciousness or desire to please, just raw energy. In an era of peace and love, he crashed the party and reminded everyone that the dark side was still there.

The morning of the day we went to the cemetery, Lauren and I were at a laundromat when a young Parisian man with long, blond hair and denim overalls came over, introduced himself as Henri, and handed Lauren an origami rose he had just made. He looked just like a "hippie" from the 1960s and, we would discover, had the same loving nature most of them strived for. We thanked him and complimented his artistry. After talking for an hour or so, he wrote down his address and invited us to dinner that evening. We accepted. That's how things worked in the 1960s.

We went to the cemetery later that day. It was very crowded. When Lauren asked someone why, we learned that we had accidentally visited on the anniversary of Jim Morrison's death, July 3rd. That was the first coincidence.

A large crowd was gathered around his grave in reverent silence. As I read his grave marker and calculated his age, I discovered the second coincidence. I was the same age then that he was when he died — twenty-seven.

As I sat by his grave, I recalled the lines from his poetry that meant the most to me at that time.

"We must tie all these desperate impressions together."

"I can forgive my injuries in the name of wisdom, luxury, romance."

"Let me tell you about heartache and the loss of god. Wandering, wandering in hopeless night."

A man with dreadlocks played "People Are Strange" on a guitar. A young girl started to cry. Her boyfriend put his arm around her. It began to rain softly, as if her sadness was affecting heaven itself.

I wondered what Jim might say if he saw us all. I imagined it might be something like, "Cheer up. I'm only dead." After all, he had referred to death as a "beautiful friend" and asked, "Can you picture what will be? So limitless and free." Unfortunately for those who loved him, he wasn't afraid of dying.

That night, we took the Metro across town to Henri's apartment. His girlfriend and another couple were there. They looked like flower children, too. We all got along wonderfully.

It was a warm night so Lauren and I sat by a window. I looked out and noticed a mural of a man's face on the front wall of an apartment building across the street. I wasn't able to make out who it was at first, but, as I focused, I realized it was Jim Morrison! I asked Henri why it was there. He said, "That's where he died." He pointed to a window and said, "That was his apartment, right there."

That was the third and most chilling coincidence. We had not mentioned to Henri at the laundromat that we were planning to visit Jim Morrison's grave that day. In all of Paris, what were the chances of ending up, a few hours later, across the street from the apartment where he died?

I looked at the window of Jim's old apartment again and saw the silhouette of a male figure passing behind the curtains. My rational mind knew it was just the current tenant, but my imagination had become unhinged. It was Jim, alive and well, pacing the floor, working on a new poem.

I looked at the portrait on the wall again, illuminated by soft moonlight, and it seemed to be smiling playfully at my bewilderment. But that feeling turned into comfort as I imagined it was Jim's way of thanking me, not just for reading his work but for getting to the soul of it. I like to believe that artists who have passed on know when someone is savoring their creations, and that they smile for a moment before returning to whatever they're doing in heaven. I hope so.

Lauren and I said goodnight to our new friends and walked down the street toward the Metro. When we reached the corner, I asked her to wait for me. I walked back to the portrait on the wall and looked up at the window of Jim's former apartment, lit with a soft, yellow light.

I tried to remember the William Blake line that inspired the name of Morrison's band . . . "If the doors of perception were cleansed, every thing would appear to man as it is, Infinite. For man has closed himself up, till he sees all things thro' narrow chinks of his cavern."

I had been living in a cavern, but for the first time in years, death didn't seem so final. Everything did seem infinite. I thought of the friend I had lost and finally felt a little peace. I closed my eyes, touched the mural of Jim's face, whispered "thank you," and walked away into the Paris night, into life.

~Mark Rickerby

Chapter 6

Angels and Miracles

Dreams and Premonitions

50

Spidey Senses

*Brothers are like streetlights along the road; they don't
make distance any shorter but they light up the path
and make the walk worthwhile.*

~Author Unknown

I t was the morning of our seventh wedding anniversary, and
my husband and I were ecstatic. I had just taken a pregnancy
test, and the results were positive!

A few months earlier, my fertility specialist had gravely
stated that, after a year of failed treatment, I "should not expect to be
a biological mother."

We decided not to tell anyone until we were sure there was no
chance of losing the baby. My first pregnancy had ended in an unexpected
miscarriage that required emergency surgery, leaving us devastated.
As happy as we were, we decided to exercise caution.

Just then, the phone rang. It was my youngest brother, Wade.
Wade and I were very close and spoke regularly. Our two older brothers
affectionately referred to us as "The Witch Mountain Twins," likening
us to the stars of the Disney film because of the way our thoughts
seemed connected. Wade and I had always joked that we had "spidey
senses." Knowing this, my husband immediately said, "Don't tell…
not even Wade."

I answered the phone as normally as I could. It was Sunday, and
Wade was confirming plans we had to meet up the following Saturday.
After a few minutes of casual conversation, Wade became serious

and said, "Can I ask you something kind of personal?' I laughed and replied sure.

Wade lowered his voice and asked, "Are you pregnant?"

I paused and answered truthfully, "According to Dr. Gill, no... maybe not ever. Why?"

Wade continued, "This is going to sound crazy. I have had this feeling all morning. It's almost like I'm remembering a dream, only I didn't dream it. I'm sitting here, drinking coffee, and it's like I just know it."

"Know what?" I asked.

"That our spidey senses are changing. You know... that thing we do. Don't get me wrong. It's not that we won't be close anymore, but more like some of that ability is being transferred to a child. Your child. I feel like you're going to have a baby soon. This sounds crazy, but I just know you are. Are you sure you're not pregnant?"

I was astonished. The moment I learned I was pregnant, Wade knew.

I had promised my husband I wouldn't tell. So I replied, "Wade, I'd love for that to be true. But I've just spent hundreds of dollars for the top fertility specialist in Houston to tell me — in his words — that I shouldn't expect to have kids. Let's just leave it at that."

Wade replied in a voice of absolute certainty, "Well, they're wrong."

Four months later, we announced we were pregnant with a baby girl. Before I told Wade, I asked him if he remembered our conversation from that day in October. He did. So it was no surprise when I told him I was pregnant that he simply replied, "I knew. But I was going to let you tell me when you were ready."

I gave birth to a beautiful baby girl five months later. And now that five years have passed, I often think about the words my brother spoke to me that day, about our "ability" transferring to a child. Wade and I still have a special bond, but like he said, it is different now. And some days, when my daughter looks at me with her beautiful, soulful blue eyes, I wonder if his prediction has already come true.

~Jolie Lisenby

51

Just a Dream Away

My grandmother is my angel on earth.
~Catherine Pulsifer

I was sitting on a wood bench in a garden filled with daisies, which were my grandmother's favorite flower. The sun was shining and felt warm on my skin. The air had a faint smell of sandalwood and vanilla. It was the unmistakable aroma of my grandmother's favorite perfume. She had passed away several years before, and I still missed her terribly.

All of a sudden I could hear her voice. It started off faint, like a whisper, and continued to grow louder and louder. "Wake up, you need to put him in his crib." She just kept saying it over and over, getting more and more frantic. Was she here? Her presence seemed so real.

The sunny sky turned dark and lightning began to shoot all around me. All of a sudden, I felt two frail hands grab my shoulders and shake me violently. I heard my grandmother's voice again: "Please wake up; you need to put him in his crib. There is not much time."

I woke up in a cold sweat. There were tears streaming down my face. It took me a moment to collect myself and figure out where I was. The room was dark, except for the glow of the television. I could hear the rain hitting the roof. I had fallen asleep watching cartoons on the couch again. I looked over at the recliner and saw my one-year-old sleeping peacefully, curled up under his favorite blanket. The thunder boomed outside and I decided that the sounds of the storm must have been responsible for my nightmare. I crawled off of the couch and went to get a glass of water.

As I entered the kitchen the lights started to flicker. I heard another loud burst of thunder and my electricity turned off completely. All of a sudden, my grandmother's words echoed through my mind. "You need to put him in his crib. There is not much time."

I walked back into the living room and went over to the recliner. I scooped my little man up into my arms. He nuzzled his head into my chest as I cradled him closer. I walked slowly to his room, navigating through the dark hallway, trying hard not to wake him. He smelled like lavender baby lotion. His eyelids fluttered and he smiled as he slept. I laid him in the crib, covered him with a blanket, and kissed him on his forehead. I whispered, "I love you more than pigs love slop." This was an old saying my grandfather had always told us. I stood there in the dark staring at him. I brushed my hand across his forehead and kissed him one more time.

As I was leaving his room, the entire house shook. There was a loud crash followed by the sound of wind and rushing water. My heart started pounding so fast I thought it was going to jump right out of my chest. I quickly looked back over to the crib. My son was still sleeping peacefully. I ran into the hallway. The wind was ripping through the house. I could feel the temperature dropping. When I reached the living room I saw a sight that brought me to my knees. A giant tree limb was sticking into the house though the bay window. It had landed right on the recliner that my son had been sleeping on moments before. There was broken glass everywhere. The wind and rain poured through the broken window. I ran over and tried to move the tree limb. I tried to push it back outside, but it was thick and heavy. I began shaking and crying hysterically. The reality of the situation hit me like a ton of bricks. If my son had still been lying on that recliner, his little body would have been crushed under the immense weight of the tree limb.

When the storm ended and the sun came back out, we inspected the tree. A bolt of lightning had hit it and severed the limb, which sent it flying through my bay window. The force and impact were enough to do severe damage to the house and ruin several pieces of furniture.

All of that could be repaired or replaced. I felt immensely grateful that my son was sleeping soundly in his crib when the branch came crashing in. I believe that my grandmother came to me in my dream that night, to save her great-grandson's life.

~Tiffany O'Connor

A Walk with Thelma

*The best reason for having dreams is that in
dreams no reasons are necessary.*
~Ashleigh Brilliant

"Y ou look radiant," I squealed, locking my arm through Thelma's as we strolled down the cobblestone sidewalk. "Look at you. You don't seem ill at all — you positively glow!"

Like a couple of schoolgirls we giggled and caught up on the past few years. It felt incredible seeing Thelma again. Thelma was eighty-nine, decades ahead of me, but our age difference didn't matter. Our friendship had blossomed from the moment we set eyes on each other.

As we walked, I felt so relieved that Thelma appeared healthier than ever. "You know, Thelma," I said, "yesterday, I had the strongest feeling I should phone you."

Although the cozy little shops beckoned us, window-shopping could wait for another day. We were too enthralled, asking questions, and catching up with each other. The path that had seemed so long suddenly ended and we found ourselves standing alone before a green pasture.

"It's that time," Thelma announced.

After hugging, we clung to each other, our eyes full of tears. I wanted to hold her forever. "I know you know, that even though I don't call as often as I should, I love and miss you a lot," I said, embracing her once more.

"I do know you love me," Thelma answered softly. "I love you too."

"We've got to do this more often," I cried. "I promise I'll come see you soon."

I'll never forget the love on Thelma's face. Her expression reminded me what I already knew in my heart, that there wasn't going to be another visit with her. Thelma's misty eyes gleamed as she grabbed my hand one last time and then gently let go as she faded away into the light.

And in that instant I woke up, brushing the tears from my face, knowing that I would never see Thelma again because I had received a call from her son, earlier that same morning, informing me that Thelma had passed away.

Upon hearing of Thelma's death, a feverish guilt consumed me all day. If only I'd followed through with visits or heeded my gut and called her the day before she died. "There's always tomorrow," I assured myself, but Thelma's tomorrows had run out and I hadn't even said goodbye. When I needed her most, Thelma's love reached me in my dream so that I could try and move past my guilt.

~Jill Burns

Dress for Heaven

I ask of life to shine meaning in everyone
who is searching.
~Aurora Hernandez

The morning after she died was unremarkable. I had slept the night through soundly, alone in my mother's queen bed, unaware of how ten hours could affect three lives. I awoke to a text from my mother. The first line read: "We almost lost our girl last night." It was the word *almost* that kept my breathing steady before I had time to register panic or dread. Or Numbness. Or whatever one might experience after finding out her little sister had died.

Almost.

For months Lisette's health had been declining in an ominously predictable way, so it was really no surprise to learn it had hit a drastic low. According to the compacted contents of a single text box, Lisette had coded—unresponsive to visual, audio, or tactile stimuli—for forty minutes, before the doctors at The Children's Hospital of Philadelphia were able to revive her.

The thing about an empty house is that it becomes that much emptier when the absences are unusual, unscheduled. It's not that I wasn't used to such times. In fact, I anticipated them through long stretches of stability, knowing from experience that *happy and healthy* were only temporary circumstances in our household. But preparation never made those times feel less hollow, less perpetually nerve-racking.

How long would they be gone? What kinds of tests would be administered? Would the results indicate the need for more surgery?

In childhood I mistook this feeling for excitement: an unexpected change that promised a sleepover at a friend's house. I also coveted the responsibility of packing Lisette's overnight bag quickly and smartly: her cleanest, full-coverage underwear, and a matching pajama set for strolls to the hospital's playroom. But now, at twenty-one, the severity of each occasion was no longer lost on me. With maturity came the realization that these "routine" trips were anything but. Until now, I had believed that her return to relatively normal health was a guarantee. Until now, processing an alternate outcome was inconceivable.

Prior to diagnosis, Lisette endured inexplicable suffering and an extreme sensitivity to light. While other babies delighted in the outdoors, Lisette wailed in discomfort until my mother blanketed her face from the sun. She knew instinctively that there was something gravely wrong with her second-born child. The doctors — as would become the norm — turned her away several times, insisting that Lisette was a normal, healthy baby girl. But as Lisette's pain increased and my mother's persistence grew, the existence of a serious problem could no longer be denied. By then Lisette's head was nearly twice the size it should have been.

When the correct diagnosis finally surfaced, Lisette's symptoms made perfect sense: Hydrocephalus is a condition caused by an inability of cerebrospinal fluid to flow freely and subsequently be absorbed efficiently, resulting in excess fluid that places an unnatural amount of pressure on the brain. Patients suffer a range of symptoms, including sensitivity to light and sound, excruciating migraines, vomiting, and lethargy. Treatment for the condition involves placing a shunt system into a ventricle in the brain, where a catheter connected to the shunt drains the excess fluid from the brain into the abdominal cavity.

Lisette had her first brain surgery when she was seven months old.

Although determining the cause of Lisette's suffering and providing a treatment seemed like a Godsend at the time, it was by no means a cure. It merely sparked the commencement of a lifelong journey — a one-way path landmarked by periodic surgeries, recurring symptoms, and eventually all-new symptoms which led to a related diagnosis. A secondary condition called Arnold-Chiari malformation surfaced when Lisette turned ten, the acknowledgement of which was slow to come as doctors attempted to lump her new complaints in with the old diagnosis of hydrocephalus. Eventual treatment for this second condition involved placing a mesh screen into the base of Lisette's skull to prevent her brain — forced downward by the pressure of the fluid — from being impaled on her spinal column.

At age twenty, Lisette had already undergone her eleventh surgery when I received the news of her rapid decline that morning.

Visiting hours were long over by the time I finally arrived at the hospital, but my mother's knack for getting on any nurse's good side made my presence a non-issue. We greeted each other warmly, exchanging reserved smiles and pleasantries as if one of us were returning from a long trip. For a few minutes we sat in the brightly lit corridor, and I listened to my mother recount last night's events in a measured, matter-of-fact tone.

"I remember watching the clock while they worked on her," she described numbly, "thinking to myself, this is the time they will write on her death certificate. 3:43 a.m."

Her voice never faltered, her eyes did not well up. She barely blinked or hesitated.

"She's sleeping now," she concluded, "but would you like to see her anyway?"

We made our way to Lisette's room. It was as dark as a space with only three solid walls would allow, the glass panels dividing her room from the hall accounting for a strange twilight glow.

She was sleeping, just as my mother had said, curled with her back to us. A tall, usually slender, girl, Lisette was about forty pounds over her normal weight then. Her illness had kept her bedridden and immobile for months. When Lisette was well, she was the quintessential social butterfly, exercising her wings on a daily basis, flitting from this or that event modeling her latest fashion acquisition. Her personality, her energy, and her wardrobe were an unstoppable force. An overwhelmingly confident, beautiful exterior masked nearly all traces of a chronic illness. But when she was ill, she lost all her energy and we knew we were about to start another round of severe health issues.

I took her in, all rounded curves and oblivion, her hands settled in relaxed fists beside her face like a child.

And the reality of watching her breathe smacked me in the chest, a hand stopping my heart in its tracks. I gasped and began to cry, never taking my eyes off Lisette's resting form. The blessing of observing her alive overwhelmed me. My mother embraced me, and the same blessing moved her finally to tears as well.

After a minute my mother ushered me out of the room so as not to wake my sister. "Do you know what Lisette told me after we got her back?" my mother asked when she regained her composure. "She said, 'I was in a room full of dresses. I found two white ones, and I just knew I had to decide between the two. I knew that making my decision would give me permission to cross over. Just before I touched the gown I had chosen, Grampy appeared.'"

Our Grampy had passed away on Christmas Eve the prior December.

"'Grampy said to me, "Honey, please don't do that. You'll break your mother's heart if you choose one." I tried to convince him to let me come with him, because I was tired of doing this. He said he understood, but that I just couldn't yet. Then I could hear the doctor's voice, calling my name, telling me to come back. And I could feel her pinching and touching me on my arms and legs.'"

Ignoring the chills that overtook me, I smiled, "Leave it to Lisette to think about fashion at a time like that."

Because humor, like a dry eye, conveyed the pretense of being okay, of courageous acceptance of the circumstances. Because humor kept my mind sheltered from examining the truth: my sister — younger, braver, uniquely fashionable, unimaginably positive — had been only one perfect white dress away from meeting God.

~Chanel Fernandez

Riding a White Horse in Heaven

The wind of heaven is that which blows
between a horse's ears.
~Arabian Proverb

There was no time to prepare. In February of 2007, while we were away on one of the very few trips of our married life, my husband Mike and I received the worst news that a parent could ever hear. Our disabled thirteen-year-old son, Jonathan, had been killed by a man who worked at the facility near our home in upstate New York. The grueling journey home felt like an eternity as we struggled to come to terms with how to tell our other son, Joshua, that his brother was gone.

We numbly walked through the preparations for Jonathan's funeral. At the same time we had to deal with a crush of media and the nightmare of trying to hold the man who killed Jonathan accountable for his actions.

It was surreal. This was the kind of thing that you saw on the news, and I never thought that something like this could happen to our family. In the midst of the darkness, however, I could hear God's voice reassuring me that Jonathan was with Him. I desperately clung to that hope.

Then, about three weeks after Jonathan's death, Mike and I had surprisingly similar dreams. Mike saw Jonathan sitting on a white horse holding a sword across his chest. He was wearing an ornate breastplate, and his hair appeared a bit lighter. He looked very handsome and appeared older than thirteen. In my dream I saw Jonathan riding full speed on a beautiful white horse. He was holding the reins in one hand and with the other he was holding a sword drawn high above his head as if riding into battle. His hair was moving up and down to the pounding of the horse's hoofs. He was wearing a shining breastplate, and his clothing was an off-white color. He looked very handsome and mature in my dream, too. He was not smiling, but his expression was one of purpose.

Mike and I marveled at the many similarities in our dreams, and we immediately knew that the Lord was giving us a glimpse of Jonathan and his purpose in Heaven. I knew that there were some scriptures in the Bible about white horses so I decided to look them up.

That's when I found it. In the book of Revelation 19:14 it says, "And the armies in Heaven, clothed in fine linen, white and clean, followed Him on white horses." We were absolutely astounded.

A week later, Mike and I attended a second memorial service held at the facility to bring closure to the other disabled kids who had known and loved our son. While at the service we noticed numerous pictures and other memorabilia set up around the room to remember him. As I was walking around the room looking at everything, I happened upon a photo of Jonathan that I had never seen before. In the photo Jonathan was leaning over a fence with a look of pure joy on his face as he was about to kiss a beautiful white horse.

My heart melted as I called Mike over to look at the amazing picture. We both instantly knew that this photo was a confirmation of the dreams God had given us the week before. Jonathan had loved horses from the time he was a toddler, and over the years we had taken many pictures of him with horses, but we had none with a white horse. We learned that Jonathan's teacher had taken the photo two months earlier during one of their outings to a local horse farm. She had forgotten all about the picture until she searched through her camera for photos of Jonathan for the memorial service.

She could never have imagined the significance of that photo to our broken hearts. We will treasure that photo every day until we are reunited with our precious son.

Three months later, the Governor of New York State signed Jonathan's Law, which gives the families of people with physical or mental disabilities access to all the records and incident reports related to them in care facilities. These records had previously been sealed. It was a great victory for the countless families of people with disabilities statewide, and a true example of how God works all things together for good. There is no doubt that Jonathan did battle in the heavens for the law that bears his name, and that he now rides with the armies of God.

~Lisa Carey

Finding the House on Balfour Street

More and more, when I single out the person who
inspired me most, I go back to my grandfather.
~James Earl Jones

Tall, gaunt and not one to suffer fools, Grandpa Balfour was one of the cornerstones of my life. He had proudly served in both world wars, was an accomplished accordion player and played the big drum in the Ingersoll pipe band. He and my grandma lived in a little house on Union Street, and every spring he tilled the ground in the back yard and grew potatoes, green onions, beans, cucumbers and carrots. My grandmother wanted to grow daisies and daffodils, but he overruled her, saying, "You can't eat flowers."

The summer I turned five I accompanied Grandpa Balfour twice a week to the local bowling green where he had a job rolling out the lawn. We crossed the train tracks, then the river, and finally went up the big hill, my small legs doing double time to keep up with his long strides. While he trimmed, mowed and rolled out the lawn, he'd leave me to play at the Thompsons' house. When he was finished, he'd stop for a cup of tea with Mrs. Thompson before taking my hand for the walk home. Sometimes we'd talk but mostly we were quiet. It was in those moments that I knew how much my Grandpa loved me.

He was a man of few words, except on the nights when he'd had

Dreams and Premonitions | 161

a few whiskies. Then he went on a non-stop talking jag, his thick Scottish brogue making him sometimes difficult to understand. He'd tell us tales — of his mother and sister and how hard it was to leave Scotland, of his first love, Jess, and how he met my grandmother Maggie. I never heard him talk about the war.

My favourite story was about the budgies. During the depression, Grandpa Joe had made extra money by raising and selling the colourful little songbirds. He told me how people would come from miles around with pennies they had tucked away, eager to have a little bit of colour and song in their otherwise grey lives. And it was true. The singing of the brilliantly hued birds that lived in shiny cages in a corner of my grandparents' living room could lift my spirits when little else could. Especially on dull winter days.

Grandpa Balfour died peacefully in his sleep at age seventy-two. I was sixteen and too preoccupied with teenage things to really let the pain of his loss sink in. My grandma no longer wanted to live in the little house on Union Street, and moved into an apartment. She gave me a few mementos of "my Joe" — his Bible, his accordion and a picture of him as a young man standing proudly with his big drum in full Scots regalia, a proud smile on his face.

Twenty-five years passed. I found myself a single mom teaching singing lessons — the love of music seeded in me by my grandpa. We lived in a small apartment and I dreamt of owning our own home. The year my daughter turned thirteen, I had enough money for a down payment and purchased a little bungalow in the east end of Toronto. After giving notice on our apartment, I began to pack in preparation for our move. We were both so excited until the call came from the real estate agent telling us that the deal on the bungalow had fallen through. Knowing I had two weeks to find a place for us to live, I went into a state of full-fledged panic.

My real estate agent pulled up every listing she had that fit the bill. The next week was a blur of driving through the city, looking at house after house. Nothing was right for us. Everything was too expensive, too small or falling apart at the seams. Seven days before we had to be out of our apartment, with no home in sight, I fell apart, thinking,

"Even if we find a place, how many people would be willing to vacate their property in such a short period of time?"

Needing to distract myself from my pain, I decided to take my daughter out to the cinema to see *Whale Rider*. In the story, the primary relationship is between the grandfather and the granddaughter, which of course, got me thinking about Grandpa.

That night he came to me in a dream. He was striding purposefully in front of me and I was running to keep up, calling out his name.

"Grandpa! Help me! My girl and I have no place to live. You've got to help. Please, please!" I woke up crying, the prayer to Grandpa Balfour still on my lips.

That morning I set out with the real estate agent, my eyes still puffy from the crying fit of the previous night. As she handed me the listings she said, "There's a new one that just came on the market this morning. It's on Balfour Street." The hairs stood up on the back of my neck.

The century-old townhouse was a bit ramshackle and needed a good coat of paint, but the bones were good, and the people were willing to move out within the week. I walked in the door and knew it was home.

As I reflect on this story, I realize that Grandpa Balfour was there for me in death as he had been in life, a quiet and constant presence. The house on Balfour Street was a safe haven for myself, and my daughter during a very difficult time. And the lesson I took from the experience has remained with me to this day, a reminder of the steady presence of the unseen hands that guide us.

~Elizabeth Copeland

56

An Owl in Winter

*Pay attention to your dreams — God's angels often
speak directly to our hearts when we are asleep.*
~Eileen Elias Freeman,
The Angels' Little Instruction Book

Familiar faces glowed in the amber lamplight of the living room. Laden with the knowledge that it was our last, tonight's cast party was more meaningful than the ones that came before it. The university was closing its doors to us and preparing to open them to a new group of students eager to embark on the theatre journey we had just completed.

Standing in a corner of the small kitchen, absorbing the warmth and laughter around me, I felt Joel's embrace. The depth of our emotional connection overshadowed any pain that may have come from the unrequited nature of my love for him. Tonight he took me in his arms, wrapped me in his warmth and my tears replaced the words I couldn't find.

"You're my Debsie," he whispered. "Look into these eyes. One day you will look into them when they're old."

Fate brought us together again twice in the years that followed. First for Joel's wedding and the second and final time for a brief lunch back in our old college town. He slid into the booth across from me, reached into his pocket and brought out a small box.

"This is for you, Debsie."

It was a rubber stamp with a picture of a tiny white kitten on its wooden top. The gift was sweet and thoughtful, the gesture laden with meaning.

The following year, Joel moved to Japan, where he would spend the next five years teaching English. We wrote regularly. His letters were filled with the new experiences of a foreign land and a different culture, while mine detailed the continued pursuit of our mutual passion for the theatre and my equally fervent dream of becoming a writer. I would come to realize, many years later, the blessings of the pre-computer age, without which, I would never have had the cherished handwritten cards and letters he sent me.

In early 1995 I received what would be my last letter from Joel. It lacked the usual playful, upbeat quality of the others as he told me of his impending divorce and plans to leave Japan. After that we lost touch and I never heard from him again.

Despite the passage of time and a multitude of life events and milestones, Joel remained a palpable presence in my life. And time, as it is sometimes known to do, shifted in my consciousness to erase all the years that separated us.

By May of 2013, technology replaced the pen and Facebook brought the past and the present together in a startling collage of old and new. Searching for Joel's page, I looked for his name among those of the old group, but he was clearly, jarringly, not there. Frustrated with my failed attempts to find him, I climbed into bed and slipped into a dream that would change me forever. In it, I was reading a newspaper, its ink staining my fingers, when someone gently told me that Joel had passed away. In an instant I realized that I was reading Joel's obituary. The cause of death was unclear but there was no mistaking the words in front of me.

When I woke, a calm, melancholy knowing settled over me, a sense that something other than a dream had just occurred. The following day I tentatively typed Joel's name into a search engine and hit send. What I saw next knocked the breath out of me. There, on my computer screen, in crisp black print, was the obituary I had been reading in my dream the night before. Joel had died of complications from surgery.

Still reeling, my feelings of loss and grief were almost immediately buffered by a strong sense of his nearness, a presence in my consciousness that was somehow more concrete than it had been during our years apart. My writing was infused with his love and support as I completed a picture book manuscript called, *Owls Can't Sing.* Preparing to approach an agent, I talked to Joel and asked for his blessing. "Please send me a sign in the form of an owl," I prayed and knew that if he could, Joel would send me an owl — a picture, a word, a trinket.

Two weeks later on a crisp February afternoon, I sat in my suburban New York living room writing a query letter, when a tapping on glass drew my attention to the French doors. There, in the bright winter light, I found myself looking into the large, round eyes of an owl. And Joel's words came back to me. "Look into these eyes. One day you will look into them when they're old." Maybe this was his way of keeping that promise.

~Deborah L. Staunton

57

Grandma's Bread

A grandmother is a little bit parent, a little bit teacher,
and a little bit best friend.
~Author Unknown

"So no behavioral shifts in school — that's a relief. He seemed happy when he told me about your cooking lesson," I said to my son's kindergarten teacher, Mrs. Flint.

"What cooking lesson?" asked Mrs. Flint.

"Didn't you teach a cooking lesson?"

"No," said Mrs. Flint.

"What? Brian told me he baked bread in school. He even described all the steps," I said, confused.

A smile crossed Mrs. Flint's face. "Did your grandmother bake bread?" she asked.

My grandmother had passed away a few weeks prior to the teacher conference. Ever since then, my older son, Brian, had been behaving in alarming ways at home. He was being extremely hard on himself. Any time he made even a minor mistake, he would cry that he was the "worst ever." Sometimes he would hit himself. He would wail every night at bedtime because he was having dreams that my husband or I would die or he would die or my younger son, Leo, would die. He missed Grandma, but death in general was rocking his happy little almost five-year-old world.

One night at bedtime, he threw a tantrum and screamed that

he would "just jump out a window!" His behavior and words were breaking my heart.

She was your typical Italian, Catholic grandma. She and my pop immigrated to New York and moved mountains to give their family a chance at the American dream. She worked hard in a curtain factory. She was a dutiful wife; she cooked like crazy, said zany things, and had no problem sharing her opinions, because obviously, she knew best. She took care of all of us. Italian grandmas take great pride in their grandchildren but take great, grand pride in their great-grandkids, and my boys felt it.

"Look-a ma great-grandson. 'E's a good boy," was a typical greeting, followed by a bear hug and wet kiss.

Her food was legendary. Homemade spaghetti, hand rolled gnocchi, lasagna, meatballs, pizza, polenta, pastina, pizelles — everything delicious that came from Italy was her specialty. Everyone had a favorite, but if you asked her what she liked best, she'd say "If you put-ta me in prison, I be fine. Just give-a me bread and I be okay."

"Bread? Really?" was my response. But as I thought about it, I realized the beauty of it. She baked her own, of course. Sometimes she would let me help her.

"Wash-a you hands. You want to poison the dough?" was her famous line every time.

I ate it toasted, with butter, for as long as I can remember. We dipped it in sauce, in oil, ate it with olives, peppers and prosciutto. It was there with every meal, nourishing us.

When I was pregnant with Brian I was extremely ill. I was diagnosed with hyperemesis and had to have IVs to get through it. I couldn't stomach anything, not even water. I felt awful and was frightened to my core that I wasn't sustaining the baby. I got on my knees and prayed for a healthy child every night. The only thing I could tolerate was my grandmother's bread. I lived on it, which meant he lived on it.

We had a family meeting over breakfast the day after my grandmother died. "Boys, I have good news and bad news," I started. "The good news is that Grandma went up to heaven to be with Pop-Pop. She feels strong and happy. She is having fun and can watch over us.

The bad news is that we will miss her very much."

"Will we ever see her again?" asked Brian.

"Someday, when we are very old and God decides it's our turn to go up to heaven, she will be there waiting for us," I replied.

I tried to reassure him that everything was okay. "It's normal for very old people to go to heaven. It's okay to miss her but you don't need to be afraid of anything happening to any of us. You will see her again someday…"

Our talks about death continued around these very logical and… hollow themes. My reassurances were not reassuring. The truth was, I was in no position to tell my son not to fear, because from the moment I was pregnant with him, I had been petrified of death. I was afraid I would die, or the boys might die, or my husband would die. I knew logically, that there was no reason to think that way, but the fear had a stranglehold on my heart.

I became a hovering, helicopter parent. I thought it made me feel in control. I felt that their happiness, not just their wellbeing, was my responsibility. I put heavy pressure on myself. I beat myself up over little things like the tone of my voice or not giving each boy enough one-on-one time. Then I had the nerve to wonder where my son's anxiety came from.

"Brian, do you remember when you told me you baked bread in school?" I asked.

"Yes, it was so fun," said Brian.

"Well, Mrs. Flint told me she never did that with you."

"No, I did it with Grandma. She picked me up in my classroom and brought me down to the cafeteria. She said to wash our hands to get the poison off," he said with a smile. "Leo was with us," he said.

"Yeah, you have to roll the dough and then you pat it. It feels squishy," added Leo.

"But first you have to sprinkle the flour on the board so it doesn't stick," Brian reminded Leo. "Then you put a towel over the dough and let it grow."

Those were the exact steps my grandmother always took. But here's the thing: my boys never made bread with Grandma or anyone else for that matter! I called my mother.

"She must've come to them in a dream. They both said the same thing. How could Brian know about the wash off the poison thing?" I said.

"Kelly, you're not going to believe this, but I keep smelling her bread," my mother said slowly. "I smelled it constantly right after she died. Now it comes and goes."

I think my grandma stayed with us, to give us peace. After Brian "made bread" with her, our conversations changed. It wasn't about being logical, or trying to control death by explaining when people die. It was about having faith that we will always be connected and that love is everlasting. We talked about leaving it up to God, trusting him as our father, so that we could let go of the worry. We started living in the present and rediscovered the joy each day held.

I landed my helicopter and began parenting with less control, anxiety and pressure. We broke out of our prison of fear. We love freely now, thanks to my grandma's bread.

~K. Seward

58

Fun Up Here

Perhaps they are not stars, but rather openings in
heaven where the love of our lost ones pours
through and shines down upon us to let
us know they are happy.
~Eskimo Proverb

I dressed my ever growing body in stretchy dress clothes and headed out for another day at the office. As I began my thirty-minute commute, I quickly drove by my parents' house two streets over and noticed my mother's black sedan parked in the driveway. I recalled she had mentioned the prior evening that she was experiencing a headache. I cracked a smile and called her to poke fun at her for playing hooky from work for a mere headache. The phone wasn't answered.

I had a new employee starting, and things were busy at work. But a couple of hours later I phoned again. There was still no answer. For reasons I will never be able to explain, I got a sinking feeling in my stomach. I called my father, and although he thought I was being overly dramatic, he drove home to check on my mother.

She was gone, at age sixty-three. A massive aneurysm had killed her.

I remember yelling, "How could this happen? I'm nine months pregnant!" I had experienced two miscarriages, and this miracle baby was days away from arriving — my mother's first grandchild.

The night after my mother passed, my best friend had a dream and she desperately wanted to tell me about it. I was not emotionally stable enough, so I politely asked her if she could share her dream with me another time.

Twelve days later, my son was born. It was surreal. I had lost my mother, and now I was a mother. I didn't know how I could possibly collect myself enough to take care of another human being. I wanted my mom. I wanted her to meet her grandson. I felt alone, and I felt intensely angry that she was gone.

Weeks went by and I tried to settle into a routine, but in all honesty, it was a very trying time.

Again my friend nagged me to let her tell me about her dream. I finally relented and said, "I will try to listen."

"In my dream your mom appeared holding the hands of two children. The boy was taller and older than the girl. Your mom said, 'Tell Nicole we are having fun up here.'"

I wept. My mother was in heaven taking care of the two children I had miscarried. I was wrong the entire time — she might not have met my third child yet, but she got to meet the first two children, the ones I hadn't known. There was a sense of relief that my children were in the hands of the best mother I have ever known.

I still grieve, and I still have incredibly difficult days, but I smile thinking about my three loves up in heaven. My angels are "having fun up here."

~Nicole Vickers

59

Sojourn of the Spirit

Mothers hold their children's hands for a
short while, but their hearts forever.
~Author Unknown

I t was a cold, gray morning in March when I woke to the phone
ringing. My heart sank. I knew it would not be good news.

"Mom has taken a turn for the worse," my sister Nancy
said, speaking in a soft voice. "She's been moved to hospice."

Within twenty-four hours, Mom had five of her six children at
her side in Aurora, Colorado. My older brother Michael traveled from
Santa Fe, New Mexico, my younger brother Richard traveled from
Michigan, and I came in from New York. The eldest, Rose, living in
California, was unable to be with us. My two younger sisters, Nancy
and Diane were living in Colorado near Mom.

As adults, we had always lived in different states, and as the
years went on we got together less and less. It would be good to see
each other, but not for this reason. Our life as a family had been a
patchwork of good times and bad, ups and downs. We had our share
of problems, not unlike other families, but we came together for Mom
and for each other.

The hospice center was beyond wonderful and I knew Mom was
in good hands. As she drifted in and out of consciousness, the nurses
met her every need and treated her like a dear friend, giving us a great
deal of comfort.

When I tried to speak to Mom, she looked my way, but with

Dreams and Premonitions |

vacant eyes. I feared she was unreachable. The nurse encouraged me to continue talking to her, "The sense of hearing is often the last thing to go," she said, squeezing my hand.

We gathered around Mom's bed and talked about happy and sad times… laughing, crying, venting. Then we each took turns having private moments with her. I told her over and over that she was beautiful and that I loved her and would miss her every day. I sensed once again that she was slipping into an unreachable darkness. Somehow I felt her fear. "Take me with you," I gently whispered in her ear. "If only in spirit, I will be forever by your side."

Mom's priest was called and we gathered around her and prayed. She was still struggling… as if she wanted to say or do something, but couldn't.

"Tell her to let go," the priest gently said. "She needs to hear it from all of you. She needs to know it's okay."

We each told her we were going to be fine, that she deserved to let go. That she deserved to be at peace. Still she struggled…

"Tell her you forgive her," the priest continued. "Ask for forgiveness in return, for whatever transgressions that may have taken place." We all looked at each other and knew in our hearts the priest was right. One by one we forgave her and asked for her forgiveness. Mom finally drifted into a calmer state. Incredibly, within a matter of minutes she slipped away softly, peacefully. Without saying it, we knew that forgiving Mom and asking her forgiveness in return was what released her. It was a powerful moment that left us silent and reflective.

Afterward, we each dealt with the loss in our own way. Michael and Diane went out to make phone calls. Richard, Nancy and I went into the family lounge. Richard slipped into the recliner as Nancy fell onto the couch. Exhausted, I sat at a table and put my head down and closed my eyes. My journey began.

I soared high above snow-capped mountains that were glistening so bright they took my breath away. Suddenly, without warning, I was driven into the earth; layers of dark soil splitting before me. I came out into bright light and looked upon a field of wildflowers dancing in the breeze. Their purple and blue colors were so vibrant, I know of nothing on this earth to compare. I was taken up, once again, high into the sky with nothing but luminous rays of light surrounding me. At that moment in time, a sense of stillness and serenity washed over me. I was at peace.

I opened my eyes and sat straight up. I noticed my brother looking at me and my sister rubbing her eyes.

"I had the most incredible dream," I said, looking at the two of them.

My sister calmly said, "Were you taken into the earth with layers of soil splitting before you?"

My brother's eyes widened as he spoke, "And did you soar above purple and blue wildflowers?"

Our mother had taken my brother, sister and me on her journey. In so doing, we knew she was safe, pain-free and in the loving arms of her God. And we were left with an indescribable feeling of tranquility and peace. Our mother gave us a gift. She took us with her just as I had asked.

I shared this experience at my mother's funeral as I gave the eulogy. Afterward, our family physician approached me and asked if I knew how lucky I was.

"In my practice," she said, looking at me intently, "I have heard stories similar to yours. Compelling stories — tangible, yet unexplainable. It truly was a blessing that you and your siblings were privileged to have had such a miraculous experience."

I believe, in the end, it's all about loving others and loving ourselves. Loving enough to forgive.

What I know for sure is the uncertainty I had while my mother was dying turned to calm and happiness after our journey. Ever since, more often than not, I have a vase of flowers on my dining room table. I always look for purple and blue wildflowers.

~Linda Ann Feist

Chapter
7

Angels and Miracles

Touched by an Angel

60

The Man Who Wasn't There

Never drive faster than your guardian angel can fly.
~Author Unknown

The cruise control was set at sixty-five miles per hour as I headed down the highway toward work. It was five in the morning and I was tired. I remember thinking that I would get a cup of coffee before my shift began.

The next conscious thought I had was that I was in some sort of terrible dream. I felt water dripping on my face and intense pain in my lower left leg. I looked up, stunned, to see rain coming through my shattered windshield. It was still dark outside and I couldn't tell where I was.

I looked down at the maroon blouse I was wearing. "I know I am dreaming," I thought. "Because I don't have a blouse this color." My mind went again to the pain in my leg. "You can't feel pain when you're dreaming, can you?"

I reached down and touched my leg and felt something thick and sticky. I brought my hand up to my face and saw blood dripping from my fingers. It wasn't a dream.

Horrified, I looked around. Somehow I had driven down a road off the main highway. There were car lights in the distance but they were too far away for anyone to notice me. I needed to get out of the car and go back to the highway to find help. Then I lost consciousness again.

When I came to, the sky had begun to lighten and I saw shattered bits of glass all over the front seat and me. Now I could see what had happened. I had somehow crashed into a cement mixer, far away from the highway.

I heard a soft voice say, "Stay in the car. Help will be here soon." I turned and saw a young man with blond curls peering at me through the window. He reached inside the car and patted my hand. I sank in and out of consciousness. Each time I awoke I remembered the words the young man had spoken and stayed in the car. As I became more lucid I remembered buying the maroon blouse the day before.

When the paramedics arrived and prepared to load me into the ambulance I asked about the young man who had called them. They pointed to a rugged looking man in a hard hat, flannel shirt, jeans and scuffed boots who was standing off to one side. I shook my head as the man approached. "He isn't the one I saw." I protested. "He isn't the one who spoke to me."

The man came closer and leaned over me. "You're in an equipment storage yard of the construction company I work for. You crashed through the fence and rammed into a cement mixer. The only reason I came by here today was because it started raining unexpectedly and we couldn't work on our scheduled project. I was just returning some tools to the shed." He shook his head. "I could barely see the top of your head because you were slumped over. I didn't know if you were dead or alive and I got too spooked to approach the car. I never spoke to you. I just called for help. There was never anyone else here until the paramedics arrived. You must have been dreaming or hallucinating." The paramedics nodded in agreement.

I later learned that I had blacked out, crossed the highway, jumped a ditch and cut across another road, crashed through a fence and knocked over a soft drink machine before being stopped by the cement mixer. I had a compound fracture in my left leg, a split lower lip that required surgery, and numerous small cuts on my face from the shattered windshield. The doctors decided that I had not fallen asleep at the wheel, because if I had, I would have woken up quickly after I went off the road. Instead, they decided I had blacked out, although they could find no medical reason for it. They also said it was a good thing I didn't try to get out of the car and stand on my broken leg, as that could have killed me.

Everyone I spoke to had the same opinion as the man from the construction company who found me. There was no young man with blond curls in the construction yard that day. My only rescuer had been the rugged fellow who ultimately called for help.

But I can see the young man's kind face as clearly today as I saw it the day of the accident. I know he was there, to comfort me and to keep me from trying to get out of the car. And I know that God sent the rain that wasn't in the forecast that morning so that somebody would return the tools to the site.

~Elizabeth Atwater

61

A Penny from Above

*Faith comes alive when the Word read from the page
becomes the Word heard in your heart.*
~Rex Rouis

I t was January 2015 and I had the baby blues. I was recovering from a C-section after being on strict bed rest at the end of my pregnancy. I hadn't lost any of my pregnancy weight and my little baby, Abbie, was in a brace twenty-four hours a day because of a hip displacement.

My husband and I were not doing well financially and we were under a lot of stress. We were living with my mother, who was having her own problems, living on a disability pension after going through breast cancer and ulcerative colitis.

We had no prospects for owning a house. What I really wanted was one with a separate suite for my mother, so that we could take care of her. We needed more room, a higher income, and a healthy baby free of her brace.

I was a bit of an emotional wreck, and I turned to a book — *Chicken Soup for the Soul: Angels Among Us* — for a change in perspective. I had always had a fascination with the supernatural and reading the stories left me in awe and wonder.

I started reading in bed one night. One of the stories was about a lady who found a penny on a day when she was missing the lucky penny that she needed for an important exam. I also read about people discovering their guardian angels and asking for signs from them. I decided to pray and ask my guardian angel for guidance.

"Guardian Angel, if you are out there please give me a sign. Things have been kind of down lately. Thank you, God, for blessing me with my beautiful baby girl. I know she is a miracle and I am so thankful she is healthy. I have been feeling really low lately and I don't know what to do. It's not working out how I hoped and my husband and I are fighting like cats and dogs! Please give me a sign that everything will work out, and keep my family healthy, happy, and safe. Amen!" I went to sleep that night dreaming of angels.

The next day, my mother and I were in the waiting area at Abbie's ultrasound appointment when my mom pointed a few feet in front of us and said quietly, "Look. It's your lucky penny."

I glanced at it and said simply, "Oh yeah," not thinking much of it.

Mom continued. "Imagine it has your birth year on it. Then it truly would be your lucky penny."

I replied, "That would be funny, but what are the chances of that?" I left the penny sitting there, but then I thought about the story I had read the night before about a lucky penny.

I got up slowly and sauntered over to pick up. I remember thinking "There's no way it will have my birth year on it." I picked up the penny and noticed it was American, not Canadian. I flipped it over eagerly to the side with Abraham Lincoln's head, searching for the date. 1986!

"Wow," I exclaimed to my mother.

"It says 1986, maybe it is my lucky penny," I thought to myself. I had never really examined an American penny before and as I looked at it more closely I saw words over Lincoln's head: "In God We Trust."

I immediately had a feeling of inner calm and gratitude, knowing this penny was meant for me, a little sign from my guardian angel. I was to trust in God. Everything would be okay.

The ultrasound appointment went well, actually better than expected! Abbie's hips were setting at a faster than average pace. I smiled at the doctor and thanked him, squeezing my lucky penny tightly in the palm of my hand.

It's been four months since I found my lucky penny and I have received lots of blessings. Things are turning out better then I could have thought or imagined.

Not long after I received my lucky penny my husband's parents offered to help us buy a house! We found the perfect home in a new development that has a park across the road, a library, aquatic center and beautiful nature trails. It even has a suite for my mother.

My husband also was offered a new job in his field without even searching. It has increased his income and has promising potential for growth in the near future. I have lost my baby weight, have more energy and feel positive about the future.

Now, if there's anything getting me down I just remember my lucky penny and remind myself to trust in God.

~Andrea K. Howson

62

My Olathe Angel

Alone is impossible in a world inhabited by angels.
~Author Unknown

I was alone in my hospital room. All the other victims from the van accident had been taken to a different hospital and my mom and sister weren't flying in until the next morning.

How did I get here? One minute I was laughing with my friends, eating a Subway sandwich in the front bench seat of the van and reveling in our speech and debate tournament successes. The next minute there was rolling and screaming and flying and now, here I was, crying and alone in Olathe, Kansas — wherever that was.

I cried some more. Why was I in a different hospital than everyone else? Was I better? Worse? Was everyone still alive? Why wouldn't anyone tell me anything?

I remembered seeing my friend Dena flying through the air. "Jeez, she shouldn't be doing that. It looks dangerous. I hope she's okay," I thought to myself, not aware yet that I was doing the same thing. It's funny what the mind does to protect itself.

And then… thud. I hit the ground… hard. I blacked out, I guess, because the next thing I knew an older woman with a charming Southern accent was kneeling over me and the sky was above me.

"It's going to be all right, sweetheart. You're going to be just fine." But I had a sense she doubted her own words. She kept looking around for help. I felt what must have been blood dripping down my face.

"Shh. Shh. Just sit real still, you're going to be fine." Again, her face didn't look as confident as her words.

My left arm felt weird. I kept trying to lift it to my eyes to get a better look at it. It was excruciatingly painful and entirely numb. Don't ask me to explain that.

"Oh, don't do that, sweet dear. Leave your hand be." But my arm wasn't right. The angles were all wrong. I couldn't figure it out. More blood dripped down by my eye. It must have looked like I was crying blood.

Now I was in the hospital bed and I couldn't roll over. There were too many contraptions all around me. I wanted my mom… or someone.

I must have fallen asleep again, because when I woke up there was a middle-aged woman sitting in the chair next to my bed. Was it a nurse? I didn't think it was my mom, but I couldn't tell. I was on a lot of painkillers and it was the middle of the night.

"Sorry! Did I wake you?" the woman asked. I shook my head no. "My husband said we shouldn't come, that it was ridiculous. But when I heard on the radio about your accident and that they sent you here to Olathe all alone, I told my husband, "Bob, turn around. We have to go see that girl. I bet she is lonely and scared. It's a three-hour drive, but I didn't care."

I didn't think it was the same woman from the crash site. Was it? I felt so confused.

"I'm so sorry this happened to you. What a tragedy. The news said some of you are really bad off. I'm so sorry. You're family will be here soon I think, right?"

How did she get in? It had to be 3 a.m. But somehow it felt okay. I felt okay.

"I wanted to bring you something, but I couldn't find the right thing. So I just brought you this cup. It's silly…"

There were cartoon characters on the outside and candy inside.

"It's more for a child. I guess I thought you were younger. Do you like it?"

I smiled and nodded, and then I must have dozed off again. I slept fitfully, but every time I opened my eyes, the woman was still in the chair next to me smiling, holding the cup. I felt somehow comforted.

"You're not alone," I heard her say before I finally fell deeply asleep.

When I awoke in the morning, a nurse was in my room doing nurse-like things.

"Feeling a little better this morning?" she asked. I nodded. "Your mom called again. She and your sister will be here by noon."

I swallowed hard, looking around the room, remembering my late night visitor. Was that woman real or just a drug-induced hallucination?

"Was there... did someone come in my room last night?" I asked.

"Nope, just me. I was on duty all night."

"There wasn't a woman who drove up from Kansas City in my room?"

The nurse laughed. "Don't think so, sweetie. You were out pretty good. I checked on you several times. Plus visiting hours were closed. No one could have gotten in. You rest now. That's the best thing for you."

The nurse left. I was alone, but felt somehow better. Who came to see me in the middle of the night?

Then I smiled. Across the room on the window ledge was a cartoony coffee cup filled with candy. The sun poured onto my face.

~Kim Schultz

63

A Desperate Situation

*The golden moments in the stream of life rush past us
and we see nothing but sand; the angels come to visit
us and we only know them when they are gone.*
~George Eliot

It was nearly midnight in a small town in New Mexico and I was terrified. I cowered in my car, on a deserted side street, while five angry young men milled around my car, shouting obscenities. My hound dog Sheba was barking furiously, doing her best to keep between the menacing men and me.

One of the men, his face twisted with rage, glared through the windshield and yelled, "I could kill that dog with my bare hands." Several replies came to my mind, but I said nothing, because I didn't want to antagonize him and make matters worse. But things did get worse anyway.

The frustrated men began pounding their fists on the roof of my car and kicking their boots against its doors. Sheba jumped from window to window, snapping in vain at the men through the glass.

I couldn't believe the predicament I was in. It had all started because I had gone out of my way to give a friend a lift home from work. After I had dropped my friend off, a clean cut young man walked up to my car and asked if I could please help him get his car started. All he needed was someone to jumpstart his battery.

Even though it was night, and I was alone with my dog, I didn't feel threatened at that point. And so I agreed to help this polite stranger get his car started. After all, I had grown up in the West, where it was traditional to lend a helping hand. Never had I refused to help another motorist and never had anyone ever refused to help me when I had car trouble. So helping this stranger simply seemed like the ordinary thing to do.

I had slowly driven my car around the corner from my friend's house, following the young man as he walked along on the sidewalk. When I saw the older model car with its hood up, I pulled my car parallel to it. Then the man opened the hood of my car and connected jumper cables from his battery to mine. Four other men suddenly came from behind a row of bushes and surrounded my car. That was when the polite young man turned vicious and ugly.

So there I sat, with my hood up and my battery attached to the other car's battery by jumper cables. Even though I still had the motor running, I was effectively trapped, because I couldn't see to drive with the hood up and I didn't dare get out of the car to close it.

I was helpless and I knew it. For the time being, Sheba was keeping the men from breaking the windows to get at me. But how long could she keep it up? She wasn't a young dog anymore — would she finally drop from exhaustion? I had raised her from the day she was born, and for nearly ten years Sheba had been my constant companion. And so I feared for her as well as for myself.

Even though I was terrified, I tried not to think about the "what ifs" — what if they broke the windows, what if they got one of the car doors open, what if they got their hands on Sheba and me.

I was on the verge of becoming hysterical and although it took every ounce of my self-control, I wouldn't let myself scream or even cry. First of all, I wasn't about to give those men the satisfaction of seeing me fall to pieces. But even more importantly, I knew that if I gave in to my emotions, I'd really be lost. I had to keep thinking clearly or I would have no chance of saving myself if an opportunity to escape did present itself.

As scared as I was, I was even angrier, and I think that helped me regain control of my emotions. I was indignant — I had gone out of my way to help that "polite" young man start his car. And this was how he repaid me?

I glanced at the gas gauge. It was nearly full, so at least I didn't have to worry about running out of gas anytime soon.

I hadn't realized that the window on the driver's side was down about three inches until I heard a low, soft voice close to my ear. Glancing at the side window, I saw the outline of a figure, but I couldn't make out the words he was saying. "What?" I asked.

"Get ready," he whispered. "I'm going to pull the cables loose and slam the hood. Then you get out of here — quick!"

I slid the gearshift into low and waited. My hands were trembling so hard I could scarcely grasp the steering wheel.

The instant the hood slammed shut I jammed the gas pedal completely to the floor and the car shot forward. My surprised attackers, in danger of being run over, leaped away from the car.

I never looked back and I didn't dare stop until I was downtown. The local movie theater had just closed and the sidewalks were full of people walking to their cars. Then, and only then, did I park my car and give in to my emotions. I leaned my head against the steering wheel and waited until my pulse slowed down to normal and my hands weren't shaking anymore. Then I drove the rest of the way home, grateful that I had escaped a dangerous situation unscathed.

I've often thought about that man who saved me and I wish I had been able to thank him, but there hadn't been time. I never even got a glimpse of his face, and to this day, I wonder what he looked like.

But I was left with a lot of other unanswered questions about that night. This quiet man, who saved Sheba and me, where did he come from? He appeared from out of nowhere; one minute he wasn't there and the very next instant there he was, standing by my window. Why was it that the other men, who were threatening me, didn't even seem to notice him? How was he able to unhook the cable and slam the hood shut right under their very noses, without them stopping him? After all, there were five of them and he was alone.

Only later did I realize that my dog never barked at the man who saved us, not even when he leaned close to whisper into my ear. This during a time when Sheba was excited, ready to fight, and trying to protect me from everyone out there. Why was it that she didn't feel the need to protect me from the man who was trying to save us? She acted as if she hadn't even seen him.

I know that each of us is supposed to have a guardian angel, and I believe mine came to my rescue that night. For me, it's the only conclusion that makes any sense.

~Connie Kutac

64

The Polar Bears

To forgive is to set a prisoner free and discover
that the prisoner was you.
~Lewis B. Smedes

Diane was the youngest of the four of us. She was a bit of a rebel, but you couldn't help but love her. She was funny, strong, smart, talented, beautiful, and passionate.

One of her passions was protecting polar bears! She was in awe that such strong, dominant animals were seen as symbols of acceptance in some cultures. Fascinated with spiritual stories, she believed as they did, that in order to survive, the polar bear allowed spirits to whiten his coat to blend with the snow. "His acceptance," she confirmed, "is a sign of his strength." Diane would tuck photos of polar bears inside random cards that she would send when she knew someone needed words of support.

No one ever thought Diane would die of an accidental overdose, much less get hooked on drugs. A crippling accident in her twenties had introduced her to pain medications and she couldn't overcome her addiction.

My brother and I had said goodbye to our parents, our older brother, and many relatives and friends, but Diane's passing released too many emotions too quickly. For years we danced around our emotions. Holidays were the most difficult.

One particular Thanksgiving would be no different. It had been a long day visiting my younger brother and his family. Somehow, we couldn't stop talking about Diane, arguing about her, trying to resolve so many unanswered questions. We were angry with her and we hadn't been able to forgive her for the way she died.

I started my long drive home from my brother's house still haunted by thoughts of my sister's passing. "It will be a long night adding to the long day," I thought.

Halfway home, I realized I had forgotten to buy a birthday card for a dear friend who never forgot mine. I only knew of one grocery store close to home that would be open and fortunately, they sold cards. So, as midnight approached, I took the exit that detoured me to the "24/7" store.

The store was practically empty, just a few shoppers filling their baskets. I had the card aisle all to myself until I felt the presence of someone next to me. She was an old woman, dressed in a turquoise and gold sari. Her face was veiled, exposing only her dark, penetrating, yet gentle eyes. The deep, weathered wrinkles that encircled them revealed she was an old soul. "Here," she said in a soft Indian accent, "I believe these cards are for you!" She handed me two cards.

I thanked her, and looked down at the cards, which were the same. On the front was a photo of a polar bear with his giant paw across his eyes. When you opened the card there were only two visible words, "I'm sorry!"

I immediately knew what this was. It was a message from Diane — her way of letting us know she was sorry and that it was time for both of us to heal and to forgive. I turned to thank the old woman again, but she was gone. I raced through the store, up and down aisles asking the few shoppers and employees if anyone had seen her. No one remembered the old woman in the turquoise and gold sari.

I knew this was no coincidence. Diane was saying she was sorry. But there was more to it. Staring at the photos of the polar bears, I remembered her symbolic story of how they accepted a white coat of fur in order to survive in their snow-covered domain. I heard my sister's voice reminding me, "There is strength in acceptance!" I knew then, her real message for my brother and me, was about acceptance.

It was the key component that was missing for our survival as well. In order to forgive and heal, we needed to accept not only Diane's way of life but also her death.

The next day, I mailed my brother his card with a lengthy note explaining how I received it. He understood and accepted the miracle that I had witnessed. Years have passed and we have healed, but my polar bear card from heaven remains on my fireplace mantle enclosed with my own personal note to my little sister: Apology accepted!

~Lainie Belcastro

65

My Mother's Warning

*What a happy and holy fashion it is that those who
love one another should rest on the same pillow.*
~Nathaniel Hawthorne

My mother and father met on a ship to Japan when they were in their mid-twenties. My mother was from the Midwest and my father from Washington, D.C. He was in the Army and was being stationed in Japan. My mother was starting a secretarial job for the U.S. Government. They fell in love and were married in Japan about a year later.

Like all marriages, theirs had its ups and downs. My father focused his life on a military career. He put himself through college, flight school, officer training school and graduate school. When I was young he was stationed in Korea and then Vietnam. Both of these assignments required that he be separated from my mother. My mother, like all good military wives at the time, stayed home and took care of my brother and me.

It wasn't easy for her. In Vietnam, my father was a helicopter pilot who regularly flew into war zones to extract other personnel who were in danger. Between his service in Korea and Vietnam, as well as the rest of his career, my father became highly decorated. As I have always understood, he earned every medal and award given by the Army, except the one that is given when a soldier dies in the line of duty.

Beginning in the year 2000, my father began developing a series of cancers. The first was pancreatic cancer, for which he was his doctor's "miracle" patient. In 2006, even though he had never smoked cigarettes, he developed lung cancer. Again, he beat the cancer. After the lung cancer, my mother confided in me that, emotionally, she could not go through another bout of cancer with my father. Watching him deteriorate and silently suffer was too hard on her.

In March 2008, I received an early morning phone call from my parents' home phone number. My first thought was that my dad was sick again. I felt relief when it was his voice on the line. But, my relief was short lived; he was calling to let me know that my mother had passed away during the night. It was either a stroke or a heart attack; we never found out for sure. The night before, she had a pain in her neck and they went to the emergency room. The hospital released her after a brief exam. My parents went home and eventually to bed. My mother passed away sometime before morning.

Three months later, my father was diagnosed with a brain tumor. Without my mom, he did not seem to have the same will to fight this cancer as he had the others. He had a lot of physical issues as a result of this latest diagnosis and I decided to spend some time with him to try to help him.

One day, I drove the ten hours to his house, arriving after dark. I spent time talking with my father before we both went to bed close to midnight. Before I went to bed, I turned on a nightlight of my mother's, which was in the guest room where I was sleeping. The nightlight was a ceramic statue of the Virgin Mary. My mother's name was Mary. She was raised Roman Catholic but had converted to the Episcopal religion as a way of meeting my Baptist father halfway. The Virgin Mary had remained important to her throughout her life.

I had been asleep for about an hour when I heard my mother's voice calling my name. I thought it was my imagination or a dream. A few minutes later, I felt an insistent tapping on my shoulder. I pulled the covers over my head in an attempt to ignore it. Again, my name was called in my mother's voice and my shoulder was tapped, as though someone was using three fingers to tap me. I heard my mother's voice saying: "Leslie, get up. Your father needs you."

I was scared. My mother was dead. I should not have been hearing her voice and I shouldn't have felt someone tapping on my shoulder. The nightlight lit up the room enough for me to see I was alone.

I got out of bed and turned on the room light. I calmed down and then realized that I should check on my dad. When I walked out into the hall I saw him right away, lying on the hallway floor. He had been trying to go to the kitchen to get a drink and had fallen.

I helped him up and back into his bed. I never told him about the voice that had woken me to find him there.

A few months later, he passed away. My parents were both buried in Arlington National Cemetery. My father's funeral was an event to see. Tourists visiting Arlington stopped to see who the important person was who was being buried. They saluted or put their hands over their hearts.

My parents loved each other dearly. Was my deceased mother looking out for my father that night? It has been seven years since then and I have never heard my mother's voice again.

~Leslie Carson Marlowe

66

The Last Message

Angels descending, bring from above,
Echoes of mercy, whispers of love.
~Fanny J. Crosby

My memory of that night comes in bright white flashes. I remember the back door opening. I remember "Silent Night" by Mannheim Steamroller playing on the radio. I remember a glass snowman filled with chocolate kisses sitting on an end table in the den. I remember Daniel's face and his anger. I remember him telling me that Julie was gone.

I remember not understanding. "Where did she go? What do you mean she's gone?" I remember my son looking me in the eye and saying, "She's just gone." And then I remember him falling to the floor.

Daniel has juvenile diabetes, so you can imagine how I felt the night the back door slammed shut and he collapsed. I was sure it was the diabetes. I remember shouting at him and screaming for someone to help.

After that, we couldn't get Daniel out of bed. He wouldn't cry. He just lay there and slept. On the second day, the principal of his school called me and told me he expected Daniel in school that day. I thought the principal was being callous.

It wasn't until I pulled up in front of the school that I understood why the principal had called. There were hundreds of students waiting for Daniel to arrive. They needed him; he needed them. They surrounded him and vanished with him into the school. For the remaining days of the school year students were constantly monitoring my son. He was never alone. Never.

Days later, letters would arrive in mailboxes addressed by Julie to various people who were important to her. In those letters she apologized for what she had done. She expressed her deep sorrow and concern for those she left behind. She urged friends to keep succeeding and wished them happy and fulfilling lives. She didn't ask them to understand why she took her own life.

I was there when my son's letter arrived. I sat beside him as he read her words written in a yellow card decorated with daisies. He folded the card and slipped it back into its envelope. I've never seen it since.

Everywhere I looked there was sadness. My son was inconsolable. I looked to heaven and cried. I begged for answers and sobbed for relief for my son.

The funeral was approaching. It was creeping up on us like a cat stalking its prey. Where to go? What to do? The mall was safe. It was normal. It was "away."

People briskly walked by chatting and laughing. Teenage girls flipped their hair and giggled. Mothers pushed strollers with sleeping children while toddlers tugged at their fathers' hands. You could smell a mixture of popcorn and cinnamon in the air. No sadness, no gut-wrenching grief. Safe.

My son, my husband and I walked down the hallway of the mall as if we were weighed down by 500 pounds of pain. We watched normalcy unfold in front of us. It hurt. I thought I saw Julie in a group of girls walking away from me. No. I just wanted to know if she was all right.

We three sat together on a bench, staring at our shoes. We said nothing. We were so tired.

I looked up. There were two men standing in front of us... just normal guys dressed in plaid flannel shirts with their sleeves rolled up. They wore jeans and what we called "Chucks," high top sneakers. The tall one stood back while the shorter dark haired one leaned forward and grabbed my hand. I recoiled, but he firmly grasped my fingers and said, "She's okay. We've been sent to tell you she's okay. She is with

God and everything is fine."

I turned to look at my husband's startled face. I looked back. They were gone… disappeared into thin air.

I saw them. My husband saw them. But most of all, my son saw them. And we all heard him.

I always thought of angels as winged spirits with halos who flutter to earth in a shining glow of light and love. Not so. These were ordinary, approachable men who blended in with everyone else. There was no heralding trumpet, no glow of a halo — just ordinary guys sent to deliver a loving, reassuring last message.

~Rebecca Newman

67

Riding with Mark

Some of the bravest and the best men of all the
world, certainly in law enforcement, have made their
contributions while they were undercover.
~Thomas Foran

In the spring of 1987, I was selected to begin training at the police academy. On that day, the first person I met was Mark. Mark was a jovial guy who had served in the Army and was now changing careers. He and I would go through the next eight months as probationary friends, studying and supporting one another. On the day of graduation, we were assigned to different parts of the state and went our separate ways.

Two years later I had taken a desk job at Headquarters, in an attempt to get back to my hometown. It was the wrong move. I was miserable in the role and questioning my career. Unbeknownst to me, Mark was working upstairs. When we happened to meet in the cafeteria. I told him of my plight.

"Why don't you join me at the Traffic Branch?" he suggested. Mark and I shared a lunch as he told me that he had met Jenny, whom he planned to marry and have children with. I had recently become a new father myself, so I applied for the transfer.

On the first day at my new assignment at Traffic Branch, Mark again met me and introduced me to everyone. As the newest arrival, he and I worked together sporadically, until I had enough seniority to partner with him. When we rode together, he started every shift by putting a photo of his daughter Elise, and later, his next daughter, Meghan, on the dashboard in front of him.

"This is why I am a police officer," he said. "This is my reason, to make it safer when they ride with me."

Mark and I had happened to solve a significant case. We put together a brief of evidence so compelling that the Superintendent wanted to showcase our work. He scheduled a press conference for the day before court.

"I can't," I told my boss. "It's my wedding anniversary, I've asked for the night off."

Mark was assigned a new recruit that night while I went to dinner for my anniversary. Later that night, a violent storm hit the city. We were home asleep when we were awoken by a lightning flash followed by an incredibly loud clap of thunder.

I arrived at work the next morning and walked into the office. Some of the other officers who would accompany us in court were unshaven and looked disheveled.

"Did you guys work all night?" I asked. "You have court this morning with Mark and me."

One of the police motorcyclists took me aside and broke the news. Mark had been killed in an accident the night before. The accident report would later surmise that he had been driving during that violent thunderstorm, had been startled by the lightning, and careened off the wet road into a tree. The officer riding with him was thrown clear upon impact — not a scratch upon him.

The rest of the morning was a blur but somehow I found myself visiting Mark's wife Jenny. She met me at the door and we cried together. Through my tears I could see Mark's daughters inside the house: two-year-old Elise sitting bewildered on the couch and eight-week-old Meghan lying in her crib. They wouldn't remember their father.

"He was here last night," Jenny said. "After the crash."

Huh?

Jenny said that shortly after midnight she woke and saw Mark standing beside Meghan's crib. She reported that Mark was quiet, just looking down at Meghan. She said that she could tell he had been in the rain as he was still in a wet uniform. Jenny said that she told him to come to bed before she rolled over and went back to sleep. At 3 a.m., when my colleagues arrived to deliver the grim news, she had not believed them and returned to check their bed where she thought Mark was sleeping.

"It was him," I reassured her. "He would never have left without seeing the girls." Mark loved his daughters more than life itself.

Mark was buried with full police honors; I was one of the pallbearers. The passing of Mark shattered me. I was unable to get past the thought that it could have been me with him. Who knows what would have happened? I moved away and distanced myself from everyone, including Jenny and the girls.

About six years later and three hundred miles away, I was on patrol when I came upon a single-vehicle accident. A car had careened off the road in a storm, the female driver trapped inside. She was in bad shape when I reached her, and she knew it.

"Please," she begged of me. "My daughters, I want to see my daughters."

I looked in the back seat of the car and saw two empty child seats.

"Where are your daughters?" I asked the driver.

She struggled to speak. "The other police officer has them. The other officer said he would take care of them. He said his name was Mark."

I looked around; there was no one. But off to the side, leaning against a gray gum tree, were two little girls. They were uninjured — not a scratch on them.

I collected the daughters and brought them to their mother. She passed away holding her children's hands. I kept the driver's last conversation out of my report. There was no police officer named Mark in the district.

Unlike Jenny, I never got to see Mark again, but I always sensed that he was still around. Every time I arrived at an accident and found an uninjured person surrounded by carnage, I always wondered if I was still riding with Mark.

~Grant Madden

68

Midnight Prayer

Silently, one by one, in the infinite meadows of the heaven, blossomed the lovely stars, the forget-me-nots of the Angels.
~Henry Wadsworth Longfellow

Last night I looked up at the sky
I wished that you were near
It's been a while since I have prayed
But God, I need an ear

I'm worried that my angel
Is too far for me to see
What if one day Heaven
Hasn't saved a spot for me?

And suddenly I heard a voice
God whispered "There's no hurry."
He said, "Your angel waits for you,
You'll never have to worry.

The stars above are porch lights
That welcome old friends home
So when it's time for you to come
You'll never feel alone.

I promise that he waits for you
So never shed a tear,
Your angel keeps his porch light on
Until the day you're here.

To remind you that he's waiting
He lights up like a beam,
And when you are so deep in sleep
He slips into your dream.

He watches you each morning,
Protects when you feel scared,
He guides you through each journey,
Gives strength when unprepared.

The sunrays are his warm hugs,
The rain is his soft cry,
For times that you doubt Heaven,
Or wish he'd said goodbye.

But angels never leave us,
Although they're not in sight,
They wake us up each morning,
and tuck us in each night.

So though he may seem far away,
When it's your time just know,
Your angel will be upon his porch,
Singing "Welcome Home."

~Samantha Nolan

Chapter 8

Angels and Miracles

Answered Prayers

69

A Voice in the Fog

If you have a mom, there is nowhere you are likely to
go where a prayer has not already been.
~Robert Brault

I've always had a "lead foot" when it comes to driving, but that night the fog was so bad that even I was creeping along at twenty miles per hour. I had just gotten back from vacation and was determined to drive to my boyfriend's house.

My mom didn't want me to go. She had a "bad feeling." I knew she was nervous because of the bad visibility on the narrow, twisting country road to my boyfriend's house. Even though Mom was notorious for her gut feelings being right, because I was twenty years old and knew everything, I went anyway.

About halfway there I regretted my decision. This fog was no ordinary cloud vapor; it seemed a white impenetrable cloak. I couldn't see more than a few feet in front of my car, and sometimes, not even the edge of the road. I was disoriented and merely guessing if I was coming upon a curve or not.

I wanted to turn around, but there were only a handful of farms on my route, and I couldn't see any lights or landmarks. The road wasn't wide enough for a U-turn and I had no idea where I was. I might have passed his driveway and not realized it.

I slowed to a crawl, not daring to stop, not daring to go faster. Going forward was all I could do. It was terrifying. I lifted prayers without words, comprised entirely of emotion. At any moment I expected a car to hit me head-on. I suppose it was good that no cars passed, but it made me feel all the more isolated.

As I crept along, a tall shadow emerged from the fog—I saw a wide tree close to the road's edge and suddenly I thought I knew where I was. I recalled one hairpin turn that had a huge tree sitting at the middle of the bend. The tree I was thinking of was near a pasture that had a gate with a little driveway leading to it. If I made it to that gate, I could sit in the driveway and wait for the fog to lift.

All this flashed through my mind as I slowly turned my car, trusting my memory that I was at the tight curve, because I really couldn't tell if the road curved or not.

Suddenly, I realized I was not at all where I hoped. There was a steep embankment right in front of me!

I yanked the wheel hard, overcorrecting, and spun out of control. I skidded off the other side of the road, through a fence and down a steep incline. With a hard bump, the front of my car hit the bottom of the hill.

I sat for a minute and assessed my damages. I seemed to be unhurt. And the car still worked when I revved the engine, although the rear window was making a rattling noise. It seemed to have been shaken loose by the impact.

But now what? I was in the middle of a field. But maybe I could find a gate and get out. I drove on through the tall grass, hearing it scrape against the undercarriage of my car.

Suddenly, like someone speaking straight into my head, I heard a clear, calm voice say, "You should get near the fence, because you never know what's in a field."

I slammed on the brakes. Had I really heard a voice? I got goose bumps. But, getting closer to the fence made good sense, so I made a ninety-degree turn back up the hill, seeking a gate that would let me out of this field. All I found was an unbroken barbed wire fence.

I parked and carefully climbed over that fence. And then I heard shouts—voices outside my head this time. Three orbs of light approached me through the fog. Three men reached me, out of breath. They all started talking at once: "We saw you go through the fence... We thought you'd stop, so we could help you… We started yelling and running as fast as we could…"

And then: "What made you turn and head back up to the fence?"

I answered reluctantly; afraid they'd think I was crazy, "Well, it was like a little voice in my head said, 'You should get near the fence because you never know what's in a field.'"

They were shaking their heads in disbelief. They assured me that no matter who was talking to me it was a good thing I paid attention.

I sucked in my breath, shocked at what they said next: "You were about two feet away from driving right into the pond… You would have drowned… That pond is pretty deep…."

It seemed unbelievable. We all agreed it was amazing that a voice warned me just in time to miss the pond. The men didn't want payment to fix their fence — they were satisfied helping me get back on the road; elated to not be fishing my body out of the water. By the time I got back in my car the fog was starting to dissipate, but the men walked along beside me, helping me navigate out of the field. As they guided me to their driveway, they showed me where I could have lost my life.

My tire tracks stopped a few feet shy of the edge of the pond. I remembered that loose and rattling rear window, and realized my car would have filled with water faster than normal. I probably wouldn't have made it. I thanked God for answering my mother's prayers — the ones I was sure she started as soon as I left the house that foggy night. And I thanked Him for the mysterious voice that saved me.

~Lorraine Furtner

70

Saved by a Strange Light

If we had no winter, the spring would not be so
pleasant; if we did not sometimes taste of adversity,
prosperity would not be so welcome.
~Charlotte Bronte

I was living in the lonely, windswept cinder hills northeast of Flagstaff, Arizona as caretaker of a remote ranch. My friends who owned the place had taken a long trip and left me in charge of their dog, cat and houseplants.

The primitive log cabin was heated by a cozy Seefire wood stove. It was situated seven miles from a paved highway, thirty-five miles from town and almost two miles from the nearest occupied dwelling. I had lived without electricity, phone and indoor plumbing before, and I loved the simplicity.

One day it started snowing pretty hard. The cabin owners had told me some people had to be evacuated in helicopters after fifty-six inches of snow fell in one night the year before. According to the forecast on the car radio, this new storm promised to be somewhat less intense, but I knew I'd probably be trapped if I didn't do something to keep the three-hundred-foot driveway clear.

I also wanted to keep the road open, if possible, because it would not be plowed. I decided that I would drive back and forth, once per hour, to the top of the north face of a lava flow about three-quarters of a mile south of the cabin. The south face would melt much faster, I knew, and the four-wheel-drive traffic from there to the paved road would help break open the rest of my escape route.

By late afternoon, I had made several round trips. The storm was showing no signs of tapering off, and I guessed that I might have to keep on going back and forth for several more hours for my time and effort already spent to have been worthwhile. As I headed out on the next run, however, it was still daylight and not too cold, and I didn't bother with boots, hat, scarf, gloves or extra layers under my jacket. After all, I would be in my nice, warm car.

I made it to the top of the lava flow and started to turn around when the rear wheels slid into loose cinder gravel. I shifted into low-range four-wheel drive and tried to get the car back on the roadbed, but all I did was sink the rear wheels deeper into the cinders.

After shoveling snow from around the front wheels and lying on my belly pulling snow from under the vehicle, my clothing was completely wet. The car would not budge, and it was obvious that the only way I'd get home was on foot. Spending the night in the vehicle was out of the question since I hadn't brought any bedding. It would have to sit where it was until I could find someone with a truck to pull it out of the cinders.

The daylight was fading as I started walking north. I'd been so preoccupied trying to free the car that I hadn't noticed how much more snow had fallen. The wind was blowing harder, too. When I reached the bottom of the lava flow, the drifting snow had almost covered my tire tracks. I trudged on until the tracks vanished. Soon I was exhausted from walking in thigh-deep snow.

It was nearly dark, the storm had turned into a blizzard, my feet and ears were freezing, and I was still at least half a mile from the cabin. Visibility was near zilch when facing north — the direction of the cabin.

I paused to gather my strength and focus my will on getting back alive. I hadn't eaten since breakfast and was faint from hunger. I thought of sitting down to rest and turned to face the south, with the wind at my back. It was then that I noticed a pack of coyotes had been tailing me. They were very close.

A wave of terror washed over me. There were five of them. I knew that if I didn't keep moving, they'd be on me in nothing flat. I stood there in the blizzard with eyes closed and head bowed, praying for help to get home safely.

When I raised my head and opened my eyes, I felt calm. Then I saw that a beam of light was shining from behind my head. I quickly turned around to look for the source of the beam. As I turned, so did the light, showing straight ahead for about fifty yards like a powerful flashlight.

I called out, "Who's there?" and kept looking around for the source of this light. The combination of terror and awe that I felt gave me a rush of adrenaline, and I started moving again.

The beam was like a beacon coming from behind my head. No one else was out there; no houses were within a mile of where I was standing. I'd seen no vehicles and heard nothing but the wind. The snow was so deep by then it would have been impossible for anything but a snowmobile or snowcat to get around, anyway, and they make a lot of noise.

I gave up trying to find the light source and just used it to spot a landmark: the top strand of a wire fence, still visible above the drifts to the north. This was the south fence line of the ranch where the cabin was. I set my course, and the beam turned itself off.

The night was black except for the reflection off the snow of a little bit of moonlight. Soon I was at the fence, and within an hour I reached the cabin. The hard work of walking through the deep snow had kept me warm enough to survive. Never had I been so happy to reach a destination!

To this day, more than twenty years after this amazing do-or-die experience, I have no idea how my prayers for help were answered that night.

~Suzu Belle

71

Trail Guides

*Let gratitude be the pillow upon which you kneel to
say your nightly prayer. And let faith be the bridge you
build to overcome evil and welcome good.*
~Maya Angelou

I climbed out of my car, barely noticing the door slam as I
headed to my favorite hiking trail. I often retreated there for
quiet contemplation and beauty. Today, I didn't smell the fall
fragrant air or take in the red-gold tree canopy above me.

All I could think was, *I've lost him for good this time.*

I blinked back tears as my sneakers crunched on the gravel trail.
How did this happen? My son had refused to finish his college applications again, just like he refused to do almost everything these days.
I'd stood in the doorway of his room, hands trembling so hard from
anger (or maybe fear of another argument) that I almost spilled my
glass of water.

"Get out," he growled from his bed.

Months of frustration boiled up. Nights of despair, poor grades.
My sunny boy, gone. Replaced by someone I didn't know. But why?

And then it happened — something that still makes me wince.
I lunged into his room, overcome with fury, and hurled my glass of
water in his face. Water dripped down his forehead and cheeks. His
eyes were wide with surprise — and hatred.

A million things ran through my mind. I needed to beg his forgiveness, salvage what was left of our love. Say something. But nothing

came out. Not a sound.

He jumped up and shoved me out. The door slammed like I was being locked away from him forever.

Help me, I pleaded silently, rounding a bend in the trail.

If divine guidance was available (which I wasn't sure I believed), I needed it now more than ever. I'd called for help before, but this time something had to change or my heart would break open and never be whole again. I was dying inside. I'd do anything to make things better. Anything.

Up ahead I saw two figures approaching with a dog. I rarely spoke to people on the trail except to nod or say hi. Walking was "alone time" that I cherished. Today, I couldn't imagine even a nod.

As they got closer, the dog strained at his leash toward me. He was a mixed breed, sable-colored with one floppy ear. Something about him, his intelligent eyes or the way he was so intent on reaching me, made me kneel to pet him.

"What a beautiful boy," I said, looking up at the two women. Both were slightly older and smiling. The dog stared at me deeply, like he could somehow see my aching inside.

"You're lucky, he doesn't usually like strangers," said the taller woman.

"He knows a fan when he sees one," I said and stood to continue on. But the dog whined and raised his paw.

I took it in both hands. "What's his name?"

"Bert," said the shorter woman. "I'm doggie-sitting for my son while he's away."

I tried to stand, but Bert whined again, and we all laughed at his puzzling behavior. Somehow the conversation flowed from there, like old friends catching up. Joan and Andie, I learned, both had sons a bit older than mine.

"I didn't think Josh would ever go to college," Joan chuckled, shaking her head. "He finally did after working construction for three years out of high school."

"Ben resisted too — thought the applications were too hard," said Andie.

"That's strange, I said, "I'm having the same problem with my son." I bent quickly toward Bert so they wouldn't see tears welling up. I couldn't blink them back anymore, like they had a life of their own. Big awful drops splashed on my shoes, and suddenly everything surged up. Right there on the open trail. In front of strangers. Bright-hued leaves falling all around.

Desperately, I swabbed at the tears with my sleeve and gulped back sobs. "How did you get him to finish his applications?" I finally managed.

"I helped him," Andie said, rubbing my arm. "Maybe I was wrong, but he needed help and I gave it to him. He's a psychologist now."

Tears spilled faster, and Andie and Joan closed around me. Bert huddled in, too. It was like being cradled in the warmest, most tender love I'd ever felt. I surrendered and let my tears flow without fear or shame.

"Our boys were just scared," Andie said. "Your son probably is, too. Give him lots of love and give him time."

Was she right? Did fear lie behind all his anger and defiance? Poor baby. Afraid to grow up, to admit how terrified he was.

Joan fished out a tissue from her pocket and said softly, "Strange, but I feel like we were supposed to meet you today."

It was like a current switched on, a vibrant, tingling certainty. Of course. It was all so obvious. I'd asked for help, for new insights and a new path, and here was my answer as clear as the trees and birdsongs around us.

I looked from Joan to Andie, and then to Bert, the one who'd insisted I stop. I had no doubt some profound helping hand had reached out to me that day. Nothing had ever seemed truer, and I knew right then everything would be okay.

I'm sure nobody noticed the change right away, but things began to shift immediately. When I got home, I pressed my face against my son's door. "Sweetie, I'm sorry," I said. "So, so sorry."

No response.

"I know you're scared about college and all," I continued. "I'm here if you want to talk."

Answered Prayers |

Not a word, but an hour later he came out. His eyes were wary, and he mumbled only that he didn't feeling like talking, but I saw it. Relief. An opening.

His life didn't turn around immediately. He ended up going to college for a year before dropping out. Three years later, he still hasn't gone back, but he talks about it often, and I feel certain he will. I'm confident he'll find his version of success.

What really changed, though, was me. I released something that day, my own fears about him, and since then a kind of magic has brought us closer than I ever imagined possible. We talk about everything — his anxieties and dreams. And I share mine. He's one of my favorite people and a tremendous human being.

I owe it all to three angels (one of them four-legged) who heeded my silent call for help one day and set me straight. I never saw them again, but whatever maneuvered our meeting on the trail is something I've come to rely on more and more. Guidance is always there, often arriving in unexpected forms if you take time to stop and listen.

~Sidney Stevens

72

Untouched

*Miracles are not contrary to nature, but only contrary
to what we know about nature.*

~Saint Augustine

M y twins were safely asleep in their beds. My mom
and I were watching a movie on TV when we
smelled smoke. About the same time we smelled
it, the furnace kicked on and our house was
quickly engulfed in black smoke. We both rushed upstairs to get
the twins! The smoke was getting thicker and I began to choke. My
mother grabbed Tami from her crib and headed downstairs. I picked
Tom up, covered his mouth with a baby blanket, and stepped out
into the hallway.

The hallway was thick with black smoke, and I had a difficult
time seeing anything through it. I placed my hand on the wall and
headed in the direction of the stairs. At the end of the hall I found the
handrail. Cradling Tom in one arm I grabbed the handrail with my
other hand and used that to guide myself down the stairs.

I was having difficulty breathing and felt like I was about to col-
lapse. I knew that if I fell down I wouldn't get out of the house, and
my only thought was to escape. I prayed to God that he would safely
lead me out of the flames.

At the bottom of the stairs I saw the glow of the fire and heard
the sound of the flames and crackling of wood burning. I could barely
see through the thick smoke, but I knew where the front door was. I

walked across the living room toward the front door as quickly and safely as possible. My fear was tripping and not being able to get back up.

Tom was crying and choking in my arms. I knew that once I got to the front door we would be safe. My only thought was "Get to the front door and get out of the house!" As I got closer I could feel the cool breeze coming through the open door. I knew that my mother must have gone out that same way, and I thanked God that she was able to get out of the house with Tami.

As I exited the front door I felt the rush of cold air hit my face. It was the middle of December in Cincinnati. It was freezing but I simply thanked God that I could breathe again and that he had allowed us to escape the fire.

Someone must have called the fire department as the trucks were already pulling up. I thanked God the firefighters had arrived so quickly. My biggest concern was the dining room, where we had important legal papers that we needed for a court case the following week.

I rushed to my neighbor's house and called someone at our church prayer chain to pray that the dining room would be spared from the fire.

In the aftermath of the fire it became evident how severe it had been. I was told by some of the firefighters that the fire was so intense that one of their trucks had sustained damage from the heat because it had been parked too close to the house. Another firefighter told me that it was truly a miracle that we escaped. He said that when the firefighters tried to enter the house through the front door, they couldn't. The living room floor had collapsed into the basement beneath the house, and he believed that my mother and I had walked across a carpet that had no floor beneath it.

The amazing thing was that the dining room remained untouched by the fire. In fact, the wax candle that was sitting on the dining room table hadn't even melted! How could it be that this fire was so hot that it damaged a fire truck parked outside the house, but didn't melt the candle that was sitting on the dining room table? The rooms on either side of the dining room were completely destroyed, but the dining room itself was untouched.

The day after the fire we found the legal papers that we had been praying for. They were completely undamaged, not even touched by smoke or water. It was as if God had placed his hand over that room and said, "This room will not burn."

I talked to the firefighters after the fire had been extinguished and they said they had never seen anything like it. It was one of the most intense and intriguing fires they had ever encountered. They had no explanation for why the dining room was untouched when the entire house should have been destroyed.

~Pam Ziebold

73

Miracle on County Road 388

*Angels are all around us, all the time, in
the very air we breathe.*
~Eileen Elias Freeman,
The Angels' Little Instruction Book

O n June 21, 2011, a maple tree fell on the van I was
driving during a thunderstorm. It landed on the roof
directly above my head and then rolled forward to
plunge through the windshield, landing on my chest
and pinning me in my seat.

In those first moments after the impact, I didn't know I was hurt.
I could hear my twelve-year-old son keening in terror in the front seat
beside me while my thirteen-year-old daughter shouted our names over
and over again from the back seat. There was thunder and lightning
and howling winds, and all I could do was pray, "God, please get my
kids out of here."

For some reason, I couldn't turn my head to look at them, but
they didn't seem to be hurt. I could see my son out of the corner of my
eye, wild-eyed and pale, and I could hear his sister moving around in
the back seat. "Climb out the window," I told her. "Run to the nearest
house and call 911 and then stay there. Stay inside, out of the storm.
Do you understand?"

"But I don't want to leave you guys!"

"We're not hurt, honey. We're just stuck."

"But… you're all bloody, Mom."

"God, please help us. Save my kids," I prayed. We were on a lonely country road with only a few houses, and no one was likely to drive by any time soon. My cell phone was lodged somewhere under the crushed dashboard. We were on our own.

Suddenly, a man spoke up from somewhere off to my left, amid the tree branches and wet leaves. "I'm here to help you, ma'am," he said.

"Get my kids out. Please."

He got to the passenger side in seconds and peered through the window at my boy. "I'm going to get your son out of here," he told me. "I need you to lean his seat back, and then I'll pull him out the backseat window."

My daughter told me later that the stranger didn't seem to notice when she grabbed his shoulder to steady herself as she climbed out the window. While she was doing that, I was struggling to move my hand those few inches to the seat release knob, which was located within reach of the driver in my minivan. I could see my fingers wrap around it, but they didn't seem to want to obey and turn it.

My son's hand closed over mine with a gentle squeeze. "I got this, Mommy," he said, suddenly calm. I watched him go back and slowly disappear, inch by inch, until he was gone.

The stranger came back to my window. "It's your turn, Ma'am," he said. "I'm gonna drag you out the same way I got your son out."

"No," I said. "Get my kids out of here. Get them out of the storm. Please." I knew it was crazy to trust a complete stranger with my children, but there was something about him that just felt safe, even if I couldn't see his face. "What's your name?" I asked him.

"Daniel Barnes. I'll take care of them."

I was alone then, although it was only a matter of minutes before the fire department showed up. It took nearly forty minutes for them to cut the tree apart and get me out of the vehicle. My neck was broken, along with other injuries that left the emergency room doctor shaking his head in disbelief — especially when he looked my children over and confirmed that they were basically unharmed.

It wasn't until several days later that I was able to read the accident report and get a phone number for the man listed as the first witness on the scene. His name was David, not Daniel, but I assumed I had just heard him wrong that night. I dialed the number with shaking hands and when he answered, I thanked him for pulling my kids out of the wreckage.

"But I didn't do that," he told me. "Your kids were already out when I got there."

"Where was the other guy?"

"There was no other guy." David explained that he had actually seen the accident take place. He had passed my van going the opposite direction and glanced up in his rearview mirror just in time to see the tree fall. It had taken him a few minutes to go around the curve and find a place to turn around and come back to help us, and my kids were standing on the side of the road with their arms wrapped around each other by the time he arrived.

The fallen tree completely blocked the road. No other cars could have come or gone.

It's a small town with only a few hundred residents, most of whom are related to each other. Everyone knows everyone else. There are few strangers in that tiny town, and no one there has ever heard of Daniel Barnes.

My son doesn't remember being lifted out through the back window. My daughter never saw the man's face. My only impression of him was of wet, dark hair and a narrow face. A calm voice.

People who weren't there that night tell me that my memory is garbled because of my injuries. They say I've confused the names "David" and "Daniel." They can't explain, however, just exactly who got my kids out of the van that night. No one seems to know who rescued them.

But I know who he was.

He was the answer to my prayer.

~A.J. Goode

A New Trust

Ask the LORD your God for a sign, whether in the
deepest depths or in the highest heights.
~Isaiah 7:11

I had just graduated from college and I went from May to July without even a single callback from prospective employers. It seemed that my skills as an English major might be useless. I was starting to doubt everything I studied and the path I pursued. "Maybe I should've chosen a safer path," I thought. My parents, who were paying my bills at the time, were starting to get anxious about my unemployment and things were getting tense between us.

One night, after spending time with friends, I pulled into my parents' driveway and decided to take a walk instead of going inside. It was late and I knew they would be asleep. The neighborhood was quiet as I walked to my old elementary school, only a couple of minutes away. The gates were open, so I let my mind wander as I looked at the building, the playground, and the playing fields. I had worked so hard to get through school, all the way up to my bachelor's degree, and yet I felt as far away from my future as I did when I was ten years old. I needed help and didn't know where to get it.

I walked over to the baseball field where I used to play and looked up at the sky. I searched for the right words, but all I could think of were curses. It had been a very long time since I looked up for answers and I had practically forgotten how to do it. Finally, more out of desperation than anger, I said out loud, "God, if you have a plan for me, I'd like to see the blueprints." I then left the school grounds and headed back home.

I decided to take a different, longer path back to the house. As I walked, I noticed almost all the streetlights were out. There was one still lit, however, and as I passed under it I noticed something shiny on the ground. It was a penny. As I picked it up, I noticed another penny, and another, and another. Searching the street and the grass I found nearly a dollar's worth of pennies scattered under this one light. I was in shock. I had never seen so much change on the ground. Somehow, it filled me with hope. I suddenly felt like everything was going to be okay, even though a dollar was not going to solve any of my financial problems. "Maybe my luck will turn around," I thought. I pocketed all the change and returned home in a brighter mood.

A week later, I saw an ad in the newspaper for a job. The position called for a writer/proofreader for a local magazine called *The Pennysaver*. I thought back to that night on the street and felt like this could be the one. I sent in my résumé, got a call three days later, and got the job by the end of August. I couldn't believe it!

I was fortunate to stay with that job for seven years before moving on to my dream job of teaching. And ever since that night, I have regained trust in the universe and how things fall into place.

Whenever I'm in doubt and feel like nothing will go my way, I look for signs, not out of desperation or fear but out of trust. I trust that anything is possible as long as I believe it is and as long as I keep my eyes open.

That night I felt like I was being watched over. In a lot of ways, I still carry that same awe of seeing all those pennies on the ground, and to this day I chuckle to myself every time I pick one up.

~Mike D'Alto

75

The House That Ernie Built

Where we love is home, home that our feet
may leave, but not our hearts.
~Oliver Wendell Holmes

My husband Fred's grandchildren squealed with delight as they leaped from the dock into the cool lake. The cousins laughed and teased each other, just as my cousins and I did when we were young. The sky was blue, the sun was hot, and the breeze was gentle. We were enjoying a family picnic with Fred's sons and their families at Fred's former home. This was a special day in an atmosphere I loved. I knew I should be happy, but I wasn't. Instead, I was numb — lost somewhere inside my memories.

Fred and I were a widower and a widow who were lucky enough to find each other after losing our spouses to cancer. When we married three years earlier, Fred sold this beautiful lake home to his son and joined me in my country house. Now, we were taking the next step. We decided that it was time to sell my house and the forty acres it sat on, and buy a smaller house in town. We wanted a place closer to medical facilities, shopping, friends, families, and church. Yet, it still needed to have big garages like the country house. Fred rebuilds antique motorcycles and has at least forty of them. He needed room for his stuff!

With those requirements, house hunting was a challenge. The real estate market was booming, and it proved almost impossible to find what we wanted. Day after day we studied the computer, but when we found one that looked interesting, it sold before our agent could show it to us. This went on for months. Finally, we gave up.

Then, Fred went online to look for motorcycle parts. Instead, he found a house that was for sale by its owner. It sounded perfect. It was meticulously built, had everything we wanted, and was even my favorite color — yellow. Plus, it had something we hadn't even dreamed of finding. Its huge windows overlooked Lake Superior, and a short walk across the scenic highway would bring us to the lake's rocky shore.

Earlier that morning, Fred and I went to look at it, fell in love, and signed the papers to buy it. We knew it was a place our friends and families would enjoy visiting. This would be *our* house. Now we wouldn't be living in houses we'd shared with our previous spouses. Fred admitted that he'd never been comfortable living in Ernie's house, and I understood. I wouldn't have been comfortable living in the home his wife Suzy designed and loved.

However, instead of being excited about our great find, I now found myself strangely preoccupied. I adored the sweet little house that Fred and I had just agreed to buy. But, I was surprised by feelings of guilt. Now I would have to sell the house Ernie worked so hard to create.

Usually a social person, I was unhappy sitting by the lake and went for a long walk. I was crazy about Fred and loved the new life we had together. It was important to me that we live in a house that made him happy. What was wrong with me? My stomach churned with unexpected second thoughts. Ernie designed the house, then he built it all by himself. Usually, he was at work all day, then worked on the house until late at night.

There were so many memories there: the sunrises over the little lake, the magnificent rock garden he created for my birthday, and the antique pump he bought from an old farmer, painted bright red, and attached to our deck to surprise me on Mother's Day. Some of his ashes were scattered by his deer stands in the woods. What would he think of me selling his creation?

Was I being disloyal to Ernie? Fred managed to keep his house in the family. I'd be selling Ernie's house to a stranger. Yet, Fred and I prayed over and over about this decision. Why was I having doubts now? I walked back to Fred's old house and joined his family for dinner.

I was quiet on the long drive home and prayed silently. I'd been praying to God about this for months, but I was still confused. I felt silly about it but I asked God for a sign.

And that's when we drove up to our mailbox and pulled out the day's mail. There was a large manila envelope that was addressed to me, had no return address, and had something heavy in one corner.

Opening the envelope, I didn't find a letter or an explanation. It simply contained a pile of 35mm pictures. They were pictures of Lake Superior and most of them had Ernie in them — sitting by the lake, walking by the lake, or simply smiling at the camera with the lake in the background. Ernie and I had gone to the big lake whenever we could. I was puzzled. Where had the pictures come from? Fred and I sat in silence, gazing at the stack of pictures.

Pictures of Ernie by Lake Superior on the very day that we bought a house on the lake. How could this be?

Then, I remembered. About fifteen years before, I sold a story, along with these photos, to a travel magazine. The story was about travel along Lake Superior's north shore, but it was never published because the magazine went out of business. These were the pictures I took for that article.

How was it possible they arrived the day we bought the Lake Superior house?

Fred looked at the pictures, then spoke gently. "What's Ernie telling you?"

When I grasped the meaning of Fred's words, I began to sob. My dear Fred held me close as I struggled to put this miracle into words.

"Ernie's telling me it's time to move on. I think he's glad I'll be living by our precious lake."

Somehow my beloved Ernie found a way to reach down from heaven. He gave me the help I needed to move on with my life.

~Lou Zywicki Prudhomme

76

Did You Love Me?

The LORD is near to the brokenhearted and
saves the crushed in spirit.
~Psalm 34:18

M y soul ached. I stared blankly at the e-mail I had received telling me my husband had succumbed to ALS. It had been ten long months since his sudden departure a few weeks after our wedding. He couldn't put me through it, he said. He couldn't watch *me* watch *him* dwindle to nothingness.

The last time we spoke he told me that when the time came, I should go to our favorite beach and celebrate him.

The coolness of the California night hit me immediately as I pulled into the hotel. The sadness of his death coupled with the last ten grueling months weighed heavy on me. I slept deeply and woke at the crack of dawn with only one thought fueling me: "Get to the beach." I quickly dressed in my running clothes and jumped into my truck. I drove the few short miles to our favorite beach and parked, inhaling the delicious salt air and letting the gentle sound of the pounding waves soothe me.

What had bothered me during those ten months was simple: How had I married someone who could leave me so easily? Did he love me? Did I not know what love was? How could I be so blind? Why did God let this happen?

I felt used and foolish. Our courtship and wedding had been

beautiful. Despite the fact that he was dying, we felt like we had it all. We truly felt God had a greater purpose for us and would see us through what was going to be a difficult time.

I remembered the laughter, the inside jokes, his love of Coca-Cola and the half empty Coke cans he would leave in the fridge. I thought about the way he would look at me and brag about me to anyone who would listen.

And then he was gone and I was alone, left to wonder what had just happened.

As I made my way from the cliff to the beach below, I was alone. The surfers were still up top staring at the waves. It was overcast and as I started to run I noticed how smooth and blank the wet sand was, the tide having just gone out. Suddenly I was sprinting, my heart beating hard and my breath catching in the cool morning air. I ran and ran until I couldn't hold back the tears any longer.

I stopped running and faced the ocean, shouting my anguish to the Lord.

"Why did this happen? I thought You had a purpose for us! Why did he leave? Did he ever love me?" I sat down in the still wet sand and sobbed.

And then I heard a voice. "Look at where you came from…"

I sniffed loudly and ran my arm under my runny nose. "Look at where I came from?" I answered angrily, "That's all I've been doing!"

The voice was still and small. "Look at where you came from…"

I sniffed again, got up, and dutifully looked at where I had come from on the beach and gasped, my hand flying to my mouth.

There was another set of shoe prints right next to mine in the wet sand. I looked around. Could I have missed seeing someone else on the beach? No, I was still alone.

Excitement rose in me, "Lord! Is it You?" I asked. "No, it can't be You. You'd be barefoot!" I exclaimed.

I bent over the prints and looked at the familiar running shoe tread of my husband's shoes in the sand next to mine, his stride longer than mine, but there! Once ALS had taken his hands, I had put those shoes on his feet so many times that I knew the tread like the back of my own hand.

I started to cry again, but this time they were tears of joy. My words were a jumble talking to him and to God.

"You did love me, you did, thank you," I sang out through the tears. "Thank you Lord for letting me know. Thank you for healing me. Thank you for this confirmation, and look Jon, your foot isn't dragging! It must feel so good for you to run! ALS can't touch you in Heaven!"

~Lily Blais

77

Nancy's Note

We are each of us angels with only one wing, and we
can only fly by embracing one another.
~Luciano de Crescenzo

It is my great privilege to be asked to speak at women's retreats. I love the opportunity to share encouragement with ladies all over the world. With my counseling background, I am often called on at these events to offer insight and help to women individually. Nancy was one of those women.

The minute she walked through the door, it was clear something was going on. Her chin and knuckles seemed to drag the ground. When the other ladies were laughing she only stared straight ahead. When they engaged in activity, she sat alone. The leader of the event noticed that Nancy seemed to be fighting back tears.

After our first session, the event coordinator, Susan, pulled me aside and asked if I could spend some one-on-one time with Nancy.

"Nancy's best friend worked so hard to sponsor her and pay her way to the retreat," Susan confided. "We both want to make sure she gets the most from this awesome opportunity."

As the women were being ushered toward a snack table, I tapped Nancy on the shoulder. "Got a minute?" I asked, beckoning her to follow me. As we walked toward a quiet spot on campus, I said, "How's it going? Are you enjoying the retreat?"

"Is it that obvious?" Nancy responded. "I told my friend I really didn't want to be here, but she has counted on my attending this weekend for eight months. She paid my entire way and she couldn't get her money back. If I didn't think it would crush her, I'd walk away right now. I'm not in the mood to listen to any inspirational speaker. No offense," she added casting a glance at me. "This has been the toughest week of my life."

"What happened?" I asked, patting the chair beside me. That's all it took. With a flood of tears, Nancy described events that would have wrecked a weaker woman.

"My husband Kal and I run a foster home for four at-risk adolescent boys. Last weekend he attended the men's version of this retreat, so I had all four boys by myself. They're a handful. I was looking forward to Monday so I could catch my breath. But on Sunday afternoon, my sister called and told me that her thirty-eight-year-old husband had committed suicide.

"My sister Karen is an emotional wreck," Nancy continued. "They have two boys, twelve and fourteen. So the minute Kal walked in the door, I drove four hours north. Karen could barely keep it together, so I had to handle the funeral arrangements and manage the boys. One minute they were crying inconsolably and the next they were acting out."

I nodded. Those grief reactions could be expected from kids that age. "You must be exhausted," I said.

"I am. The funeral was Thursday. Karen wanted it done quickly to get closure for herself and her boys. I got home just in time to come here."

"You were there for your sister. Who was there for you?" I asked.

"Kal would have been, but he had to care for our boys. So it's just been God and me dealing with this. I don't know about Him, but I'm drained." She laughed and cried at the same time.

"I'm glad you haven't lost your sense of humor. I probably would have by now. Nancy, I think the events of this weekend could be just what you need. I have a prayer exercise to suggest. I think it will help you dump some of your grief and stress, so you'll be ready to receive all the hope and help this weekend has to offer."

I placed my hand on Nancy's shoulder and prayed a lengthy prayer to help her off-load her stress and sob out her immediate grief and pain. When I was done, a look of relief came over her. Then she asked if we could pray for her sister as well. She and I took turns praying for her sister and the boys. Time seemed to stand still as we lingered in God's presence in prayer.

Over an hour later, we returned to the group, and Nancy was ready to join in. She listened, laughed, and learned with the other women. Later that day, she thanked me for taking the time to pray with her.

"It was my pleasure," I said, hugging her.

The week after the retreat, I sent Nancy a card to let her know I was still praying for her. It had a picture of a lamb resting serenely in the arms of Jesus. Inside, I wrote this verse of encouragement from Jeremiah 29:11: "'For I know the plans that I have for you,' declares the Lord, 'plans for welfare and not for calamity to give you a future and a hope.'" I signed it, "Praying for you — Linda."

Two years passed. I was living in a twenty-foot travel trailer with my husband and three teenagers, two dogs, and a cat. We were building a new home on six acres at the end of the world. In order to save money, we had moved to the property with no phone and no power except a generator that I had to pull-start every day in the pouring rain of an El Niño winter. As if that weren't enough, my twelve-year-old daughter, Ashley, needed to have emergency heart surgery. We literally would have to live in UCLA's cardiac unit for a couple of weeks. I was trying hard not to fall apart.

As I stopped at the post office to pick up our mail before heading to LA for this fearful ordeal, I noticed an envelope with Nancy's return address. Nancy and I had not talked for two years! We hadn't shared as much as an e-mail since I sent her that card.

I opened the envelope and found the very card that I had sent her. She had crossed through her name and written my name instead. There was a note at the bottom saying, "I don't know what's going on in your life right now, but you have been heavy on my mind. I felt led to pray for you and send this card back to you."

She could not have known all that I was experiencing. It was nothing short of a miracle that she was thinking of me and praying for me at a time when I needed it most. Nancy's note let me know that I was not alone, that God had heard my prayers and was prompting folks miles away who I barely knew to keep me encouraged.

~Linda Newton

78

Mom Found a Way

A mom's hug lasts long after she lets go.
~Author Unknown

I was one of the first to arrive at the cemetery on the day of my mother's funeral. I wanted to make sure the director had placed the memorial wreaths and flowers just so, that enough folding chairs had been set up beside the gravesite for those who needed them, that the stand on which the guest book and pen were to be placed was easily accessible, and that the framed collage of photographs that traced my mother's eighty-nine years of life had been given a place of prominence.

I wasn't disappointed; the funeral home had done a wonderful job. Even nature had cooperated by giving us a brilliant sky and mild temperatures, despite it being early February. My only dismay came when I noticed a smattering of white feathers scattered across the lawn beside the gravesite.

"Ugh," I groaned. With no time to spare and no practical way to clear the messy space before the others arrived, I could only hope that the mild breeze would eventually clear them away.

Yet, as I steeled myself to face the next few difficult hours, the strange presence of those white feathers also gave my grieving heart a sense of comfort. So, I picked up a nice one and placed it in the pocket of my skirt. I thought I would save it to press alongside a yellow tea rose from one of the wreaths—a remembrance of this day.

During her last weeks of suffering ill health, when both of us knew she had precious little time left, I would often ask her, "What in the world am I going to do without you, Mom?" My mother was the wisest, most loving, nurturing person I'd ever known. I couldn't imagine my life without her in it. "You're my best friend," I told her, my heart breaking.

"Look," she said, in that practical, knowing tone of hers that never failed to steady me. "I will always be near. Always. If after I'm gone there is a way, any way possible, I promise I'll let you know I'm around and watching over you." Then she would flick a hand and change the subject, as if to put the matter to rest.

Several weeks later, white feathers began to show up in the oddest places, such as the carpet in my office or the corner of my closet. At first I didn't make the connection. I was too preoccupied, too busy missing my mother. But one day in early spring, thinking exercise would help cheer me up, I took a morning walk despite the snow on the ground. With each step, I thought about how much I missed my mother. I murmured a silent prayer. "Lord, please tell Mom hello for me, and because You know my heart so well, tell her how much I miss her."

Then, for some reason, I looked down. There, on top of the snow, lay a flawless white feather.

"Oh!" I said, startled. And all of a sudden, I knew. I understood. A rush of emotion rippled through me, and my mind flew back to the day of the funeral when I'd discovered all those white feathers at the gravesite, those many times afterward when I'd found tiny white feathers in all those impossible places. And I remembered my mother's words as she assured me she would always be with me, and that if there were any way possible, she would let me know it.

I turned the feather in my hand, marveling at it through a blur of tears. God had heard the cry of my heart and had answered in a way that I couldn't possibly misunderstand — through that lovely white feather. With God's blessing, my mother was saying hello right back.

Since then, white feathers have made many appearances during significant times — those times when having my mom by my side would have meant the world to me. Once last summer on a trip to France, I visited a small art gallery in Avignon. The woman who owned it had dedicated the gallery to her deceased artist father, and she'd filled the rooms of her ancient renovated stone house with his many drawings and paintings. Because I, too, grew up with an artist father, the woman's heartfelt devotion to the gallery had made me especially sentimental toward my own deceased parents. How wonderful it would have been if they'd been there to share this lovely place with me.

Stepping out into the sunlight to wait for the others in my tour group to assemble, I looked toward a flowerbed where lavender bloomed. There, in the black soil beside those fragrant fronds, where I couldn't miss it, fluttered a delicate white feather. My mother and the Lord had done it again.

Over the months that followed, I found white feathers everywhere. For instance, I found one miraculously stuck to a vertical kitchen cupboard on Thanksgiving Day while I was preparing the turkey for our first holiday dinner without my mother. One day while thinking about my mom, out of nowhere a white feather floated past as I vacuumed my living room. And once I found a slender white seagull feather while walking into the post office where I planned to mail a birthday card to one of my mother's good friends.

Who can explain such things? I can only marvel at these little white gifts. I have so many now that I keep them tucked safely away in a decorated rosewood box. And each time I add another white feather to the pile, my heart swells with emotion and sweet assurance that all is right in the world, that love is the very thing that makes the impossible possible.

My mom kept her promise.

~Paula L. Silici

Angels and Miracles

Faith in Action

79

Heavenly Possible

"For I will restore health to you and heal you of your
wounds," says the LORD...
~Jeremiah 30:17

I sat numbly with the occasional tear slipping down my cheek.
I kept replaying the doctor's words: "I believe it is cancerous,
although it seems to be a strain I have not seen before."

The tumors were on my tongue, and part of it would
have to be removed. I was told it would severely impede my speaking
ability and there would be little to no chance of singing again. This
was devastating to a pastor and a singer.

I couldn't remember a time in my life when I had not been singing.
My first solo was at age three. I never had any training, but I let my
heart guide my voice and they seemed to make a good team.

I had joined the church to sing in the local Christian choir as
a young girl. After that, I joined worship teams, Christian bands,
appeared in musicals and even went on mission trips which focused
on spreading the news via song. Now my songs would be silenced
forever. How could God use me if I was silenced?

I had the surgery and went through two painful months of recovery.
And then tumors returned. I went to another doctor, and had more
surgery and lost more of my tongue. Now there was no chance of
singing and even speaking would be difficult.

I remember speaking to a dear friend before the surgery, asking
her what I should do. Deb, in all her wisdom, said, "Be the first."

"What?"

She reminded me of the struggles I had overcome my entire life. I had already survived two other kinds of cancer. She told me I was strong and that I needed to be the first to do what the doctors said couldn't be done. Be the first to speak well. Be the first to sing. Just trust God, believe in myself and do it!

Upon waking after surgery, I had a nurse approach me, laughing. She said that before I went completely under the anesthesia someone had commented on the size of my breathing tube. They were worried about it scarring my throat. Apparently I sat straight up and pointed to the doctor and said, "Look here, buddy, I am a preacher and I am a singer. DO NOT harm my throat; I have work to do."

I should have known then that God had a plan.

Unlike the first surgery, my recovery from this one seemed to be on fast forward. I was forming words again after days instead of weeks and months. Within a week I found myself trying to sing again.

Shortly after that was Christmas. I found myself in the back pew of a church where I didn't know anyone. The music to "O Holy Night" began to play. Remember my first solo at age three? It was to that song. This had to be a sign. I closed my eyes and at the same time opened my heart.

I asked God to allow my spirit to sing even if my mouth couldn't. Then the words spilled out. When the song was over, I opened my eyes and discovered that people were staring at me. So much for hiding.

I apologized profusely for singing too loudly. But the people were crying. They said they had never heard singing like that — that it was like angels were backing me up. I explained that they were and then gave my testimony.

The lady in front of me was dealing with cancer and had asked God for a sign. She got it through me.

When I returned to my surgeon for a follow-up, he and his intern began asking my husband questions. Finally I smiled and began answering them. The intern looked quickly at his chart, thinking he had the wrong one. He then asked, "Didn't you just have some of your tongue removed?"

I smiled and said yes. Then he looked at the doctor and said, "Should she be able to speak?"

The doctor replied "No," and smiled.

I looked at the intern and said, "What is medically impossible, is Heavenly possible."

~Pastor Wanda Christy-Shaner

80

A Special Message

Angels can fly directly into the heart of the matter.
~Author Unknown

My father's surgery would begin in two hours. His health situation — long marred by high blood pressure — had very quickly advanced from problematic to urgent when an ultrasound revealed ninety-nine percent blockage of his carotid and femoral arteries. His cardiologist was amazed that my dad had not already suffered a massive stroke, and surgery had been scheduled so quickly that I could not make it home to Texas in time from the East Coast.

I needed to put on a brave face for my daughter, Brinnley, who was four years old. Brinnley and my dad had a very special relationship. To say that Brinnley loved her "Pop" would be the greatest understatement of all time. Because of it, I had not spoken of his health issues. But as I proceeded to go about our normal morning routine, I noticed that Brinnley was being unusually quiet. I grabbed a cup of coffee and looked over at her.

"Brinnley, are you okay honey?" I asked gently.

Brinnley did not reply. She looked at me, then walked out of the kitchen and headed toward the living room.

My husband, who was frantically getting ready to leave for work, called over to her, "Good morning, Monkey!"

Again, Brinnley acted as though she hadn't heard us. My husband and I looked at each other quizzically and asked, "What's that about?"

Both of us followed her into the living room where we found her at the coffee table. She had gotten her notebook and crayons and begun drawing a picture. We sat down on the couch and attempted to speak to her, but she continued to draw the picture in silence. She seemed so different this morning, not her usual bubbly, chatty self. Instead, she was so focused on her work that it was as if she were in a trance, coloring feverishly to finish by a certain time.

When she finished, she dropped the crayon and stared at the picture. Then she picked up her notebook and walked over to me. "Mommy, this is for you."

I couldn't breathe when I looked at the picture. It was the human heart, perfectly sketched in bright Crayola colors to include chambers and arteries. It was unmistakable.

I took a deep breath and looked into Brinnley's eyes. She was smiling, her beautiful blue eyes locked onto mine.

"Brinnley, what is this?"

Still locked on my gaze, she replied, "Pop is going to be fine, Mommy." And just like that, she turned and walked away, as tears began to stream down my face.

My husband, who had not yet seen the picture asked, "What's wrong?" I handed the picture to him and heard him whisper, "Oh my God," as he placed his hand on mine.

To this day, I don't know how to explain the picture, or how Brinnley knew that my dad would be okay, other than to recognize I observed something extraordinary. After all, she was only four years old… how could she possibly know how to draw something as complex as a human heart with such amazing detail?

I learned later there had been major complications during the surgery, and my father had almost lost his life. It wasn't until a few days later, when I was able to speak to him briefly that he said one thing, "Give a hug and kiss to my angel Brinnley." I felt only then that

I truly understood what happened. I am certain it's a miracle that my dad survived and, even more, that my daughter was able to get his message to me when I needed it most.

~Jolie Lisenby

81

Three-Dollar Miracle

We all have a guardian angel, sent down from above.
To keep us safe from harm and surround us
with their love.
~Author Unknown

I braced myself against the biting spring wind as I walked through the pharmacy's sliding doors into the parking lot. I stuffed my empty hands into my coat pockets. They were empty, too. Disgusted, I shook my head. What had my life come to? I didn't even have enough money to refill my prescription. The time had come to admit it. I was broke.

How quickly I had stepped over that line. One day I was holding a paycheck and the next day I was holding a pink slip. Twenty-two years of employment hadn't meant much when my company decided to cut costs. With a mortgage and plenty of other bills to pay, I blew through my savings in no time. Now, here I stood, unable to purchase a simple necessity for the lack of three dollars.

My feet felt leaden and I stood outside that pharmacy for a long time, despite the gusting wind, pondering my dilemma. I felt so desperate, I even entertained the idea of asking the next customer who walked toward the pharmacy for the three dollars I needed.

My late mother would have taken a different tack, I thought, as I stood there contemplating my next move. Mom had long subscribed to the notion that we are each assigned a guardian angel — ready to help out in tough situations, waiting to be asked for assistance. Mom made no apologies to anyone about her firm belief and much to the amusement of many naysayers had actually given her guardian angel a name.

I had been one of those naysayers. Yet at that moment I felt so hopeless, a cry came from deep inside me: "I've tried to do everything right. I worked hard and now I have nothing to show for it. I'm scared. If my guardian angel is really out there," I pled, "please help me." Then I tipped my head down to keep the dust in the air from blowing into my eyes. And right in front of me, three dollar bills floated directly toward my feet.

While my practical side prefers to maintain a healthy skepticism about such things, I no longer count myself among the doubters. That experience in a windy parking lot seems like proof positive that I do have a guardian angel. I've been pondering names for her for quite a while now. I'm not sure, but think I'll call her "Mom."

~Monica A. Andermann

82

God Laughs

The most beautiful thing we can
experience is the mysterious.
~Albert Einstein

One of the most astounding occurrences that I've ever witnessed at my church happened when I was hosting a group from out of town. The group included Jean, Lynette, and Audrey.

When Sunday came they decided to go to my church. It was an ecumenical group. Jean was a Roman Catholic, Audrey was a Quaker, Lynette did not attend church, and I was a Presbyterian.

As we went into the church, Lynette commented "I haven't set foot in a church for over thirty years. The ceiling will probably come down."

I almost always sit in the back row, but they marched in and sat right in the front row so I joined them there. We had just settled into our seats when we heard a loud crash. A chunk of one of the ceiling lamps fell down right in front of Lynette. Never before in the more than fifty years I have attended that church had such a thing happened. Furthermore, there are about thirty seats in the front row, yet the chunk fell directly in front of Lynette.

Although I am a medical doctor, I do like numbers. My undergraduate major in college was biostatistics. Probability is of special interest to me. The probability of our sitting in the front row is fairly small. The probability of a piece of a light fixture falling when one had not fallen in the previous fifty-plus years is extremely small. The probability of that piece falling in front of our row and in front of Lynette, the person who made the joke, and right after we sat down, is infinitesimally small.

Coincidence or the hand of God, you'll have to make up your own mind. If it is the hand of God, He surely has a sense of humor. Maybe He was sending a message to Lynette: "If this is what it takes to make you believe, I will do it."

~Doris V. Schoon

83

Ask and You Shall Receive

*Prayer at its highest is a two-way conversation and for
me the most important part is listening to God's replies.*
~Frank C. Laubach

I was planting flowers one May, and watching our four-year-old son ride his bicycle on our farm by himself. I worried that he would always be playing alone with no siblings by his side. My husband and I endured years of infertility treatments before realizing that God's plan for us was adoption. We adopted our first son as a newborn, and he was a dream come true! But, we had always hoped for a house full of children.

When our son was two, we updated our paperwork and put our names back in the waiting "pool" along with hundreds of other couples hoping to adopt a child. I prayed daily that God would add to our family. But, I was becoming impatient and even our son was starting to question the wait.

"Mom, when do you think I will have a little brother or sister?" he asked that evening. With sadness and frustration in my heart, I replied, "You will have to ask God about that."

Later that night, my husband arrived home, and I told him about our son's questions and my response to him.

So, he asked our son if he had asked God.

"Yes!" our son replied. "He said it would be on Thursday."

I tucked our son in that Monday night and quickly forgot about his divine prediction.

A few days later, I was busy preparing supper when the phone rang. I vaguely recognized the name on the caller ID. Where had I seen that name before?

"Is your husband home, too?" the pleasant voice on the line asked. "Can you call him to the phone? I have some exciting news to share," she said.

It wasn't registering yet, but I hollered for my husband to come to the phone. I was on the phone in the kitchen, and my husband picked up the phone in the office a few rooms away.

The call was from our adoption agency. The caseworker was calling to tell us that a baby boy was born on Monday — the same day my son sent up his prayers. The baby boy's birth parents had decided on an adoption plan and picked us to be the adoptive parents!

I couldn't see my husband, but I could tell by his trembling voice that he was starting to cry.

"It's Thursday," he said, choking back tears of joy. He had remembered our son's prayer.

My knees went weak, and I almost fell to the floor. Just as God had told my son. It was Thursday, and this one phone call was about to change our lives forever.

The birth parents wanted to meet us the next day! I'm a planner who doesn't generally like surprises, so this was extremely stressful but in the best way possible.

We drove to meet the birth parents three hours away on Friday. By Saturday, we were a family of four!

And, God had even more surprises for us that year as He decided to add to our family again just eleven months later by sending us a daughter, too.

~Kristine Jacobson

A Thousand Cranes of Hope

Cranes carry this heavy mystical baggage. They're icons of fidelity and happiness. The Vietnamese believe cranes cart our souls up to heaven on their wings.
~Mitchell Burgess

A visit to the hospital is rarely a pleasant one. Its distinctive smell of disinfectant is never welcoming to the senses. Its white walls with the occasional splash of colour — seemingly an attempt to lift the spirits of the crestfallen souls that enter — is never encouraging enough.

As I made my way to the ward, I took a deep breath and practised a smile. After all, nobody needed another miserable face in the room.

As I entered the ward, I overheard my relatives making plans for a funeral. My grandfather had been in a coma for almost a week, with a discouraging diagnosis from the doctor. "It's only wise to make plans now," my uncle said.

I wondered. Was this really the end for him?

My grandfather was a distant figure in the family. A man of very few words, his stern demeanour made him seem unapproachable.

However, I saw him in a different light. Raised at my grandparents' place since young, I forged a very close relationship with them. While my grandmother played the role of bad cop, my grandfather and I were partners in crime. He would sneak me downstairs for ice cream when

Grandmother was in the bathroom, while I secretly added more sugar in his morning drink because he had a sweet tooth that Grandmother disapproved of.

But as I grew older and moved back in with my parents, Grandfather returned to being the quiet and lonely man everyone else saw.

I wanted to awaken this quiet man. I did not believe it was his time to go.

I had an idea. I had read about paper cranes and wishes coming true. For every one thousand folded origami cranes, we get a wish granted by the gods. Absurd as it sounds to the adults, I managed to convince my sisters and cousin to carry out this sacred plan. My family believed in Buddhism, while my cousin's family believed in Christianity. We therefore believed that with combined powers, any wish would come true. We had to act fast so that before death could claim him, God would save him.

In between classes, I was folding origami cranes. Before bedtime, I placed them all in a jar. Watching the jar fill up day by day was akin to filling up the hope in our hearts. Every origami crane was accompanied by a little prayer that my grandfather would open his eyes to see the world again.

The last few cranes were completed at the hospital. We left the jars of origami cranes by his bed and said a final prayer. This was it. Would God save him?

A week later, he was still in a deep sleep. That night, I bawled my eyes out lamenting the gods for not granting our wish. The one thousand origami cranes had not delivered our wish to the gods. We only had one wish — was that too much to ask for?

Just when all hope seemed lost, a call from my aunt one afternoon changed everything. She wanted us to come to the hospital immediately — my grandfather was awake.

A visit to the hospital is rarely a pleasant one. However, this time, I was greeted by the scent of flowers that visitors brought, and thank-you cards from discharged patients pinned on the staff notice board. I stepped into my grandfather's ward and saw him holding our jar of origami cranes. This man of few words looked up at me and said, "My good girl, thank you."

~Pebbles H.

85

Angel in Charge of Lost and Missing Things

If the only prayer you said was thank you,
that would be enough.
~Meister Eckhart

I have an "Angel in Charge of Lost and Missing Things." No, really! I do! It all began one evening in Chicago when I was meeting friends at a neighborhood restaurant. It was a clear, but frigid evening. After enjoying a satisfying dinner, I reached for my keys, only to discover that the chain was broken, and the car key gone. Panicked, I emptied my purse and pockets, while everyone searched the restaurant. All to no avail.

My friends and I carefully retraced my steps back to the car parked a block away. It was quite dark, so I was glad that I had parked beneath a streetlight. As we approached, I noticed something glistening in the snow a foot or so from the front passenger door. It was my key sticking straight up in the frosted snow.

I couldn't believe my luck. Had anyone else found the key, they could have started my car and driven away.

"Somebody up there likes you!" my friends called as I drove off. Mulling that over, I decided that perhaps I had been blessed by a special, "Angel in Charge of Lost and Missing Things."

Years later, after moving to Santa Fe, we learned to keep our four cats inside, safe from both the harsh terrain and local coyotes. One day, Charles called me at work, panic-stricken.

"Talia is missing! I've searched the house… behind furniture, under the bed, in closets… calling and calling, but…"

After calming Charles down, I suggested he lock the other cats in one room, open the front door, and sit on the floor in the middle of the house quietly calling her to him. Upon hanging up, I went into a private office, closed the door, and implored my special angel to bring her home.

About ten minutes later, Charles called back.

"I did as you suggested, and a few minutes later Talia was tapping my arm. She's curled up in my lap now as if nothing happened." Agreeing that she had probably been hiding, we both laughed and hung up. Yet, I couldn't let go of the feeling that an angel had intervened on our behalf.

A few months later, Charles told me that the safety clasp on his heavy 18-karat gold bracelet must have broken, and the bracelet was missing. We searched everywhere, but came up empty. He was devastated, as it was both a financial and sentimental loss.

Later that evening, while taking a shower, I put in a special request to my angel to help us locate Charles's bracelet. We had a large bathroom with an enclosed shower and steam unit. Once the water was shut off, the steam subsided, and I noticed something glimmering at my feet. In the midst of the parting fog, sitting upon the drain, was the missing bracelet. I fetched Charles and pointed to the floor of the shower. His jaw dropped.

"But I checked the shower! This doesn't make sense!"

"I asked my Angel in Charge of Lost and Missing Things to help us," I confessed.

"Your what?"

"I know it sounds silly, but I think I have a special angel helping me locate missing objects!"

Over the years, we both grew to depend upon my angel. Any time something was missing, one of us would simply say, "Angel in Charge of Lost and Missing Things, please stand over my lost [fill in the blank] until I can return safely to it."

The number of items that have been retrieved in this way is really quite impressive, and includes articles of clothing, more jewelry, house keys, files, pens, and even my pedometer more than once.

One time in San Francisco, I decided to walk a half-mile home after an evening function, high heels and all. Having forgotten to pick up groceries earlier, I bypassed my house and challenged the area's steep hills towards Whole Foods, another half-mile away.

Arriving hungry and tired, I realized that one of my favorite shawls, which I had wrapped loosely across one shoulder, was gone — lost somewhere along the way. My options were to either hike back up and down the hills, or place my loss in more competent hands. I opted for the latter and petitioned my angel to come to my aid.

"Oh, Angel in Charge of Lost and Missing Things, I know I must be causing you no end of extra work, but I'd really appreciate it if you could reunite me with my silk paisley shawl after I finish shopping."

Then, free of worry, I turned confidently toward the task at hand. Emerging from the store an hour later, I hoisted my bag in my arms and began the trek home. I soon spotted my shawl sitting upon a curb across the street, seemingly invisible to the eyes of passers-by who walked right past it. Not even feeling the need to hasten my pace, I crossed the street and picked it up as casually as if I were collecting my wrap from a theater's cloakroom. Of course, I didn't need a claim ticket, because my angel was thoroughly familiar with the item's owner, notorious as I was for losing things.

Things haven't changed much. Just a few minutes ago, I realized that yet another lovely earring had leapt from my ear to join the "lost and missing," so I alerted Charles to keep his eyes open for it.

"Didn't you call upon your angel?" he asked, chuckling as he began the familiar search for treasure throughout the house.

"Well, of course I did," I responded indignantly. I quietly suggested to my angel that it would be a blot upon his record if he failed to deliver while I was writing a story touting his dedicated service.

Not to worry though... I see Charles coming this way holding the dangling bauble. He's shaking his head and smiling. To tell the truth, I think he's studying to become an angelic apprentice. Not a bad idea in this household, as it probably offers unlimited employment opportunities.

So, next time something of yours disappears, simply concentrate on asking for the assistance of your own "Angel in Charge of Lost and Missing Things." I'll bet he has been nearby waiting for an assignment.

And the best part? The only payment you'll ever need is a simple "Thank You, Angel in Charge of Lost and Missing Things. Thank You!"

~Sue Ross

86

Spiritual Healing

True healing involves body, mind and Spirit.
~Alison Stormwolf

I heard the patient voices of many people chanting, the slow, rhythmic beating of an Indian drum, a piercing screech of a passing Eagle, and I saw his face and what lay beyond his eyes. He is a Shaman, taught in the ways of the Santa Clara Pueblo and Mescalero Apache, and it is his beliefs that brought an understanding that day — the day we almost lost my brother.

"Everything that we cannot explain, everything we cannot understand, and everything we cannot put a name to makes up Creator," the Shaman explained. I stared into his brown-flecked eyes, forgetting his roughed up appearance for a minute. I forgot that he needed to shave the darkening stubble off his narrow face and round chin. I forgot that he needed to comb his curly dark hair, which fell just below his shoulders.

His curls partly covered a hand-beaded feather — white and grey. They also masked the three earrings he wore in only one ear: two turquoise and silver studs, one dangling silver feather. He is always covered with jewelry. He loves it. Square-cut turquoise rings sat on the middle finger of his right hand. Three other silver rings encircled his fingers close by. An amber necklace as large as the paw of a mountain lion blended with his medicine pouch. They rose and fell on his chest as he prayed. I smelled burning sage.

I was eighteen and living in Southern California when my family got the call that my brother in Oregon had an industrial accident at work. The doctors told us he was not going to live. I had already decided he was dead. That's how bad my grief had been. The trauma to his head was so bad that his body and mind went into a coma.

I remember his room in the Intensive Care Unit was so sterile, so blank. White walls, white bed sheets, white floor. It was so startling. Life is supposed to have color. I stared at my brother, lying silently in his bed, half propped up as if he were in a good position to watch a game on the television. His head was swollen to his shoulders.

A tracheotomy tube stuck out of his throat below his chin and was attached to one of the many machines beeping consistently in his room. There were two IVs in one arm, and one in the other, and fixed into the top of his head were two of the cruelest, coldest wires I had ever seen, monitoring what brain waves they could find. The machines continued to beep bitter automated beeps. Where was my twenty-year-old brother in all of this? Where was he while his body looked like this and the machines had control of his life?

Now the Shaman had stepped into this room full of horrors.

"Eagle is the direct messenger to Creator and his people," he explained. "Prayers offered and spoken with an Eagle's feather go swiftly up to Creator. The sacredness of this animal and all its parts is to be deeply respected always." I wondered at the Shaman's knowledge at his thirty years of age. No college degree, no full-time job with benefits, no trace of disdain or worry on his face. He gives it all to Creator when he has to. He can stand in his cut-off jean shorts, faded black X-Men T-shirt, and leather sandals, and give all his sorrow, pain, and despair back to Creator. This is what he does.

I watched him perform the simple ceremony in the Intensive Care Unit of the Oregon hospital. My injured brother's own medicine pouch lay wrapped around his ankle, the only available place left on him to put it. The tiny, leather fringed pouch so brown against his pale white skin, sat as his anchor, the stuff within it put there by him. The pouch is him. I saw the Eagle's feather come out of the Shaman's bag. It was almost three inches long, two inches wide, with a quill that had been encircled by beading in a zigzag pattern of silver, black, and red. He began to run this silken feather up and down my unconscious brother's body, praying as he did so. He chanted in almost silent whispers. I began to pray silently to myself as he worked.

"When there is trauma to the head so bad that a man becomes unconscious, it is believed that the soul leaves the body. It then becomes vulnerable to any outside forces that wish to come and fill the vacancy. The medicine pouch is our protection. It is our anchor for our soul," the Shaman explained. His strong words of clarification prevented the hospital staff from removing the pouch from my brother's ankle.

The doctors had no hope and told us what they felt was the truth. It was unlikely my brother would survive. The two-ton pipe that landed upon his face would take not only his life, but my family's as well.

The whole week the Shaman stayed, brushing his prayers over my injured brother's body. It was my mother who called the Shaman to help my brother's injured body and disconnected spirit.

The Shaman is my oldest brother Lael, and although I don't understand how our injured brother was able to wake up within a week of his horrific accident, he did with our brother chanting next to him.

The doctors were astonished. He came back to us, minus his sense of smell and the vision in his left eye. There is no answer to how he survived when things were so dark and hope was almost gone.

The look in Lael's eyes tells me enough, however—that Creator heard the prayers. So today, my brother lives and my oldest brother dances.

~Melissa Maglio

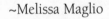

87

Turning to Mom

Because I feel that, in the Heavens above, the angels,
whispering to one another, can find, among their
burning terms of love, none so devotional as
that of "Mother."
~Edgar Allen Poe

I was finding lots of things as I looked through the old cedar chest. Ornaments that I made in elementary school — could that really be fifty years ago? Cards I had received and stashed away, cards Mom had received and stashed away before me. That chest held two intertwined lifetimes of memories. Finally my eye caught the glint of the coil-bound notebook that I had been searching for. I knew the pages contained the comforting words I needed.

It had been a long and strange day, and I was seeking comfort. Earlier that day, I completed the final tests in a long litany of pokes, prods, and X-rays. Now I needed something to calm me as I waited for the verdict. I felt alone — abandoned, even. I needed the loving assurance that only a mother can give, and that was why I was poring through that chest.

Mom had faced similar moments as she journeyed down her own cancer path decades earlier. I had experienced her journey by her side, and then laid her to rest.

What I was seeking now were *her* thoughts as she waited for "the news." That's what I knew she had tried to write about in this notebook that I had bought for her. Peeling back the cover now, I was eager to learn from her wisdom and was immediately struck by the dearth of words. So few pages had been filled — and two of them were in my own handwriting. This surely wouldn't be enough to hold onto. But then I began to read…

> *Dear Mom,*
> *This isn't anything fancy, but this type of scribbler is just what I use for my journal. I think your idea for writing your experiences/ thoughts/revelations down is a really good one. It will likely help you a lot and, who knows, it may end up helping other people. But I think you should do it for yourself first — writing can be very therapeutic.*

I looked up from the notebook, struck that the person "it may end up helping" turned out to be me. I didn't think of this at the time I had purchased it, of course, but this simple notebook and the few pages that had been used were a gift. To myself.

I turned the page to reveal my mother's entries.

> *August 8, 1995*
> *I finally got started to write. 2 weeks ago today July 25 I had surgery removing my left breast — let's go back to June 26 at doctor's for annual check-up. Whole world changed. Found lump in my breast and she explained it was very suspicious and she made appointment for many tests. She asked how I was? I said, "You tell me." Things moving very fast now and surgery is in a few days. She said I was taking it very calmly. It was then I realized the same calm (my guardian angel?) that I got when Bob's diagnosis was revealed. She said about steps I'd go through anger, denial, etc. I had remembered this from Bob's experience, too, and left it in God's hands. With my doctor's warning and God's guidance, I was calm.*

There it was. That calm that enveloped her in that moment remained until her end. That's what I remember most about that long-ago time, and what I craved to feel now. With her few simple words, that's what she was providing. When was the last time I had put God first? My daughter, my obligations to family and friends, deadlines and commitments, busyness of life — that's what fueled my days. But heeding this guidance from heaven, that's what was needed here for me right now. Her journal continued to describe the logistics of the next few weeks, the appointments and tests, and her continual reminder to herself of her "heavenly guidance."

Told my kids and what a shock it was for them. They are trying to take it in stride, I can see, but I'm sure they remember this happening with their Dad nine years ago. At this time I prepare myself for the worst. If it was my time, I had lived so much longer than Bob, had raised four children who were well-established, had seven grandchildren and I had a lot to be thankful for. I'm not afraid to die, because of all the people I love who have gone before me. Very conscious of suffering I might go through, but also know that God wouldn't give me anything I couldn't handle.

And that was it. A few paragraphs that, in this cellar on this day so many years after she wrote them, felt to me as though she was holding my hand. I sat quietly with her words, feeling reminded of my own gifts. I, too, loved my life and felt grateful. I calmly looked down to read the short final passage, in my own handwriting:

Thank you for living as long as you did. Thank you for loving as well as you did. Thank you for teaching all that you did. Thank you.

A heavenly conversation with my mother. A message of comfort, delivered to myself through the years. My mother had spoken to me, at my own long-ago behest, and her voice was never more clear.

And just then the phone rang and I turned to look calmly in its direction. I was surrounded by angels and I felt strong.

~Sandy Kelly

88

Along for the Ride

A dragonfly to remind me even though we are apart,
your spirit is always with me, forever in my heart...
~Author Unknown

"Energy never dies. It only changes form." That's what my minister Ben kept telling me after my mom died. I would go to him in tears because I was desperate to feel a connection to Mom. He would just grin and insist that she was still there, somewhere, in a different form. His attitude irritated me.

"Several months after my aunt died, my uncle was jolted awake in the middle of the night to the sound of clanging pots and pans," I told Ben. "He went to investigate and found his wife standing in the hallway. He said they talked for half an hour!"

To be frank, I'm pretty sure I'd pee my pants if I found Mom cooking in my kitchen at 3 a.m. At the same time, I'd love to see her.

"My neighbor lost her spouse two years ago and she said that sometimes she'll be driving down the road and a peacefulness washes over her because she can feel her husband beside her in the passenger's seat," I said. "Why won't Mom come sit with me?"

"Her spirit may come in a way you don't expect," Ben said. "You can't anticipate it. Just be open to it."

Summer came and my family headed to my parents' lake cabin in northern Michigan — the same one I'd been going to since I was eight years old. I had always loved going to the lake so I could go boating, waterskiing, and swimming. This year, however, I dreaded it.

Sure enough, the moment I set foot on the wooden dock, I recalled Mom's squeal — the one she used whenever she was sprayed in the face with lake water. As I took the blue canvas off the Sea Ray, I thought of the hundreds of rides Mom had taken while relaxing in the stern of the boat. Mom, always sporting a cool pair of tinted sunglasses, would stretch out her tanned legs, propping them up on the side of the Sea Ray, her feet crossed at the ankles. This enabled her to bronze her body but still catch a cooling breeze.

My stomach knotted, knowing that Mom wouldn't be joining us on the boat this summer or ever again. That's what was so difficult for me to wrap my head around — the finality of it all. How could it be that I would no longer get to experience Mom's' playful spirit?

"This summer will be awful," I thought to myself. "Mom's gone. The magic's gone. The joy is gone."

"Hey, Mom!" my nine-year-old son Kyler hollered as he sprinted down the path toward the water. "Can we take a boat ride?"

My two-year-old chimed in. "Please, Mommy! Can we?"

I lifted Trevyn into the boat.

"Sure," I said, flipping on the blower.

"Might as well," I thought. "I have to get these 'firsts' over with sometime."

I took a deep breath as I clicked the boat into reverse, backing it off the hoist.

The motor gurgled in the shallow water as we slowly maneuvered past the buoy. As I helped the boys tighten the straps on their life jackets, Kyler pointed to the left of my head and announced, "Hey, Mom — look!"

A dragonfly was hovering near my face and then landed on my shoulder.

I giggled as its delicate wings tickled my skin. I didn't think much of it. It buzzed off in a flash and we continued making our way out of the cove.

"Is everybody ready?" I asked before pushing down on the throttle. "Okay, hang on!"

Just as we were about to speed up, the dragonfly returned. This time it landed smack dab in the middle of the seat on the back of the boat. Despite the strong breeze that made its wings flutter, it remained. The kids sprinted toward it and I was sure their sudden movement would scare it off, but it didn't budge.

"That's the spot where Mom always sat," I told the boys.

"That's right!" Kyler said.

I remembered reading that the dragonfly symbolizes transformation and significance and that they often appear to carry a message.

Could it be that Mom was trying to tell me that she was still with us? And not just on this boat ride but always? I was skeptical and yet intrigued at the same time.

The lake was like glass and so the boys asked me to speed up a bit. I pushed down on the throttle: 15 RPMs, 20, 25. We occasionally hit a whitecap or boat wake and as water sprayed up on all of our faces, I heard Mom's familiar squeal, only coming through my sons' mouths this time.

I glanced back. The dragonfly was still with us. I didn't know how it was hanging on. I thought of the times an insect clung mightily to my windshield only to lose its grip once the vehicle picked up speed. I wondered how this little guy was able to stay put. I could only imagine it was because he was enjoying the ride.

Throughout that summer, a dragonfly joined us on numerous boat rides — always on the middle of the seat in the stern of the boat. After the third time, the boys started greeting the insect each time they saw it.

"Hi, Grandma!" they hollered.

"Energy never dies," Ben had said. "It only changes form."

I tapped the throttle as I piloted the boat out of our cove.

"Love you, Mom," I whispered into the wind.

~Christy Heitger-Ewing

89

The Teddy Bear

Forgive, not because they deserve forgiveness, but
because you deserve peace.
~Author Unknown

Earl's crossed arms and permanent grimace told everyone in the room he didn't want to be there. Meanwhile, Kim wiped away tears as she expressed her desire for a happy marriage with a husband who managed his anger.

The couple was attending a Cleansing Stream seminar, led by Church on the Way in Van Nuys, California. Earl, sporting a two-day stubble on his chin, was a bear of a guy — an angry, burly man with an intimidating scowl. Kim, on the other hand, radiated warmth and faith.

During a portion of the seminar held at a hotel, Earl and Kim joined three other couples for informal counseling and prayer. I was part of the Cleansing Stream's leadership team and I began with routine questions: "Where did you meet? How long have you been married? What do you do for a living?"

Earl grunted a few answers between complaints about this "inquisition," but I could see right through his bravado. Something was bothering him.

Kim said that if Earl didn't get help soon, the marriage would be over. Years of belligerence and shouting had taken their toll.

The session concluded with a time of prayer. With my eyes closed, I kept seeing a fuzzy brown teddy bear with a plaid bow around its neck.

I wondered if I hadn't gotten enough sleep the previous night. What did a teddy bear have to do with this guy and his deep-rooted anger?

As the meeting broke for lunch, a leader asked if Earl felt any differently. "I never believed in any of this prayer stuff anyway, so the answer is no," he replied. "I only did this for my wife."

I leaned over to my husband and said, "I know this sounds crazy, but the Lord wants me to buy Earl a teddy bear."

My husband rolled his eyes, but after twenty-nine years of marriage, he had learned that my spiritual antennae usually picked up the right signals. "Okay, let's go find one."

At a nearby market, which happened to be having a sale on teddy bears, I found the exact bear I envisioned: a furry brown bear with a plaid bow around its neck. I purchased the bear and found a gift card too. I wrote a note explaining that God had told me to give Earl the bear, although I didn't know why.

When the seminar regrouped in the hotel ballroom, I found Earl and Kim sitting toward the back. I walked over and handed Earl the brown paper bag holding the bear and card. When he lifted the bear out of the bag, Earl clutched it to his chest and his shoulders began heaving uncontrollably. Tears rolled down his cheeks. People couldn't help looking his way.

After pulling him aside for a few minutes, the seminar leaders asked Earl to approach the podium in the front of the room. He did, clutching Kim and his teddy bear.

"I would like to thank the group for praying for me today," he stammered. "Something happened here today, and it happened because a lady bought me this teddy bear. You see, no one in the whole world knows what this teddy bear means to me. When I was a little boy, I had a very cruel father who regularly beat me. One day I disobeyed him and, for my punishment, he took my favorite teddy bear to the back yard incinerator, where he burned it right before my eyes. I was so crushed, so hurt, that I never forgave him. I realize today that God knew my unforgiveness caused great anger in my marriage. Now that God gave me back my teddy bear, I can start healing."

Dabbing at my tears, I sat in awe of God's tender grace and unfailing love.

~Judith Ann Hayes

Chapter
10

Angels and Miracles

Love that Doesn't Die

90

The Third Sunday in August

Sometimes our grandmas and grandpas
are like grand-angels.
~Lexie Saige

Trembling, I knelt on the playground in front of my four-year-old son. "What did the old man say to you?"

"Move!" my son shouted. "And then he poked me with a stick." He jabbed his little fingers into his ribs to demonstrate. But he couldn't have been telling the truth. We were at our family reunion, for goodness sake. No one would hurt him there.

When I was a kid, I counted down the days until that reunion. Every August, on the third Sunday, rain or shine, the extended family gathered at the same private grove in the town where my grandparents lived. The place always seemed as much a part of the family as the attendees — like hallowed ground. The facilities there were, and still are, rustic at best. But that was what we loved about it.

For my cousins and me, one of the best things about the picnic grove was the playground. Nestled beneath hundred-year-old oaks that soared fifty feet in the air, and arranged helter-skelter on uneven rocky ground, the equipment seemed like it had sprung up in the middle of a forest somewhere and we'd just happened upon it.

The swings were suspended from heavy chains before plastic sleeves prevented pinched fingers; the merry-go-round was unforgiving wood and threw kids off like a bucking bronco; and, when waxed up properly, the bump in the middle of the mile-high aluminum slide would send us into the air.

We cooked our meals on a huge outdoor fireplace. Grandfather Russell arrived early in the morning to chop the wood and start the fire so it would be good and hot by lunchtime. By the time we all arrived, he'd have set up a lawn chair near the fireplace where he would listen to the Phillies game on the radio while he smoked his pipe, tended the fire, and observed.

It was always a magical day, in a place where we could run free, safe from the outside world. I don't think it occurred to any of us kids that things would ever be any different. But they changed quickly.

The year Grandfather Russell died we set up his chair and his radio in tribute and tried to go on as usual, but there was a heaviness in the air. A loss of innocence, in a way. We did the things we always had, but it just wasn't the same.

By the time I got married and had a son and took him to the reunion for the first time, I viewed the rustic charm of our location differently. Instead of being a fun adventure, it seemed like a hassle. The food wasn't appropriate for a toddler, the fireplace was a hazard, and the playground was a deathtrap. Instead of seeing it like something out of a Disney movie, it seemed like something the Brothers Grimm dreamed up. And since the relatives in my grandfather's generation had followed his lead in quick succession, there weren't as many family members and the air seemed thick with emotional memories.

The reunion became a time to mourn. I dreaded it. But for my son it was all new. The thing he loved most? The playground, of course. He explored, but I couldn't watch. That outdated equipment was so dangerous!

"Let him go," my relatives urged when he ran to the sliding board. "You did it by yourself when you were a kid."

But what if he fell? What if he scraped his tender little shin on the serrated metal rungs climbing up to the top? And it was windy that day. What if he got pelted with a hail of acorns and let go?

I held my breath. His maiden voyage went well, but the second time around he hit that bump and caught some air. He flew off the slide and was propelled forward a few steps before falling face-first in the dirt, just the way I had once upon a time, just the way all of my cousins had.

He picked himself up and dusted himself off, but that was his last trip down the slide. He decided to kneel at the bottom and drive his toy cars up it like a mountain. Good. He was happy and I didn't have to worry. I was sitting about twenty-five feet away from him, talking to relatives, when all of a sudden my son jumped down from the end of the slide and ran like his hair was on fire.

Before I could even get to my feet, a deafening crash shook the ground. A limb from one of those mighty old oaks had broken off and fallen on the bottom of the slide, precisely where my son had been playing with his cars. The echo still rang through the grove when I reached him.

He wasn't hurt. He wasn't even scared. I was terrified and shaking. "How did you know that branch was going to fall?" I asked him. "What made you run away?"

He shrugged his shoulders. "An old guy told me to move."

"What old guy?"

He shrugged again. "Rusty. He poked me with a stick and told me to move."

I'd been watching him like a hawk. There was no old guy around. No one poked him with anything. And no one was named Rusty. But why did my four-year-old son smell like he'd been smoking a pipe?

It couldn't have been what I was thinking.

By now, other relatives had gathered around. It took two grown men to move the oak branch off the slide. My son remained calm. It never occurred to him that he could have died — that the branch would have hit him if he hadn't run away.

I was shaken, and we left the reunion early that day. That night, I quizzed my son again about why he'd moved before the branch fell, but he never changed his answer. "Rusty poked me with a stick."

The next year, when we went back to the reunion, I watched and I waited. I sniffed around for my grandfather's pipe. I looked for a sign that he was around, but there was none. Why had he come last year and not now? Maybe the answer was simply because we needed him last year and this year we didn't. Or maybe the answer was that he was always there, observing the way he used to, and when his great-grandson was in danger he was able to act.

I wondered, too, how many other long-gone relatives patrolled that picnic grove. More than a few, I'd guess, given that none of us has ever suffered more than a quickly forgotten bump while playing there, despite the ancient and dangerous playground and all those old trees.

I still go to that reunion every year. Now I go for two reasons: to see the relatives that I still have, and to feel closer to those I don't. Maybe the air really is magical there, laden with memories, awash with the kind of love that transcends death, alive with connections that will never end.

~Tracy Falenwolfe

91

All in Good Time

Time is a physician that heals every grief.
~Diphilus

After my father was gone I visited Mom more frequently. Eventually we began sorting through Daddy's belongings and Mom gave me his watch.

"You take this, Annie. I know you will appreciate having it someday."

She placed the watch in my hand and my fingers closed around it. I recalled him slipping the watch over his calloused hand every morning as he descended the stairs to start his day.

"Thanks, Mom," I said, trying not to cry.

I put that big watch on my wrist even though its large face and its extra wide band looked comical on me. I didn't care. My father wore it every day and I resolved that I'd wear it every day, too. And there it stayed no matter the occasion. When I went to bed I'd slide my arm under the pillow and listen to the rhythmic tick, tick, tick that eventually lulled me to sleep.

On the first anniversary of Dad's passing, I noticed the watch had stopped at the exact time of his death—5:17 p.m. It occurred to me that this might be Dad's way of telling me it was time to move on. I put the watch in my jewelry box.

During that second year after his death, I helped my mother downsize. She gave away or sold most of her furniture, readied the house for sale, and found a new place to live in a retirement community.

Even though she would be without Dad, Mom was looking forward to making new friends in the retirement community.

I didn't realize it at first, but slowly the cloud of grief was lifting from my heart, too. Mom and I would often end up in a fit of laughter recalling one incident or another with my father. Still, I wanted answers. I needed to know he was happy even though he'd moved on. I prayed often for his peace and happiness but accepted that I'd never know for sure.

Mom was well settled into her new life and carrying on as best she could when we neared the second anniversary of Dad's departure. I hadn't thought of the watch in months. Then, one day, I came across it in my jewelry box. I picked it up and discovered to my astonishment that not only was it running, but it was also showing the correct time and date. How could that be? It had stopped cold right on the very first anniversary of his death. I'd looked at it a few times since it had initially stopped and the time and date had never changed. Yet now it was keeping perfect time.

Dad's watch continued to run perfectly, never losing a minute, for the next ten years. Watch batteries just don't have that kind of longevity.

When that watch came roaring back to life long after it had stopped, Daddy was letting me know loud and clear, "Don't worry about me, Annie, I couldn't be happier." Of this I have no doubt.

~Annmarie B. Tait

92

Christmas Comfort

Grandmas hold our tiny hands for just a little
while, but our hearts forever.
~Author Unknown

My mother had passed away in October and I was bereft. Our fifteen-year-old daughter Jessica was despondent, too. Her Mimi had been her world.

We had run away to out-of-town relatives for Thanksgiving, and now we faced our first Christmas without my mother. To make it more painful, Jess's birthday was Christmas Eve. My husband suggested we escape to New York. What could be more festive than the holiday lights and Broadway shows?

We had gone to the theatre that night, had enjoyed a late supper afterward, and had returned to the hotel exhausted. Our room had a wonderfully inviting king size bed, which the three of us shared. Robert fell onto his side and was deep into dreams before Jess and I had washed our faces. I crawled into the middle with Jess to my right. She had been unusually quiet and I knew she was missing her grandmother when I heard her whisper, "Mom, would you please 'tickle-scratch' my back?"

"Sure, sweetheart." My mother had been the world's best back-scratcher. She had the lightest touch and the greatest endurance anyone could ever imagine. How many nights had that gentle hand lulled me to sleep, her fingers barely sweeping over my skin from shoulder to shoulder and across my neck? Unfortunately for Jess, I had inherited neither the instinct nor the patience to do it the way Mama had done. But I would try.

Jess turned her back to me, and, as I lifted my arm toward her shoulder, the atmosphere in the room seemed to change. It became cooler — not unpleasantly so, but cooler and different. Where it had been completely dark the minute before, there was now a soft glow around us, and then, something, or someone, took my hand and guided it over and around my daughter's back. It was as if my hand had become the object on a Ouija board. I did nothing. My delicate movements were totally involuntary and foreign to me. My own hand was weightless and tireless. I had no control over where or how to touch her — or when to stop. Eventually, my hand moved to the top of her left shoulder and patted it twice. With that, the session ended, and the darkness returned.

I brought my hand back to myself and pondered what had just transpired. A few moments later, I thought I heard Jess sniffle.

"Are you still awake, honey?"

"Uh huh. Mom, Mimi was here, wasn't she?"

"It seemed that way. Why do you say so?"

"Somehow the room felt different, strange. And the way you scratched me felt just like her. You never have done it for so long. And then the signal that you were through."

"Signal?"

"You tapped me twice on the shoulder. That's what she always did when she was finished."

"I don't remember her doing that. Hmm, I guess that really was Mimi letting us know she is still with us and she is okay." With that Jess hugged me and fell fast asleep.

We could not have had a better Christmas present.

~Grace Givens

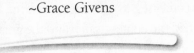

Guiding Me Through the Storm

I cannot think of any need in childhood as strong as
the need for a father's protection.
~Sigmund Freud

Black-bottomed clouds heavy with rain obscured the moon. Leaves hung limply in the humid air. We were in for a crackler, as my dad used to call the big thunder and lightning storms that cause serious damage to trees and property, but I wasn't overly concerned. It was a quick ten-minute drive to the south end of town and my meeting. At worst, my flip flop–covered feet might get wet. An umbrella would keep the rest of me dry.

A couple of hours later the conference room windows rattled in their 100-year-old wooden frames. Small broken branches from the big oak trees that lined the street outside struck the rippled glass with rapidly increasing force. The noise escalated. Conversation stopped. The meeting was hastily adjourned. Everyone hurried out into the storm, hoping to reach home before it got any worse. Except for me.

I walked over to the wall of windows. The rain obscured everything but the puddles of standing water and the swirling leaves and branches on the sidewalk immediately below. Yes, my feet were going to get wet, but thank goodness I didn't have far to drive.

The old building's oversized front door was difficult to open on even the driest of days so I gave it a harder-than-usual shove, hoping it would pop open on my first try. Immediately, the wind grabbed the door and slammed it all the way open against the brick wall. My umbrella skittered off into the night as I wrestled the door closed. Cold water dripped down my back. Wet leaves sucked at my feet and water splashed onto the backs of my calves with every step I took. Conditions were deteriorating rapidly.

One block. Two blocks. I drove north toward home. My SUV rocked side to side, buffeted by the wind. I sensed when I passed a familiar convenience store, but I couldn't see the entrance. The wipers couldn't clear the rain fast enough. I was happy no other cars were on the road around me.

Five blocks. Six blocks. The thunder boomed non-stop. Suddenly a brilliant flash of light filled my vehicle and I heard an explosion. Lightning hit a tree less than a block in front of me and pieces of tree flew like missiles through the night. I slammed on the brakes. The smell of burning wood filled my nostrils as the trunk of the tree tumbled across the roadway in front of me. My hands trembled as I guided the SUV down a nearby side street.

Rain pelted the driver's side window and branches scraped against the side of my vehicle. I fought the wind to stay on the road. I knew I was only blocks from home, near one of my town's gorgeous parks, but I couldn't see any of it through the downpour.

Then my headlights reflected off something in the road ahead of me. A tree, its trunk more than three feet in diameter, blocked my way. I backed up a hundred feet and turned down another side street. Large branches littered the road. I drove over them, not willing to stop or turn around yet again. Slowly and carefully I bumped over one branch after another, wincing as they scraped the undercarriage. I gripped the steering wheel.

Within minutes I saw another tree blocking my path. I stopped. It was too big to drive over and too large to drive around. I was more than twenty minutes into a drive that typically took ten, and I was not much closer to home than when I started.

The storm surged around me. The trees were weapons tonight.

I prayed out loud for safe passage home as I reversed direction again.

Thunder rumbled. Lightning crackled. I saw a glow in the road ahead. Electrical wires — live ones — sparked on the blacktop. I took a deep, unsteady breath.

"Turn around, Darlene. Double back. Two streets," I heard my dad say.

I obeyed. My dad never led me the wrong way.

But my dad had died three months earlier!

"Wind down your window. That way you'll hear the wires hissing even if you can't see them," he said.

I powered down my window and hung my head out so I could hear better. The rain poured down like some sort of a berserk faucet, but I drove on. Dad was with me.

HISSSSS.

Another wire down!

"Dad!" I yelled.

"You can do this, kid. Keep going."

Rain dripped off the ends of my hair and traced paths down my face, but I kept driving, my head out the window listening for a telltale hiss. Soon, though, I was out of options, trapped in an area of a few square blocks, surrounded by downed trees that were too large for me to drive over or around.

I had to make a choice: Stay in my SUV until the storm blew through, hoping I wouldn't get hit by a falling tree or blowing debris. Or walk the rest of the way home. In flip flops. I didn't hesitate, even though I knew old growth trees lined the sidewalks between home and me. I shut off the engine and opened the door. I stepped into the rain and wind and began one of the longest walks of my life.

"You got this, kid," Dad said.

I flip flopped my way around downed trees, over branches and through puddles, all the while listening for the telltale hiss of a downed power line or the crack of a breaking branch overhead. I slogged through it all, and fifteen minutes later, I unlocked my front door. I was safe.

The next day I learned that I had driven through the hardest hit area of my town at almost the peak of the storm. Weather experts called the storm a microburst, which is like a treetop tornado. It left near-total devastation in its wake. I drove through it. I walked through it. And I did it with the help of my dad. And the bonus? I got to hear his voice just one more time.

~Darlene Sneden

My Angel-in-Law

The guardian angels of life sometimes fly so high as to
be beyond our sight, but they are always
looking down upon us.
~Jean Paul Richter

The psychic medium paced the studio, his shaggy white hair flowing behind him. He pursed his lips, listening to an internal dialogue that forty hopeful people could not hear. We were all there for essentially the same reason — to connect with a lost loved one.

He paused, his eyes closed, and then offered clues to the audience as to whom he was channeling. We were instructed to raise our hands if the details resonated with any of us. He gravitated toward different sides of the room as if by radar, divulging additional details until he could single out the person whose loved one was communicating from the other side. The room was full of mourners looking for solace, and a glimpse into what world, if any, their loved ones now inhabited. At least I know I was.

While I believed in the power of psychics, many in the room did not. They wore cynical scowls, and the medium encouraged their doubt. He welcomed skeptics, and hoped to prove his genuine gift by providing specific information that no one else could know. He acknowledged that his industry was full of charlatans, preying on believers who'd pay any fee for a message, an image, or some hope. It was easy enough to fool them. Most anyone could proffer vague details that desperate people would interpret as personal. Who didn't know someone who'd had a heart attack, walked with a limp, or had passed in a tragic accident? Grief made people gullible.

I'd been to this medium's group readings on other occasions. I'd lost a brother, both sets of grandparents, and several friends. After my brother died suddenly, I sought answers through psychic reading in order to make sense of the loss. This particular psychic had "read" my brother with such clarity that I hoped to re-experience some of the comfort, spiritual nourishment, and peace I'd previously felt. I knew I might not get a personal reading this time, as there were only so many he could squeeze into the allotted two hours.

What I never imagined was that I would hear from someone I'd never met.

My mind flashed to three years earlier, as I lay in the recovery room, struggling to breathe against an invisible weight on my chest. While I'd been told that the transfer surgery to implant three fertilized embryos had been textbook easy, I nonetheless knew something was wrong. In that moment, I couldn't think about the years I'd struggled with infertility, the multiple failures, the pills and shots, and the crushing monthly disappointment. I just needed to breathe.

My body had hyper-stimulated from the fertility drugs, producing twenty-three eggs in a single month, and it would take a while to recover from such a taxing feat. Awash in hormones, continuously breathless and tremendously uncomfortable, I was on bed rest for a month. That rest gave me the opportunity to think, obsess, and pray. I hoped to become pregnant and I yearned to recapture who I'd been before the infertility. My happy, busy life had been invaded by the pain and frustration of infertility, and it was all consuming.

I gradually recovered from the hyper-stimulation and learned that I was carrying twin boys. It was a high-risk pregnancy that eventually returned me to bed rest because the boys were positioned very low and they needed more time to develop their lungs before they could safely be born.

Again, with hours to fill the day, I read through baby rearing books and name books. We'd intended to name Twin A after our grandfathers, and Twin B was to be named after my husband's mother, who had died when he was ten years old. I often stared at pictures of my husband as a little boy with his mom, and could feel their profound sadness while she grew sicker and succumbed to a diabetes-related illness. I'd already formed a bond with my unborn boys and could not fathom a separation like my husband endured with his own mother. I wished that I had known my mother-in-law, and that she could be a part of the miracle that was taking place. I was pleased to honor her memory with our child's name.

When I delivered two healthy five-and-a-half pound boys we were overjoyed. Unfortunately, that joy was tempered by the temporary paralysis that I experienced in both legs, lasting for six weeks after their birth. I could not pick up my babies when they cried; I could not walk to them and watch them sleep in their matching bassinets. I was dependent on others to bring the boys to me, and I worried that our bond would be hampered by my temporary disability.

I never considered that I wouldn't recover; I simply had to. My babies needed me, and we had a life to lead that did not involve my using a wheelchair, walker, or cane. Despite my new-mother fatigue, I had physical therapy each day until I was able to walk without assistance. Sheer determination to be the mother I wanted to be for my babies helped me regain the use of my legs.

I recovered and was happily raising my twins when my brother passed. His death cloaked me in a depression that only the toddlers could lift me from. The psychic had helped me before. I was there again to see if my brother's spirit was still around me.

The group reading was almost over when I heard the psychic mention that he was communicating with a woman who had been a teacher and was diabetic. I, along with several other people raised my hand. He approached my general vicinity, throwing more details, until there were only a couple hopeful hands raised.

"Who has the twins?" he asked.

My spine tingled as I called out that I did. He approached me and asked if I knew someone who'd been scalded in the bathtub. I held my breath. That particular incident was very traumatic for my husband. He witnessed his mother, who'd lost sensation in her foot, unknowingly step into the blistering water. It was the beginning of her decline.

"Yes, that was my mother-in-law," I whispered.

He nodded, looking up.

"She wants you to know that she watched over you when you were pregnant and afterward with your legs."

It was in that moment that I realized she did know me, and loved me. She was a part of our lives in her own way, and I was enormously grateful.

I'd finally met my mother-in-law.

~Shanna Silva

95

Double Exposure

A mother's love runs deep and its
power knows no limit.
~Author Unknown

The last time my mother was at our house was Thanksgiving Day. She had been diagnosed with advanced stage cancer two months earlier, and she was already showing signs of weakness. So instead of the usual "Thanksgiving at Grandma's house," we decided to have it at ours.

By the time everyone arrived, the house smelled of turkey and stuffing, and the tables looked festive and inviting. It was a good day for my mom and dad, with a house full of children and grandchildren. We ate and laughed about times growing up. Then, while the kids played, we put the football game on TV and played pinochle with my dad.

It was nice for us to see my mom dressed up and out of their house for a change. She spent most of that day sitting in the comfortable rocker in the living room. We took lots of pictures that Thanksgiving.

After that day, Mom's condition worsened quickly. She died two weeks later, just before Christmas. It was the first of many holidays and special occasions without Mom there to celebrate with us.

Time lessened the grief, but we still missed her very much. She and my dad had always been there for their grandchildren's birthdays, school events and special times in their lives, and my dad still came. One of those special occasions arrived the following spring.

Our youngest daughter made her First Holy Communion, which

is a special celebration in our church. I got out the white dress and veil that my mother had bought for me when I made my First Communion. I washed it and hung it out to dry. The lace sparkled in the sun. I replaced the yellowed ribbon and sewed a new white slip. How sad, I thought, that Mom would not be here to see her granddaughter on this day. Sarah was especially close to her grandma and grandpa. She had spent a lot of time with them before she started school, since they babysat her when I returned to work. It would be the only First Communion of our six children that my mom would miss.

We had lots of family over that day and, as usual, we took lots of pictures with family and friends. I was anxious to see the pictures, and quickly took them in to be developed. This was back before digital cameras, when you had to load the film into the camera, and then take the film to the drugstore to have the pictures developed.

When I picked up the photos I opened the folder, and for a moment my heart almost stopped. Right on top was a picture of Sarah in her communion dress sitting on the arm of the rocker, and next to her, sitting in that comfortable rocker, was my mother! The picture was a little fuzzy, but there was no mistake — it was Sarah and her grandma, on the day that she made her First Communion.

When I got over my initial shock and looked through the rest of the pictures, I realized that the photos had been double-exposed — communion pictures taken on top of Thanksgiving pictures. In the time that had passed there were holidays and birthdays when I had taken other pictures. But somehow I had missed taking in this one roll of film from Thanksgiving. And I had re-used that roll of undeveloped film on that day, thinking it was a new roll of film.

What were the odds! But that day in May, my daughter's picture was taken sitting next to her grandma. It was as if my mother was sending a message from heaven saying, "See, I haven't missed anything! I've been right here beside you all the time."

~Peggy Archer

96

I Get Misty

A song will outlive all sermons in the memory.
~Henry Giles

My grandmother loved music and played the piano and the organ, and my mother played the piano as well. But she needed the sheet music for everything she played except for the song "Misty," which she knew by heart. It was a running joke in our family that every time we visited someone with a piano, at some point, my mother would sit down and laughingly ask, "Anybody wanna hear 'Misty'?"

My parents were married for forty-three years, taking up the RV lifestyle in their mid-fifties and traveling around the country. They settled in Longview, Texas, and bought a small house there. One night, my mother began to feel ill. She'd been plagued with respiratory problems most of her later life, and my father took her to the hospital. She was admitted for the night. The next morning, as my father was preparing to leave to visit her, the hospital called to tell him that my mother had passed away.

My father was shattered. I booked the next flight to Dallas, rented a car and headed to Longview.

Later that evening, I suggested we go out to dinner, if for no other reason than to get out of the house. He agreed, and off we went.

From the subdivision where my parents lived to the "restaurant row" of Longview was about a ten-minute drive. We ate dinner and tried to make conversation with each other. As we got in the car, I told my father that I wanted to make a stop at a convenience store to grab some diet soda. On the drive back, we began discussing the various things we needed to get done as far as a service, notifying out-of-town relatives, and other arrangements. As we talked and drove, I passed at least five or six different convenience stores, telling myself, "I'll stop at the next one."

Finally I came to an intersection that was also the turn-off to get to their subdivision. There was a store there, so I pulled in and got out, realizing that this was my last opportunity to grab some soda.

I opened the door and walked in, and as I did, I heard music coming from a radio behind the counter.

It was Johnny Mathis singing "Misty."

I froze. And then I smiled, realizing that it was my mother reaching out to me one more time, asking if I wanted to hear "Misty."

~Greg Moore

97

A Heavenly Message

Unable are the loved to die. For love is immortality.
~Emily Dickinson

M y mother died in 2005, but she continues to visit with me very frequently. She suffered an agonizing death over five months from the effects of lung cancer.

After her diagnosis I spent time with my mom every day until her passing. During this time we made promises and gave one another comfort, shared laughter, tears and memories. We went through drawers and closets and turned trinkets into treasures and artifacts into legacies. We talked about life and we talked about death and the possibility of an afterlife. Mom promised that she would visit from that other world.

"But how will we communicate?" I asked.

"Our bodies are just pulses of energy; paranormal experiences are just pulses of energy that manifest themselves in some way through networks," was her explanation. "I think we will be able to communicate through all things electrical," she whispered through quivering lips, her eyes welling with tears.

A friend of mine, whose sister had succumbed to cancer the previous month, came to visit my mom. "Do you think your sister knew when she was going to die?" my mom queried.

"Absolutely," he replied. "The day before she died, my sister asked her husband to call their children and tell them to come to the hospital as soon as possible. When the family had gathered my sister closed her eyes and passed away. She definitely knew when she was going to die," he explained.

As happens with stage 4 cancer, my mom's health deteriorated very rapidly. She was bedridden and she could not eat as her mouth was filled with thrush. Frail as she was, she continued to be an emotional paragon of strength, dispensing kindness and wisdom.

"It's a funny thing, this life," she said. "We started out so very poor, but your father and I worked, scrimped and saved. Now I have this big house and I can only exist in one room. The refrigerator is full of food and I cannot eat. I have a new car in the garage that I can't drive and money in the bank that I'll never spend. It's not what you accumulate in this world that is important, it is how much we love one another that counts. Have no regrets, my darling," she rasped.

As I sat holding her hand on December 31st Mom whispered to me, "Sweetheart, I think it's time for me to change my address."

Did she know that death was imminent? I could barely speak, trying to choke back tears as I made the appropriate phone calls to the necessary medical agencies to get Mom to the hospital. The stretcher service arrived and with decorum and grace my mother bade her home goodbye as she was wheeled out into the waiting van.

Mom remained lucid and interacted with us for a couple of hours after her arrival at the hospital and then quietly slipped into a very deep sleep. At midnight, fireworks rocketed across the sky and welcomed 2005. The window of her hospital room provided the perfect vantage point for the shimmering explosions of color and light as they burst into the midnight sky. In her slumber, I knew she could not see the symbols of gaiety and hope. My fingers encircled her soft, limp hand as I watched the sky alight with glimmering streaks of gold, silver, green, red and blue. I wished that the comets could whisk her skyward to heaven and bring a painless peace for her soul.

When my sister came to relieve me from my watch, I went home and had a fitful sleep. My deceased grandma and grandpa came to me in my dreams. Did they come to comfort me or was I thinking of them because I felt impending death? Were they letting me know that they were ready to welcome their daughter to heaven? Was their visit a premonition, or was I simply having a dream?

I got out of bed, and welcomed the new day — the New Year — with a shower. Then I brewed a pot of coffee and put a bran muffin into the microwave oven to defrost. I keyed the appropriate buttons, and suddenly, there was a short burst of flames and a puff of smoke inside the cavity of my two-month-old microwave oven. The flame vanished and the smoke dissipated. Then the microwave oven ceased to operate.

Moments later the phone rang. My sister sobbed on the other end of the line. "She's gone."

The day my mom died, I plugged a miniature candle-shaped night light into an electrical socket in my bedroom. It illuminates when the room is darkened. After getting into bed and extinguishing my bedside lamp, I would watch its steady glow and feel my mother's warmth envelop me. It glowed steadily in the darkness for about one year. Then it stopped lighting in the darkened room.

Soon after, it began to flicker in the dimly lighted room, just before I turned off my bedside lamp. I would watch it for extended periods of time and as soon as I turned off the lamp, the flickering ceased. I would turn the lamp back on and the flickering resumed. Was my mother trying to communicate with me? How could I possibly interpret the intermittent flashes of light?

One evening, I was having dinner with my father-in-law who had been a Flight Lieutenant in the Armed Forces. One of his "secret missions" was working out of Duluth, Minnesota, following up on reports of UFO sightings. Although he could not share any details of his mission, the conversation turned to the subject of Morse code. He joked that perhaps the aliens would communicate with us in Morse code. I didn't know much about Morse code, but he explained to me that it was used to communicate information as a series of on-off tones, lights, or clicks. Each letter or numeral was represented by a unique sequence of dots and dashes.

Using my computer I researched Morse code. For months I studied the series of dots and dashes until I understood the sequencing. Then, for days I watched the tiny electric candle flame flicker in my dimly lit bedroom. Finally, I was able to follow the flickering with some semblance of order: ".. .-.. --- ...- . ..-"

I copied the signals onto a notepad and after several attempts realized that I was writing the dashes and dots over and over again in the same pattern. I studied the pattern, trying to find a beginning and an end. "I-l-o-v-e-u" — the symbols repeated over and over again. I leaped from my bed and put my trembling fingers over the flickering light. I love you too, Mom.

~Sheryn Smith

98

Pennies from Paula

A strong friendship doesn't need daily conversation or being together. As long as the relationship lives in the heart, true friends never part.
~Author Unknown

When my best friend, Paula, passed away eight years ago, my daughter had a difficult time working through the loss. McKenna was ten years old at the time and Paula was like a fun aunt to her. She would see or hear from Paula at least a couple of times a week. Paula was my backup sitter and a true comfort to McKenna when I was going through my divorce.

When Paula went into the hospital for her second transplant in 2007, I really did believe that she would sail through the procedure just like she had before. There was nothing in Paula's history with the disease that would make me believe anything different. She had been a fighter and a survivor since the day that she was first diagnosed with cancer.

When I realized that Paula would not be coming home from the hospital, I tried to prepare McKenna as best I could. My daughter had already experienced great loss when my grandmother passed away. But as McKenna reminded me, GG, short for Great-Grandma was older and that was what happened when people got old. Paula, on the other hand was not old, so death should not have been a possibility.

Telling McKenna that Paula had died was one of the hardest

things I have ever done. There were tears, yelling and lots of sleepless nights. McKenna was afraid that if Paula could die young, so could I. I did my best to assure her that was not going to happen, but I know that she did not fully believe me. We prayed a lot.

During this time, I tried to keep McKenna busy so there would be less time to worry. I had her enter an art competition at my work. Students were asked to make something out of a generic, small box. McKenna decided to make a wishing well. It was really quite cute and she added pennies as part of the décor. When explaining her thoughts behind her "box art" creation, McKenna remembered what I had told her about finding pennies. I had told her it meant that someone in heaven was thinking about you. Her wishing well was actually a tribute to her friend Paula.

This simple piece of art seemed to do the trick. McKenna was feeling better and we were finding pennies everywhere… inside the house, the car, on walks, in parking lots, her room, my office, etc.

Then one night, when I was having a hard time falling asleep, I felt a presence in my room. I remember this feeling of peace and a swirling light hovering at the door. I was not frightened and I immediately knew that it was Paula.

The next morning when I woke up, before I could say anything about last night's "visit," my husband Joe said to me, "Paula was here last night." I asked him why he thought that. Joe is blind so I was pretty sure that he did not see the same light that I did. He then said that when he got up to go to the bathroom, he passed her in the doorway. He said that he felt a presence as he was walking by and immediately knew that it was Paula.

Needless to say, I was a little surprised when Joe shared his encounter with me. However, when I got out of bed and headed out of the room, I found a penny on the floor right where I saw the light. I knew that my dear friend had indeed stopped by.

~Laura Dailey-Pelle

99

Elmo Takes a Nosedive

Brothers and sisters are as close as hands and feet.
~Vietnamese Proverb

My brother Ralph's death shattered my world. Losing him so suddenly knocked my feet out from under me because he was my lifeline, my confidant, my best friend, and my support through some trying times.

Ralph and his wife, Martha, had moved to my town after his retirement. After Martha's death, Ralph and I became even closer than before. I did what I could to help him through his loss like he'd done for me so many times.

He and I loved to go to the local auction in our small town. At one particular auction, a laughing Elmo figure from *Sesame Street* was up for bids. I raised my hand. Nobody else wanted him, so I won the bid. When they brought Elmo to our table, Ralph flipped a button on the bottom of Elmo's foot, and the fuzzy red character began laughing, shaking and walking toward me. We couldn't find the button to turn him off, and everyone in the entire room was laughing right along with Elmo. Ralph and I laughed so hard that night that our stomachs hurt.

From that day forward he and I had a daily routine of sending each other a text message with a picture of Elmo attached. Elmo was our way of saying "smile" to each other. The morning of Ralph's death I received his usual message asking me how things were going, with a picture of Elmo's smiling face. I replied that all was well, and returned that picture to him. There was nothing in our conversation to indicate that he was not feeling well. But later that day he had a fatal heart attack.

My grief over Ralph's death consumed me. I couldn't get it out of my mind. I missed him and his crazy antics. I missed having someone care about me enough to inquire about my wellbeing every single day of the week. I loved all four of my brothers, but for some reason Ralph and I were cut from the same mold. He was five years older than me, but we remained close even after both of us were grown and married with families of our own.

I was thinking about him one morning about two weeks after his death as I loaded hay into the golf cart to take to the pasture for the horses and donkeys. As I approached the pasture, I noticed something unusual. A helium balloon from some unknown source had landed just inside the gate, and a small breeze caused it to move back and forth across the grass. I noticed that there was a string attached to it, so my best guess was that a child had accidentally let go of it somewhere, and it had lost most of its helium and taken a nosedive into my pasture.

Because plastic can cause great harm to horses and donkeys if ingested, I opened the gate and walked in to retrieve it. As I approached it, the balloon suddenly rose into the air just out of my reach. That's when I noticed it. Elmo. The balloon had Elmo's smiling face on it.

Was Ralph sending me a message? Was he telling me to "smile" as he did every morning?

"Ralph, is that you?" I asked.

Just as I asked that question, the balloon did a curtsy, then flew back up. It rose higher and higher, flew over the fence, and headed toward the barn. The horses came out of their stalls, snorting and prancing, as it flew toward their paddock. Up it went, over the top of the barn, across the next pasture, and headed toward the hundred-year-old oak trees in the distance. I figured it didn't have enough air in it to keep it out of the tall trees, but I was so wrong.

Elmo's smiling face kept climbing. Every so often the balloon dipped down as though it was waving to me, but then it would right itself and climb higher. It approached the trees, but then it seemed to stop. It danced there in the air for several minutes.

Then over the tops of the tall trees it went. When it reached the top, Elmo's face took a bow, then continued on its journey, disappearing from my view. It went out of my life as quickly as it had come in.

"I got your message," I said as tears flowed down my cheeks. All the pain and emptiness I felt poured out. I was completely drained.

Suddenly the tears stopped and a smile came across my face. I remembered the night of the auction when we first bought Elmo, and the laughter he brought to us.

"I know you want me to smile, but it's been so hard to do since you've been gone. But I promise you that from this day forward I will give it my best shot."

More than two years have passed since Ralph's death. Every time I think of that unexplained helium balloon it brings a smile to my face.

~Carol Huff

Look for My Spirit in the Light

We shall find peace. We shall hear angels. We shall see
the sky sparkling with diamonds.
~Anton Chekhov

I'd stumbled through four months without my son. As I walked to my car, trying not to cry until I was inside it, I could already picture what would happen when I got home. I'd walk through the door, drop my bundles on the way to the living room, and crumble into a fetal position on the couch where I would stay until bedtime.

I managed to make it to my car without bursting into tears. That was a first. Had I reached a turning point? Was this the start of that longed for "getting better" people kept promising?

My route home from work had changed since the accident. The backcountry road I used to take was off limits to me. I hadn't been on it after they called and told us to come to the crash site. Since that night the haunting vision repeatedly jolting me from sleep was of the tree with the crumpled car wrapped around it.

On this day my car approached the crossroad we'd travelled the night of the crash, following the glow of lights from the orchard we'd been instructed to report to. And then I heard a voice: "Go to the tree."

"What? I'm not going to the tree," I quickly said out loud.

"Go to the tree," I heard again. It sounded like it was coming from the passenger seat beside me.

My panic at the thought of doing so overshadowed the wonder of what was happening as I argued yet again, "I am not going to the tree. There is no way I am going there."

"Turn here. Go to the tree," came the directions from a presence I could feel but not see.

"Fine. But I'm not staying there long."

As I turned onto the road, a vision flashed before my eyes of rotating lights from emergency vehicles, an ambulance pulling away while another stayed, cars lining the shoulder and the street sign we parked under. Now, months later, I pulled my vehicle to a stop once again under the same sign.

I crossed the road and walked toward the tree. There were displays of affection lying at its base. Even though a few bags of memorabilia from this makeshift memorial were delivered to my home a few weeks earlier, more items had appeared at the base of the tree. As my eyes lifted to the trunk, noticing the scar and missing bark caused by the impact, I noticed writing where the bark should have been. People had written words of love and friendship. My son's name was everywhere I looked amidst those words.

I didn't feel a sense of darkness as I'd dreaded. Instead, I felt the outpouring of love for my son.

As if on cue, a truck pulled to the shoulder beside me. Two of Donovan's friends approached me hesitantly. They said they had felt an unexplained pull to come to the tree also, their reluctance matching my own.

"Martha, what are you doing here?" one of them said.

"I don't know. For some reason I feel drawn to this tree today," I said. "This tree has haunted me for so long and I never thought I'd come here. But as I stand at this spot, I realize this is not where Donovan's spirit is. When you two walked up my heart knew his spirit's in you, carried within his friends."

The boys shared a few stories of past visits they and others had made to this place where their friend died. They'd felt his presence there, through unexplained breezes in the leaves of the tree and other signs. My daughter had shared with me that on her first visit after the crash, she'd heard a wind chime hanging from one of the branches start to ring as she approached but stop upon her return to the car. As she turned to look back one last time, the wind chime began its melody again.

As I drove home, and replayed the afternoon's events, I heard a voice as clearly as if it came from the radio itself: "Mom, look for my spirit in the light, not in the darkness."

"Donovan, where are you?" I asked. And then I felt a calm that I hadn't felt for four months. I left something at the tree that day — the thought that Donovan's spirit was there. Now, instead, I know that his spirit is within the hearts of those who surrounded his days, who now shed light on mine as we share our memories.

~Martha Tessmer

On Butterfly Wings

*Love is like a butterfly: It goes where it pleases
and it pleases wherever it goes.*
~Author Unknown

After the motorcycle accident that claimed the lives of my daughter and son-in-law, my husband and I moved our grandchildren into our home. Overnight, my husband and I went from being retired grandparents to full-time caregivers and legal guardians for our heartbroken grandchildren. Cari was ten and Michael only six when they lost their mom and dad. While we all were grief stricken, Michael took the loss especially hard and withdrew into himself.

Not long after the accident, I ran into an acquaintance who offered her condolences and then asked if I'd received a message from Julie from "the other side."

I asked what she meant.

She confided that after her mother passed away, her mom's spirit visited her in her dreams and made its presence known to her in unexpected ways.

I must've appeared skeptical because she smiled knowingly and patted my hand. I don't recall her exact words, but I do remember her look of certainty when she told me that someday Julie would send a sign to let me know she was nearby.

Nodding, I mentally noted the woman's comment. Although I hoped one day to get a "sign" from Julie, raising my daughter's children kept her memory alive every day.

Staying busy helped put my sorrow and self-pity on hold. My husband and I focused on creating a stable, loving home and familiar routines for Cari and Michael. For the remainder of the school year, I drove our grandchildren back and forth to their schools—Cari to her fourth-grade elementary class and Michael to kindergarten at a cross-town campus.

By the end of the summer, we enrolled both children in our parish school so they'd be closer to home and able to spend their school days in the same building. I volunteered in the cafeteria, on the playground, and in the library to reassure them, as well as myself, they would have someone who loves them close by.

My days were filled with carpooling, helping with homework, and taking our grandchildren to sporting events, practices, birthday parties, and other activities. If a note came home asking for field trip drivers, I signed up.

A year after the accident, I chaperoned a group of Michael's first-grade classmates to the Sophia M. Sachs Butterfly House. Dressed in matching bright red casual-day T-shirts and blue jeans, Michael and the handful of boys in my group entered the Butterfly House with a sense of wonder and adventure.

Swarms of multi-colored butterflies greeted us as we meandered through the lush garden. While most of the lovely insects flitted around briefly before darting off to the garden's fragrant tropical flowers, an orange and black Monarch anchored itself on Michael's shirt and clung there.

My grandson's big brown eyes grew wide as he checked out his colorful passenger. While we continued our garden tour, the other boys waved their arms, trying to get the Monarch to fly away; it refused to budge. Word spread, and even more classmates and chaperones gathered around to see Michael and his determined hitchhiker. Uncomfortable with all the attention, my shy grandson quickened his pace and wiggled his shoulders, but the winged wonder refused to abandon him. It wasn't until we headed for the exit that the magnificent Monarch finally fluttered away.

In church one Sunday some time later, our pastor talked about how butterflies are symbols of resurrection and renewal. With a jolt, I recalled the bright and beautiful Monarch that refused to leave Michael's side and remembered the woman's words of assurance that I'd one day receive a message from my daughter. A sense of serenity spread over me with the belief that Julie had sent a sign during Michael's field trip to the Butterfly House.

Although Julie's physical presence is gone, her spirit lives on. On the wings of one of God's most delicate creatures, my daughter sent assurance that she will always be close by, watching over her beloved family, helping us find peace and grace in life's special moments until we're reunited again.

~Donna Duly Volkenannt

Meet Our Contributors

Monica A. Andermann lives and writes on Long Island where she shares a home with her husband and their little tabby Samson. Her writing has been included in such publications as *Woman's World*, *Sasee* and *Guideposts* as well as many *Chicken Soup for the Soul* books.

Peggy Archer is the author of picture books for children, including *Turkey Surprise*, a *New York Times* bestseller. Besides writing, she enjoys walking, line dancing, and time with her grandchildren. She and her husband have six children and eleven grandchildren. They live in O'Fallon, MO. Visit her at peggyarcher.com.

Elizabeth Atwater and her husband Joe live on a horse ranch in North Carolina. They both enjoy horses, gardening, reading, and of course, writing.

Ruth Barmore received her Associate of Arts degree in 1990 from Cecil College in Maryland. She is an honorably discharged Air Force veteran, the wife of a career Air Force husband, mother of two sons, and proud grandmother of two. Ruth enjoys sewing, quilting, traveling and writing. She plans to write mysteries.

Barbara Bartocci is an author and professional speaker who has given motivational talks throughout the U.S. and Canada. She has had nine books published, including the national award-winning *Nobody's Child Anymore: Grieving, Caring, Comforting When Parents Die,* and she is completing her first novel.

Lainie Belcastro has many titles in the arts, but her most treasured title is mom to her daughter Nika. Together they created the trademarked storytellers, Mrs. Terra Cotta Pots & Twig, who plant dreams for children! Lainie, a published writer, has signed with a children's book publisher. She plans to live "happily ever after!"

Suzu Belle is a single sixty-something nomadic adventurer from Winnipeg. She enjoys working out at the gym, swimming, sunbathing, hot springs, growing food, cooking and taking care of animals. E-mail her via suzu@inbox.com.

Born and raised on Cape Cod, **Kristine Benevento** has lived in two countries and three states as a military spouse. Currently living in Vermont, she enjoys family get-togethers and anything her husband and sons are involved in. A former firefighter and EMT, she holds a B.A. degree in Emergency Services Management.

Lily Blais works in risk analysis but writing is her passion. Her first novel is complete and she is currently submitting it to literary agencies. Time with family and friends means the world to her and she has just welcomed into the world her first grandchild.

Jill Burns lives in the mountains of West Virginia with her wonderful family. She's a retired piano teacher and performer. She enjoys writing, music, gardening, nature, and spending time with her grandchildren.

Christy Caballero lives among the trees in Northwest Oregon with kitties and a Greyhound. She has earned national awards in journalism and four Maxwell awards from the Dog Writers Association of America. E-mail her at 7swans@earthlink.net.

Barb Canale's books include *Prayers & Playfulness: Daily Devotions for Young Families* (2016 AmorDeus Publications), the award-winning *Prayers, Papers, & Play* for college students (2013), *To Have and To*

Hold for married couples (2014), and *Hope and a Whole Lotta Prayer: Daily Devotions for Parents of Teenagers* (2015).

Ria Cantrell writes under a pen name. She is a best-selling author of historical romances. Ria was born and raised on Long Island but now enjoys living on the sunny gulf coast of Southwest Florida with her British rock-star husband. Ria is also a classically trained vocalist.

Lisa Carey has written a book about Jonathan and her family's journey through tragedy, and hopes that book will be published soon. She and her husband Mike and son Joshua live in upstate New York where they fight for the rights of the disabled. You can view the horse photo on YouTube. E-mail Lisa at Jonathancareyfoundation.org.

Sue Carloni is a freelance writer who lives in Wisconsin. She has had 150 articles, stories, and poems published in magazines for children and adults. She loves to read and take walks in the Wisconsin state forests. As a member of the Hawks Inn Historical Society, she volunteers on their archives committee.

Sharon Carpenter earned her B.A. degree in History and English at Jacksonville State University, and her M.A. degree from the University of Memphis. She teaches middle schoolers in Memphis and tries to avoid Elvis Week. Her biggest fans are her husband Jesse and three incredible kids who turned into amazing adults.

Pastor Wanda Christy-Shaner runs a Facebook page called "Good News Only," a site developed for prayer and praise. She has been previously published in the *Chicken Soup for the Soul* series, as well as *War Cry*. She is an award-winning speaker, actress and adrenaline junkie. E-mail her at seekingtruth65@yahoo.com.

Elizabeth Copeland is an author and theatre artist. Her novella, *JAZZ — Nature's Improvisation*, won the 2014 Ken Klonsky Novella

Contest and was shortlisted for the 2015 ReLit Award. Other works are published in *Forge Journal* and *Circa,* among others. She lives in Sackville, New Brunswick with her husband, Glenn.

Doug Couch earned an Ed.D from The University of Kansas and retired from the University of Central Missouri as Director of Academic Advising. He and his wife, Peggy, have four children and twelve grandchildren. Doug passed away in October 2015, and this piece demonstrates that his greatest joy was his family.

Dwight Crocker has worked at George Junior Republic with at-risk youth for the past seventeen years. He enjoys hunting and fishing and spending quality time with his wife and daughter. He would like to thank Daisy Townsend for writing this story. It wasn't possible without her.

Mike D'Alto received his Master's of Creative Writing degree from Queens College in 2013 and a Bachelor of Arts degree from Hofstra University in 2007. He teaches English at Suffolk Community College and tutors high school students for standardized tests. He enjoys writing poetry and one-act plays.

Laura Dailey-Pelle received her master's degree in Health Care Administration from Central Michigan University. She works at a hospital in southeast Michigan as Director of Radiation Oncology and Healing Arts. Laura enjoys walking, reading, writing, photography and spending time with her family.

John Elliott is a forty-four-year veteran of Israel's Mossad and the CIA's Special Operations Group. For nine of those years he was assigned to Interpol in Lyon, France. Fluent in six languages, he is an on-air contributor for the BBC, and is also a public and motivational speaker.

Tracy Falenwolfe lives in Pennsylvania's Lehigh Valley with her husband and two sons. She is a member of Sisters in Crime, Mystery Writers of America, and the Kiss of Death Chapter of Romance Writers of

America. She's been published in several anthologies. Learn more at www.tracyfalenwolfe.com.

Linda Feist, a Buffalo, New York native, resides in North Florida. Retired, she is now pursuing her first love, writing. Her debut story at age seven, "Apes in the Attic," received critical acclaim from her mom. That was it… she was hooked! Linda believes our greatest assets are our children and our elderly. She plans to write about that.

Chanel Fernandez is a graduate of Rutgers University living in central Florida and pursuing her love of the arts via every possible avenue. Currently, Chanel is busy growing a brand called Graphted Designs, which incorporates her multiple passions, using fashion design and editorial photography to realize her visions.

Betsy Franz is an award-winning freelance writer and photographer specializing in nature, wildlife, the environment and both humorous and inspirational human-interest stories. She is dedicated to encouraging others to see, appreciate, and protect the wonders of nature around them.

Lorraine Furtner enjoys exploring writing in all forms. She's a playwright, storyteller, and former newspaper columnist whose poetry has appeared in *Imaginary Gardens* and Foundling House, an online journal. She lives with her family in East Tennessee and is working on a novel and a children's picture book.

Grace Givens has only recently begun writing about the many serendipitous occurrences in her life. A veteran performer, she is a cancer survivor who sings through her exams, tests and treatments. She and her husband Robert reside in Houston, TX. E-mail her at gracegivens@gmail.com or view her at youtube/gracegivens/survive.

A.J. Goode studied English at Blackburn College and Central Michigan University. She is a romance writer, humorist, and proud member of

Romance Writers of America. She and her three children currently live in Southwest Michigan, where she also enjoys quilting, reading, and baking. E-mail her at AuthorAJGoode@gmail.com.

Robbi Ann Gunter received her Chef certification from George Brown College in Toronto, Canada. She studies ancient wisdom and quantum physics with spiritual Elder, Grandmother Pa'Ris'Ha. As a Sun Dance Ceremonialist, she is devoted to uplifting consciousness. Robbi is an entrepreneur and writer in Kingman, AZ.

Pebbles H. writes leisurely on her personal blog at pebblesinthesun. wordpress.com and professionally as a marketer. Armed with an over-imaginative mind and her love of languages, Pebbles hopes to publish her poetry collection and write children's books that will inspire all.

Lane Elizabeth Hall is a native of Atlanta, GA where she currently resides and works. She enjoys dancing, singing loudly in her car, and struggling to teach herself how to play the guitar. Her aspirations include seeing the Northern Lights, hugging a Redwood tree, and having a personal library in her own home.

The Norwegian adventurer and Mount Everest summiter **Siv Harstad** has a business background and is known for her unlimited source of courage, enthusiasm and how she transforms challenges into achievements. She's an international speaker, helps people with her leadership methodology, and takes people on amazing adventures.

Judith Ann Hayes loves to write! She is an avid reader. Her older daughter is a registered nurse and her younger daughter is a make-up artist; both are happily married. Judith is a very proud grandmother. She loves to spend time with friends, but her greatest joy is having fun with her three grandchildren.

Christy Heitger-Ewing is a freelance writer living in Avon, IN with her husband and two sons. She is a columnist for *Cabin Living* magazine and writes regularly for Christian magazines. Her book *Cabin Glory* (www.cabinglory.com) was a grand prize winner. Visit her website at christyheitger-ewing.com.

Stan Holden has been an art director and cartoonist for most of his career. Known for his out-of-the-box thinking, he was able to parlay his creative talents into the business world. His inspirational business book *Giving Candy to Strangers* has helped tens of thousands of people from around the globe connect with others.

Andrea Howson is an aspiring writer living off the West Coast of Vancouver Island in Victoria, British Columbia. She is a doting wife, and mother of a beautiful little girl who inspires her every day. Andrea enjoys painting, kayaking, hiking and being in the outdoors with her family.

Carol Huff is owner of Sudie Belle Animal Sanctuary in Hartwell, GA. Most of her writing inspirations come from her rescued animals. Aside from her animals, she enjoys gardening, horseback riding, and sleeping. E-mail her at herbiemakow@gmail.com.

Kristine Jacobson is a mom of three, a farmer's wife and a writer. She has a degree in news-editorial journalism from the University of Nebraska–Lincoln and has worked at daily newspapers and in nonprofit public relations. She enjoys reading, biking, walking, scrapbooking, camping and nature.

Susan Maddy Jones is a freelance writer living in Arizona. Visit her blogs about emotional intelligence, overcoming adversity, authenticity, life balance, appreciating nature, hiking, camping, travel, and teardrop trailers at swimminginthemud.wordpress.com and teardropadventures.com. E-mail her at susan.jones326@gmail.com.

Sandy Kelly is a communications specialist from Alberta, where she has enjoyed a successful career as a reporter and nonfiction writer for over twenty years. Her lifelong love affair with the written word has made her an avid reader and dabbler in fiction writing, and she is currently working on her second novel.

SuZan Klassen is a freelance writer and artist. Her adult children have given her three grandchildren so far. SuZan enjoys traveling with her husband. Join her via her "Travel Light" website at suzanklassen.com.

Karin Krafft is a Norwegian immigrant to the United States. She lives in Portland, OR where she spends most of her free time writing. Three days a week she has the privilege of caring for her fifteen-month-old granddaughter. Karin enjoys, reading, walking, swimming and spending time with friends and family.

Jolie Lisenby received her Bachelor of Arts degree from University of St. Thomas in 1996. She resides in Southern California with her husband and daughter, where she enjoys the outdoors and continues to pursue her love of writing.

DeLila Lumbardy has had ninety articles published and in 2016 published her first book, *Bound by Secrecy*, available on Amazon. She is currently working on the sequel to the Christian novel. She blogs monthly on her website. She loves living in the Black Hills of South Dakota.

Australian born author **Grant Madden** immigrated to the USA in 2005 and currently resides in El Cajon, CA. Grant's cover stories have appeared in *Sailing*, *Cat Sailor* and the *San Diego Reader*. This is his fifth story to be included in a *Chicken Soup for the Soul* anthology. Learn more at grantmadden.com.

Joyce Styron Madsen has done corporate and medical research and written children's stories and articles. She is an animal welfare advocate, rescue dog foster mom, humane society volunteer, and handler for

Lila Comfort Dog. She usually writes surrounded by her four former puppy mill dogs. E-mail her at joycestyron@sbcglobal.net.

Melissa Maglio works as a librarian in the Bay Area and lives with her husband Mario and their three cats: Mia, Mittens, and Fluffy.

Joshua J. Mark is an editor/director and writer for the free online history site, Ancient History Encyclopedia. His nonfiction has also appeared in *Timeless Travels Magazine* and *History Ireland* and his short fiction in *Litro* and *Writes for All,* among others. He lives with his wife Betsy and daughter Emily in upstate New York.

Leslie Marlowe received her B.A. degree in Political Science from the University of Florida and her J.D. from Nova Southeastern University. She has three adult children, a dog and a cat. She loves hiking in the mountains. Leslie enjoys writing and hopes to publish a novel soon.

Katie McKenna is a fundraiser and stand-up comedian living in Brooklyn, NY. She runs a blog called *Small Bites and Little Victories.* She plans to become a motivational speaker to use her experience to help others who have experienced trauma. Her story in this collection was adapted by the author from her book *How to Get Run Over By a Truck.* Copyright 2016 Katie McKenna. Used by permission of Inkshares.

Marsha Warren Mittman has had numerous poems and short stories published in various journals and anthologies, including two other *Chicken Soup for the Soul* books. She's received a half-dozen mid-west poetry awards, and distinctions in two short story competitions. Her second chapbook, *Patriarchal Chronicles*, is forthcoming from Finishing Line Press.

Greg Moore has spent his life in broadcast radio; he is frequently heard on morning radio shows across the country as a creator of comedic vignettes and parody songs. He lives in Oklahoma City.

Lava Mueller is a Creative Writing instructor at the Community College of Vermont. She is also a seminarian at Andover Newton Theological School where she learns about angels and miracles in a most academic and scholarly way. Lava lives in Vermont and loves being part of the *Chicken Soup for the Soul* series.

Rebecca Newman received her Bachelor of Arts, *summa cum laude*, and Master of Arts degrees from Hollins University. She is the mother of a brilliant son and creative daughter, and the grandmother of seven children. She enjoys creative as well as nonfiction writing and heirloom sewing.

Linda Newton is a counselor and the author of *12 Ways to Turn Your Pain into Praise*. She frequently speaks at retreats, conferences, and seminars in the U.S. and abroad. Visit her online at LindaNewtonSpeaks.com, and check out her Facebook page at facebook.com/answersfrommomanddad.

Lynne Nichols retired from teaching after thirty years. Her experience spans all grade levels from first to eighth, including a year in Victoria, Australia as an exchange teacher. She now divides her time between Naples, FL and Taos, NM. Interests include scuba diving, time with her grandchildren and reading.

Diane C. Nicholson is a writer/photographer and longtime vegan. She and her husband Harry recently opened Twin Heart Animal Sanctuary in Tappen, BC. Follow them at Facebook.com/twinheartsanctuary or contact her via e-mail at mail@twinheartphoto.com. Diane is a regular contributor to the *Chicken Soup for the Soul* series.

Samantha Nolan received her Bachelor of Arts with a focus in English from Queens College, CUNY in 2014. She resides in Long Island and works in New York City. Samantha enjoys traveling and writing whenever she has the chance. She hopes to publish novels in the future.

Carolyn C. O'Brien owned and operated an independent bookstore in Mississippi for sixteen years. She now lives in lower Alabama with her husband and a Russian Blue cat that came with the house.

Tiffany O'Connor, Ph.D., holds a Doctorate in Philosophy and a Master of Business Administration degree. She is an accomplished freelance writer. Tiffany is married to her high school sweetheart and is the mother of two amazing boys. She chronicles her experiences raising boys at hashtaglifewithboys.com.

Nancy Emmick Panko is a retired pediatric nurse. She is a frequent contributor to the *Chicken Soup for the Soul* series. A member of the Cary Senior Writing Circle and The Light of Carolina Christian Writers group, she is the author of a soon-to-be published fictional novel, *Guiding Missal*. She and her husband live in North Carolina.

Carol Greenley Papenthien lives in Iowa with her husband. This is her first time writing for publication and she finds the experience exciting. She enjoys golfing and baking pies for family and friends.

Jeannie Powell loves a good mind-body-spirit discussion and is anxious to share unusual happenings, which have felt a lot like angels and miracles. She enjoys writing about life's important details that often go overlooked. Her first book, *Life Simplified*, will be published in fall 2016.

Kay Presto has stories published in a variety of *Chicken Soup for the Soul* books. She's an award-winning television and radio broadcaster and photojournalist, covering motorsports. She has recently completed a middle-grade novel, and is currently writing several children's books. E-mail Kay at prestoprod6@yahoo.com.

Lou Prudhomme is a teacher, writer, grief counselor, and volunteer chaplain with a Bachelor of Arts and a master's degree from the University of Minnesota Duluth. She is the mother of four and grandmother to fifteen, with homes in Minnesota and Florida. No day is ever long enough to do all that she loves to do.

Sandy Alexander Reid has taught high school English in St. Louis for thirty-nine years. She is the mother of three sons and collects flamingos. She uses the story "My Heroes" to introduce herself to her students every year and asks them to write a story of their own, introducing themselves to her.

Mark Rickerby is a frequent contributor to the *Chicken Soup for the Soul* series. He is also the head writer for *Big Sky*, an upcoming Western TV show, co-author of his father's memoir *The Other Belfast*, and a voice actor and audiobook narrator. He also wrote and sang fifteen songs on a CD for his greatest achievements, his daughters Marli and Emma.

Sue Ross finds stories in everything she does, reveling in language that lifts and inspires. It is rumored that Sue's first word gave her such satisfaction that she said it twice... "Author! Author!" Holding a B.A. degree in English, Sue has recently completed her first novel, titled *Golanski's Treasures*. E-mail her at kidangel@me.com.

Jessie Santala has a master's degree in Creative Writing from the University of Denver. She works as a personal assistant and a photographer. She is married to the love of her life and is the mom of two precious babies. She finds time to write in her "free" time.

Doris Schoon received her M.D. from the University of Minnesota, interned in Brooklyn, NY, and worked two years in New Mexico for Presbyterian missions. After ten years in general practice, she specialized in ophthalmology. Her last fifteen years of practice were at the VA Long Beach hospital. She lives in Anaheim, CA with her dog Sheba.

Kim Schultz is a published author, playwright and actor. Her recent memoir *Three Days in Damascus*, about falling in love with an Iraqi refugee, is being released fall 2016 with Palewell Press. Learn more at kimschultz.net and thisauthenticstory.blogspot.com or via Twitter @kimschultz1.

K. Seward, M.S. Ed., is a children's book author and her articles, poems and stories have appeared in magazines and devotionals for kids. She lives in New York with her husband and two sons. She is thrilled to be a part of this *Chicken Soup for the Soul* anthology as she has been an avid reader and fan since she was a teenager.

Paula L. Silici is continually astonished by her spiritual experiences and loves to write about them. She lives with her husband Frank near Denver, CO. E-mail her at psilici@hotmail.com.

Shanna Silva is an author, freelance writer and Tony-nominated producer. Her work is found in the *Multiples Illuminated* anthology, on Kveller, and her first children's book, *The Passover Scavenger Hunt*, will be published in early 2017. E-mail her at shanna@2ndchapter.net.

Sheryn Smith is a retired educator. She enjoys writing, cooking and spending time with family and friends. In her "first life" she published five best-selling cookbooks. Currently she is working on writing about her adventures in China, where she taught English for a brief period.

Darlene Sneden is a writer and editor living her dream in Montclair, NJ. Married to her high school sweetheart, Darlene is known as Mom to two wonderful young adults. She is an empty nester who finds adventure around every corner. Read her blog at adventuresofamiddleagemom.com.

Kimberly Sokolofsky lives in Boiling Springs, PA with her husband and three boys. Kim leads the children's ministry at her church, and also works with children with autism. Kim enjoys traveling with her family, hiking, and being involved in her community.

Toni Somers lives in Springfield, MO with her husband of sixty years and two Miniature Schnauzers. Somers' poetry, fiction, and memoir have won local and national awards and been published in *Today's Woman* magazine, *Chicken Soup for the Soul* books, and in four anthologies. E-mail her at txlaughinggull@gmail.com.

Deborah L. Staunton's work has appeared in *The Sondheim Review*, *Mothers Always Write*, *Sheepshead Review*, *Meat for Tea* and *The MacGuffin*. She has written child development materials for Harcourt Learning Direct and her essays "Promises Kept," "An Owl in Winter," "Anything Could Happen," and "Shoes" placed in various contests.

Sidney Stevens has an M.A. degree in journalism from the University of Michigan. Her essays and articles have appeared in *Newsweek*, *Travel & Leisure*, *Sierra*, and Mother Nature Network. She also coauthored four health books and enjoys yoga, hiking, reading, traveling, creating art and volunteering. E-mail her at sstevens@epix.net.

Kelly J. Stigliano lives in Orange Park, FL with her husband Jerry. They have five children and two granddaughters. A member of Word Weavers International, she has been published in magazines and anthologies, and actively blogs at *Mentoring Moments for Christian Women*. Kelly travels extensively as an inspirational speaker.

Annmarie B. Tait resides in Conshohocken, PA with her husband Joe Beck. Annmarie is published in several *Chicken Soup for the Soul* books, *Reminisce* magazine, *Patchwork Path*, and many other anthologies. She also enjoys cooking, crocheting, and singing and recording Irish and American folk songs. E-mail her at irishbloom@aol.com.

Martha Tessmer taught technology for thirty-five-plus years at colleges and corporations. A master's degree in Education, combined with the tragedy of her son's death, launched an unexpected ministry as a nationwide public speaker and author. Her passion is to touch lives through lessons her family learned on their trek.

L. Thorburn received a Master of Education degree from The College of Saint Rose. She works for the state as a trainer for local social services offices across the state. She is an avid camper, biker, and a first-degree black belt in Tae Kwon Do.

Mary Vela is an award-winning author whose work as an editorial assistant led to monetary awards and selection as "Civilian of the Year." A number of her picture books won Book of the Year awards and two short stories received Honorable Mention from *Writers Digest*. Find her books at www.readingforfun.net.

Nicole Vickers lives and works outside of Chicago. She has a three-year-old son, Kade, with another little boy on the way. Nicole enjoys spending time with her family, reading, and daydreaming about becoming the next great American novelist.

Shereen Vinke walked her way through college, taught for a couple of years, and now spends her days chasing her husband and their three children. When she is not making use of the blessing of walking, running, biking, and other leg-related activities, she enjoys reading, writing, and creating artwork.

Donna Duly Volkenannt lives in Missouri with her husband and grandchildren. Her work has been published in multiple genres and has won several awards, including the Erma Bombeck Global Humor Award. While completing her first novel, she blogs at donnasbookpub. blogspot.com.

Following a career in Nuclear Medicine, **Melissa Wootan** is joyfully exploring her creative side. She enjoys writing and is a regular guest on *San Antonio Living*, an hour-long lifestyle show on San Antonio's NBC affiliate, where she shares all of her best DIY/decorating tips. Contact her through facebook.com/chicvintique.

Amy Catlin Wozniak shares her life with her soul mate, four children, two grandsons, and a Great Pyrenees named Scarlett O'Hara, who has absolutely no problem living up to her namesake. She resides in Northeast Ohio, where she reads and writes stories that reflect God's hope. E-mail her at amy@catlinwozniak.com.

Pam Ziebold is a retired wife and mother and has experienced an awesome life of answered prayers. She wrote this story because she felt God wanted His people to know He still hears and answers our prayers.

Meet Amy Newmark

Amy Newmark is the bestselling author, editor-in-chief, and publisher of the *Chicken Soup for the Soul* book series. Since 2008, she has published 134 new books, most of them national bestsellers in the U.S. and Canada, more than doubling the number of Chicken Soup for the Soul titles in print today. She is also the author of *Simply Happy*, a crash course in Chicken Soup for the Soul advice and wisdom that is filled with easy-to-implement, practical tips for having a better life.

Amy is credited with revitalizing the Chicken Soup for the Soul brand, which has been a publishing industry phenomenon since the first book came out in 1993. By compiling inspirational and aspirational true stories curated from ordinary people who have had extraordinary experiences, Amy has kept the twenty-three-year-old Chicken Soup for the Soul brand fresh and relevant.

Amy graduated *magna cum laude* from Harvard University where she majored in Portuguese and minored in French. She then embarked on a three-decade career as a Wall Street analyst, a hedge fund manager, and a corporate executive in the technology field. She is a Chartered Financial Analyst.

Her return to literary pursuits was inevitable, as her honors thesis in college involved traveling throughout Brazil's impoverished northeast region, collecting stories from regular people. She is delighted to have come full circle in her writing career — from collecting stories "from the people" in Brazil as a twenty-year-old to, three decades later, collecting stories "from the people" for Chicken Soup for the Soul.

When Amy and her husband Bill, the CEO of Chicken Soup for the Soul, are not working, they are visiting their four grown children.

Follow Amy on Twitter @amynewmark. Listen to her free daily podcast, The Chicken Soup for the Soul Podcast, at www.chickensoup. podbean.com, or find it on iTunes, the Podcasts app on iPhone, or on your favorite podcast app on other devices.

Thank You

We are grateful to all our story contributors and fans, who shared thousands of stories about the miracles and angels in their own lives. We had more than 5,000 submissions and it was all hands on deck to read them, with Susan Heim, Ronelle Frankel, Mary Fisher, Barbara LoMonaco, Kristiana Pastir, and D'ette Corona narrowing down the list to a few hundred finalists.

As always, we had way more great stories than would fit in this volume, and many of them will end up appearing in future Chicken Soup for the Soul titles.

Associate Publisher D'ette Corona continued to be Amy's right-hand woman in creating the final manuscript and working with all our wonderful writers. Barbara LoMonaco and Kristiana Pastir, along with outside proofreader Elaine Kimbler, jumped in at the end to proof, proof, proof. And yes, there will always be typos anyway, so feel free to let us know about them at webmaster@chickensoupforthesoul.com and we will correct them in future printings.

The whole publishing team deserves a hand, including Senior Director of Marketing Maureen Peltier, Senior Director of Production Victor Cataldo, and graphic designer Daniel Zaccari, who turned our manuscript into this beautiful book.

Sharing Happiness, Inspiration, and Hope

Real people sharing real stories, every day, all over the world. In 2007, *USA Today* named *Chicken Soup for the Soul* one of the five most memorable books in the last quarter-century. With over 100 million books sold to date in the U.S. and Canada alone, more than 200 titles in print, and translations into more than forty languages, "chicken soup for the soul" is one of the world's best-known phrases.

Today, twenty-three years after we first began sharing happiness, inspiration and hope through our books, we continue to delight our readers with new titles, but have also evolved beyond the bookstore, with super premium pet food and a variety of licensed products and digital offerings, all inspired by stories. Chicken Soup for the Soul has recently expanded into visual storytelling through movies and television. Chicken Soup for the Soul is "changing the world one story at a time®." Thanks for reading!

Share with Us

We all have had Chicken Soup for the Soul moments in our lives. If you would like to share your story or poem with millions of people around the world, go to chickensoup.com and click on "Submit Your Story." You may be able to help another reader and become a published author at the same time. Some of our past contributors have launched writing and speaking careers from the publication of their stories in our books!

We only accept story submissions via our website. They are no longer accepted via mail or fax.

To contact us regarding other matters, please send us an e-mail through webmaster@chickensoupforthesoul.com, or fax or write us at:

Chicken Soup for the Soul
P.O. Box 700
Cos Cob, CT 06807-0700
Fax: 203-861-7194

One more note from your friends at Chicken Soup for the Soul: Occasionally, we receive an unsolicited book manuscript from one of our readers, and we would like to respectfully inform you that we do not accept unsolicited manuscripts and we must discard the ones that appear.

Chicken Soup for the Soul.
Hope & Miracles
101 Inspirational Stories of Faith, Answered Prayers & Divine Intervention

Amy Newmark
and Natasha Stoynoff
Foreword by John Edward

Good things do happen to good people! These 101 true stories of wondrous connections, divine intervention and answered prayers show miracles and good happen every day, giving hope whenever you need it most. You will be amazed and uplifted as you read these inspiring stories. Great for everyone — religious and not — who seeks enlightenment and inspiration through a good story.

978-1-61159-944-2

More Hope and Inspiration

The National Bestseller with Real Stories from Real People

Chicken Soup for the Soul

Messages from Heaven

101 Miraculous Stories of Signs from Beyond, Amazing Connections, and Love that Doesn't Die

Jack Canfield,
Mark Victor Hansen,
and Amy Newmark

When our loved ones leave this world, our connection with them does not end. Sometimes when we see or hear from them, they give us signs and messages. Sometimes they speak to us in dreams or they appear in different forms. The stories in this book, both religious and secular, will amaze you, giving you new knowledge, insight and awareness about the connection and communication we have with those who have passed on or those who have experienced dying and coming back.

978-1-935096-91-7

to Brighten Your Days

Chicken Soup for the Soul

Angels Among Us

101 Inspirational Stories of Miracles, Faith, and Answered Prayers

Jack Canfield,
Mark Victor Hansen
& Amy Newmark

Celestial, otherworldly, heavenly. Whatever the term, sometimes there is no earthly explanation for what we experience, and a higher power is clearly at work. In this book of 101 inspirational stories, contributors share their personal angel experiences of faith, miracles, and answered prayers. You will be awed and inspired by these true personal stories from people, religious and non-religious, about angel guidance, miraculous intervention, and love from beyond.

978-1-61159-906-0

More Bestselling Books

Chicken Soup for the Soul®

Touched by an Angel

101 Miraculous Stories of Faith, Divine Intervention, and Answered Prayers

Amy Newmark

Foreword by Gabrielle Bernstein

Seen or unseen, angels are in our midst! These divine guides, guardian angels, and heavenly messengers help and guide us when we need it most. In this collection of 101 miraculous stories, real people share real stories about their incredible, personal angel experiences of faith, divine intervention, and answered prayers. You will be awed and inspired by these true personal stories from religious and non-religious, about hope, healing, and help from angels.

978-1-61159-941-1

to Deepen Your Faith

Changing your world one story at a time®
www.chickensoup.com